Historically Black Colleges and Universities

Historically Black Colleges and Universities

Charles L. Betsey

editor

Transaction Publishers
New Brunswick (U.S.A.) and London (U.K.)

Library of Congress Catalog Number: 2008009453
ISBN: 978-1-4128-0782-1
Printed in the United States of America

Library of Congress Cataloging-in-Publication Data

Historically black colleges and universities / Charles L. Betsey, editor.
    p. cm.
  "The papers in this special book grow out of a session held at the
annual meeting of the National Economic Association"—Introd.
Includes bibliographical references.
  ISBN 978-1-4128-0782-1
    1. African American universities and colleges—Congresses. 2. African
Americans—Education (Higher)—Congresses. I. Betsey, Charles L.

LC2781.H57 2008
378.73089'96073—dc22   2008009453

Dedication

For their support, encouragement, and inspiration
I thank my mother, wife, and sons
Margaret Betsey, Margaret C. Simms, Eric Randolph,
Josh Betsey, and Dan Betsey

Contents

Introduction

Because of the history of enforced racial separation in the United States, until recently the vast majority of people of African descent who received postsecondary education in the United States did so in historically black institutions. Beginning in the 1830s, public and private higher education institutions established to serve African-Americans operated in Pennsylvania and Ohio, the Border States, and the states of the old Confederacy.[1] The 1954 Supreme Court decision in *Brown v. Board of Education* that overturned *Plessey v. Ferguson* provided the legal foundation for African-Americans to (among other things) attend previously all-white public elementary and secondary schools and led the way for integration of segregated public institutions of higher education.[2]

Subsequent to the passage of the Civil Rights Act of 1964, states began to more actively pursue mechanisms to increase black enrollment in previously all-white schools or face the loss of federal funds under the provisions of Title VI.[3] The increase in enrollment of African-American students in predominately white colleges and universities that occurred over the succeeding decades led some (including government officials at the state and federal level and some notable scholars) to conclude that HBCUs were superfluous and not deserving of continued support.[4]

HBCUs are a diverse group, including public and private, four-year, and two-year institutions, co-educational and single-sex institutions, research universities and professional schools, and vary in size from several hundred students to over 10,000. Prior to *Brown*, 90 percent of African-American postsecondary students were enrolled in HBCUs. Currently the 105 HBCUs account for 3 percent of the nation's educational institutions, but they graduate about one-quarter of African-Americans receiving college degrees.[5]

There has been a renewed interest over the past several years in the role, accomplishments, and future of Historically Black Colleges and Universities (HBCUs), and a corresponding burgeoning in scholarship on the topic. The interest has been motivated

1

by several events including the widely publicized financial and accreditation difficulties at Morris Brown College,[6] continuing litigation involving efforts to assure compliance with court decisions in *United States v. Fordice* (that reaffirmed the obligation that state governments that previously operated dual systems of higher education have to provide equal higher education opportunities to all citizens), and the United States Supreme Court cases involving the University of Michigan's use of race in admissions decisions.[7]

The competition that HBCUs currently face to attract and educate African-American and other students presents both challenges and opportunities. Despite the fact that numerous studies have found that HBCUs are more effective at retaining and graduating African-American students than predominately white colleges, HBCUs have their detractors. Perhaps because of the increasing pressures on state governments to assure that public HBCUs receive comparable funding and provide programs that will attract a broader student population, several public HBCUs no longer serve primarily African-American students.

Several commentators have suggested that in the changing environment some HBCUs will not survive, particularly those that are financially weak. Given the pressures facing public HBCUs in terms of financing and waning public support, some have focused on private HBCUs and asked whether they are perhaps most likely to be able to adapt to the changing environment and "continue to [s]tand and [p]rosper."[8]

The papers in this special book grow out of a session held at the annual meeting of the National Economic Association and represent an attempt to contribute to the continuing examination of HBCUs and their role in U.S. higher education. The papers by Betsey and Price investigate the question of faculty productivity at HBCUs; and, in the case of Price, the role of outside funding from the National Science Foundation. The Wilson and Swinton papers deal with student achievement at HBCUs. Wilson looks at student achievement at HBCUs relative to that of Black students elsewhere, while Swinton considers the effect of the SEE program at Benedict College on student achievement. Gasman examines the media coverage that Morris Brown College received about its accreditation and financial woes and discusses media coverage of HBCUs more generally. Gasman also provides a bibliography of recent research on HBCUs that we hope will be useful for others interested in pursuing research in this important area.

The papers included in this volume touch upon only a small subset of the issues confronting HBCUs. Hopefully, they will stimulate discussion and further research, especially among economists, around questions pertaining to the future of Historically Black Colleges and Universities.

This volume would not have been possible without the dedicated involvement and persistence of Rhonda Vonshay Sharpe, Assistant Editor of the *Review of Black Political Economy*. I also wish to acknowledge the dedicated editorial staff at Transaction Publishers, particularly Andrew McIntosh and Daphne Kanellopoulos, for their role in making the current publication possible.

Charles L. Betsey
Guest Editor

Notes

1. Cheyney University (1837) and Lincoln University (1854) in Pennsylvania and Wilberforce in Ohio (1856) were all founded prior to the 1860s.
2. Brown v. Board of Education, 347 U.S. 484 (1954); Plessey v. Ferguson, 163 U.S. 537 (1896).
3. P.L. No. 88-952, 78 Stat. 241.
4. Jencks, C., and D. Riesman, "The American Negro College," *Harvard Educational Review,* 37 (1967); for an early discussion of the issues see special issue "The Future of Black Colleges," *Daedalus,* Summer 1971, Volume 100, No. 3.
5. United Negro College Fund.
6. See Marybeth Gasman's article in this issue for a discussion.
7. Grutter v. Bollinger, 539 U.S. 306 (2003) and Gratz v. Bollinger, 539 U.S. 244 (2003).
8. William G. Bowen, foreword in Drewry H.N., and H. Doermann, *Stand and Prosper: Private Black Colleges and Their Students,* Princeton, 2001.

The Effect of Attending an HBCU on Persistence and Graduation Outcomes of African-American College Students

Valerie Rawlston Wilson

I. Introduction

In America, higher education often provides additional opportunities for political, social and economic empowerment. According to the Census Bureau, individuals with a bachelor's degree now earn almost twice as much as high school graduates. While college completion rates for African-Americans between the ages of twenty-five and thirty-four have increased tremendously (130 percent) from 1970 to 2000; they continue to lag behind those of whites by nearly thirteen percentage points,[1] contributing also to a persistent earnings gap.

The Higher Education Act of 1965 defines Historically Black Colleges and Universities (HBCUs) as institutions of higher learning established before 1964 whose principal mission was then, as is now, the [higher] education of black Americans. All institutions classified as HBCUs are accredited or making reasonable progress toward accreditation by an approved accrediting body. HBCUs have played an important role in narrowing the education and earnings gaps by providing the opportunity for a college education for a significant number of African-Americans, especially during the period of segregation. Furthermore, low tuition costs have enabled many HBCUs to provide a college education to those who would have been unable to afford one otherwise. Tuition rates at the thirty-nine United Negro College Fund (UNCF) member HBCUs are approximately 52 percent lower than comparable schools.

There are 105 institutions classified as HBCUs, representing 3 percent of all institutions of higher education in the United States. HBCUs currently enroll 15 percent of all black college students and produce roughly one-third of all black college graduates.[2] Although most HBCUs are

5

small, have a relatively high percentage of disadvantaged students, and lack many of the resources available at mainstream institutions, even among HBCUs there are differences in financial endowment, tuition costs, fields of study offered, and academic selectivity.

Notwithstanding their limited resources, HBCUs have done a remarkable job of educating many of this country's African-American professionals. At either the graduate or undergraduate level, HBCUs have educated some 75 percent of all African-American Ph.D.s, 46 percent of all African-American business executives, 50 percent of African-American engineers, 80 percent of African-American federal judges, and 65 percent of African-American doctors. However, as state and federal budgets tighten, questions regarding the efficiency of a post-segregation "dual" university system could become increasingly important, as would empirical evidence regarding the importance of HBCUs in the educational attainment of African-Americans. Unfortunately, this is an area of research that remains largely unexplored.

In this chapter I examine whether there are unique benefits to African-American students who attend HBCUs by comparing four-year persistence rates, and six-year graduation rates of African-American students at HBCUs and Traditionally White Institutions (TWIs). I also consider some of the channels through which these outcomes may vary. In particular, I consider differences in financial aid packages as well as social and academic environments.

Section II presents a summary of the literature followed by an explanation of the theory of persistence as well as the empirical model and methodology used in my analysis in Section III. Section IV presents a description of the data, including summary statistics. I discuss the estimation results in Section V, provide an extension of the analysis using an alternative data set in Section VI, and conclude with a discussion of all the results in Section VII.

II. Review of the Literature

In 1992 the state of Mississippi was ordered to justify or eliminate any policies that "substantially restrict a person's choice" of institution or "contribute to the racial identifiability of the eight public universities" (*United States v. Fordice*, 1992). Ironically, though this case was initially aimed at ending segregative practices at public predominantly white institutions, the continued existence of public HBCUs in Mississippi (and possibly throughout the country) as predominantly black institutions was called into question as well.

Prior to this case, there were few studies offering empirical evidence of the ways in which HBCUs have affected human capital attainment among African-American youth since the American educational system was legally desegregated. Among the empirical studies that have been done, three basic questions seem to dominate: (1) What is the value of HBCUs to American society at large? (2) Are African-American students who attend HBCUs more likely to graduate from college than their counterparts at TWIs? (3) What effect does HBCU attendance have on post-baccalaureate outcomes?

Morse, Sakano, and Price (1996) used administrative data from three schools in North Carolina—North Carolina A&T (an HBCU), UNC-Greensboro, and UNC-Chapel Hill (both TWIs)—to compare the value of these schools as welfare-enhancing projects. While they found that all three schools were welfare-enhancing, in terms of return per dollar of appropriation, and impact upon labor earnings in the state, North Carolina A&T, the HBCU, ranked the highest. In terms of the social welfare gain, they also found that as HBCUs close, the equilibrium stock of human capital decreases, implying that HBCUs have a social value measured by increased output that would not occur otherwise.

Ehrenberg and Rothstein (1994) compared the college completion behavior of African-American college students at HBCUs to their counterparts at TWIs using the cohort of students from the 1972 National Longitudinal Survey of High School Students (NLS-72). Unlike previous studies, Ehrenberg and Rothstein allowed the decision to attend an HBCU to be endogenous, and then controlled for this decision in their estimation of the probability that students who entered college within three years of their high school graduation (in 1972) had graduated from college by 1979. The authors concluded that the average probability of graduation by 1979 for African-American students who attended HBCUs was twenty-one percentage points higher than those who attended TWIs.

The findings on whether HBCU attendance improves post-baccalaureate outcomes, such as future wages and graduate school enrollment, are mixed. Ehrenberg and Rothstein concluded that HBCU attendance did not increase the probability of graduate enrollment, nor did it have a significant effect on future wages. The authors' estimates of the 1979 wages of HBCU graduates were 7 percent to 11 percent lower than those of TWI graduates, but the difference in wages was not statistically different from zero.

Constantine (1995) finds evidence to the contrary. Her analysis of the effect of HBCU attendance on future wages of African-American students differs from the Ehrenberg and Rothstein study in two important ways. First, Constantine uses the multinomial logit college choice model developed by Manski and Wise (1983)[3] to model all of the choices available to high school graduates (that is, no four-year college, four-year HBCU, four-year non-HBCU) as opposed to limiting the analysis only to students who attended four-year institutions. Second, the wage observations used by Constantine were taken later in the careers of those sampled than those used by Ehrenberg and Rothstein.[4] Constantine's results reveal an 11 percent increase in wages associated with attending an HBCU without controlling for B.A. attainment by 1979.[5] When the author interacts HBCU attendance with B.A. attainment, the estimated effect of HBCU attendance is reduced to 6 percent, and the effect of B.A. attainment from an HBCU is 3 percent, neither of which is statistically significant.

Largely absent from the existing literature are studies of persistence and graduation behavior among HBCU students. A second major shortcoming is the fact that there is a lack of information on patterns of higher education attainment for African-Americans who have graduated from high school and attended HBCUs since the seventies. The majority of studies are based upon data collected from older cohorts of students, such as those from NLS72. The role of financial aid in the educational decisions and attainment of African-American college students has also received limited attention in the literature.[6] Given that over two-thirds of African-American college students receive some type of financial aid this is a topic worthy of closer examination.

This chapter contributes to the existing HBCU literature by using event history modeling to address three basic questions: (1) Compared to their counterparts at TWIs, are African-American students who attend HBCUs more likely to experience an interruption in enrollment before the completion of a degree? (2) How do individual and institutional characteristics affect the persistence behavior of African-American students? (3) Are African-American students at HBCUs more likely to graduate within six years than those at TWIs? The next section describes the model of persistence used in this analysis.

III. Empirical Model and Methodology

Unlike previous studies of HBCU attendance, the model of persistence used in this study incorporates duration dependence. Human capital theory proposes that the decision to enroll in college is similar to an investment decision in which one chooses to make the investment only if the present discounted value (PDV) of the benefits outweigh the PDV of the costs. As an extension of this idea, the decision to persist or continue enrollment represents a multi-period investment in which the decision to continue enrollment in each subsequent semester is affected by the cumulative investment in time and resources, or duration of previous enrollment. In order to model such a multi-period investment decision I adopt Cox's popular proportional hazard model. The hazard function, h(t), is defined as

$$h(t) = h_0(t)e^{\beta'X(t)} \qquad (1)$$

where t is the duration variable, $h_0(t)$ is the baseline hazard at time t, X is the vector of explanatory variables, both constant and time-varying, and β is the vector of coefficients to be estimated. Though the underlying persistence process is defined in continuous time (a student may decide to leave at any point in time), durations in the data are measured by academic terms or semesters. Therefore, it is necessary to implement the discrete time equivalent of Cox's model, called the complementary log-log (cloglog) model.[7] Since enrollment is determined at the beginning of the term, when t terms are observed, the actual duration interval is [t, $t + 1$) terms. In this single event framework, failure to enroll in term t, given enrollment in all previous terms, will be called a *first* stopout.[8] The probability of a first stopout in interval [t, $t + 1$) is defined as

$$P(t \leq T < t + 1 | T \geq t) = 1 - \exp[-\exp(\beta'X(t) + \gamma(t))] \qquad (2)$$

where the $\gamma(t)$ are the logarithm of the integrated baseline hazard pieces, $\log(\int^{t+1} h(u)(du))$, summarizing the pattern of duration dependence in the interval hazard. The probability of enrollment for exactly t terms is then given by

$$P(t \leq T < t + 1) = P(t \leq T < t + 1 | T \geq t) \times P(T \geq t) \qquad (3)$$

where

$$P(T \geq t) = \prod_{x=0}^{t-1} [1 - P(s \leq T < s + 1 | T \geq s)] \qquad (4)$$

is the probability of enrollment in all terms prior to term t.

For a sample of N individuals labelled $i = 1, \ldots, N$, each with an observed duration of t_i terms and censoring indicator c_i, with $c_i = 1$ for a stopout and $c_i = 0$ for a censored observation (no stopout), the sample likelihood is given by

$$L = \prod_{i=1}^{N} \{[P(t_i \leq T \leq t_i + 1 | T \geq t_i)]^{c_i} \times [P(T \geq t_i)]\} \qquad (5)$$

$$L = \prod_{i=1}^{N} \{[1 - \exp[-\exp(\beta'X_i(t_i) + \gamma(t_i))]]^{c_i}$$
$$\times \prod_{s=0}^{t_i-1} [\exp[-\exp(\beta'X_i(s) + \gamma(s))]]\}. \qquad (6)$$

The baseline hazard is left unspecified and the likelihood function is estimated using a semi-parametric estimation procedure similar to that used by Meyer (1986). By doing so, I am able to simultaneously estimate β and the $\gamma()$'s. This approach prevents inconsistent estimation of β due to a misspecified baseline hazard and provides a flexible (nonparametric) estimate of the baseline hazard.

In addition to the proportional hazard model described above, I also specify the decision to leave college in each term using linear and non-linear (probit) discrete time, discrete choice panel data models. For the panel data linear probability and probit models, the probability of first stopout is specified by equations (7) and (8) respectively.

$$P(t \leq T < t + 1 | T \geq t) = \beta'X_i(t) + \gamma(t) \qquad (7)$$

$$P(t \leq T < t + 1 | T \geq t) = \Phi(\beta'X_i(t) + \gamma(t)) \qquad (8)$$

The corresponding likelihood function is

$$L = \prod_{i=1}^{N} \prod_{s=0}^{t_i} \{[1 - P(s \leq T < s + 1 | T \geq s)]^{1-d_{is}}$$
$$\times P(s \leq T < s + 1 | T \geq s)^{d_{is}}\}, \qquad (9)$$

where $d_{is} = 0$ if $s < t$, and $d_{is} = c_i$ if $s = t$. These alternative specifications are estimated in order to test the robustness of the proportional hazard estimates.

Before estimating each of these models, the data set was converted from its original format, containing one row of data per person, into one in which each person contributes t_i rows, where t_i is the number of time periods (e.g., terms) person i was at risk of stopout. Term $t = 0$ corresponds to the fall 1995 semester. Each subsequent term, $t = 1, 2, .$

. ., 7, represents the first, second, . . ., and seventh semester (excluding summer terms) after fall 1995, up to the spring 1999 semester, at which point the data is right-censored.[9] If person i never experiences a stopout within the observed period of analysis, the binary dependent variable d_{is} = 0 for all of person i's spell terms ($s = 1, \ldots, t_i$). If a stopout is observed for person i, the binary dependent variable d_{is} = 0 for all but the last of person i's spell terms ($s = 1, \ldots, t_i - 1$) and $d_{it} = 1$ for the last term ($s = t_i$). Expanding the data set in this way results in as many as 2,590 observed person-term records for the 469 individuals in the BPS sample. Dummy variables for each term of enrollment are included in the equation for non-parametric estimation of the baseline hazard in each interval.

The decision about whether to stopout in any given term is modelled as a function of individual characteristics, family background, high school academic performance, local labor market conditions, and a binary variable indicating HBCU status (1 = HBCU, 0 = TWI). Individual and family background variables include gender (1 = male, 0 = female), family income, whether the student is from a single parent or broken home,[10] and a series of dummy variables representing parent's highest level of education. High school academic performance is measured using SAT scores and cumulative high school grade point average. High school academic performance provides a measure of academic preparation for college. Average weekly earnings for the manufacturing industry and unemployment rates for the student's home state are included as measures of local labor market conditions in each term. Since the proportional hazard model allows for the use of time-varying variables, unemployment rates and average weekly earnings are allowed to vary with time and are updated each year.

The baseline specification of this model assumes that there is no unobserved heterogeneity and that HBCU attendance is exogenous. There are two potential problems with this specification of the model. First, ignoring the presence of unobserved heterogeneity will generally lead to biased coefficient estimates. Second, HBCU attendance is likely to be endogenous with respect to subsequent college going behavior. I will address the former by modeling individual time-invariant random effects, and I control for the potential endogeneity of HBCU attendance by using an instrumental variable approach.

I begin by estimating overall differences in persistence between HBCU and TWI students based upon individual background characteristics at the time of initial enrollment. I then seek to decompose the effect of attending an HBCU by controlling for differences in various institutional characteristics, financial aid, and social integration at the individual and institutional level.

IV. Data

This analysis is based on data for three cohorts of students. The first cohort consists of those who began their postsecondary education in the fall of 1995, the second consists of those who began in the fall of 1982, and the third consists of those who began in the fall of 1980.

Data for the 1995 cohort are taken from the restricted use files of the Beginning Postsecondary Students (BPS) Longitudinal Study which was implemented by the National Center of Educational Statistics (NCES). Baseline data for BPS cohorts are drawn from the National Postsecondary Student Aid Study (NPSAS), a program that collects financial aid and other data on nationally representative cross-sectional samples of all students in postsecondary institutions across the United States. BPS then follows these students at two to three year intervals for at least six years.

Data for both the 1982 and 1980 cohorts are taken from the High School and Beyond (HSB) Survey, also implemented by NCES. The cohort that began college in 1982 consists primarily of students from the sophomore cohort of HSB, as well as those from the senior cohort of HSB who didn't enter college until 1982. The cohort that began college in 1980 consists entirely of students from the senior cohort of HSB. Both cohorts of students were initially interviewed in 1980, and three follow-up surveys were conducted at two year intervals up to 1986.

From the 1995–96 BPS cohort I draw a sample of 469 African-American students between the ages of 17 and 21 who enrolled for the first time at a four-year postsecondary institution at the start of the 1995 fall semester, and participated in all three waves of the survey (NPSAS 95/96, BPS 98, and BPS 2001). Within this sample, 146 of the students attended one of fifteen HBCUs.[11] Combining both the sophomore and senior cohorts from HSB I obtain a sample of 816 African-American students, also between the ages of seventeen and twenty-one, who began their postsecondary education at a four-year institution in the fall of 1982 or the fall of 1980, and participated in all four waves of the HSB survey. In this sample, 244 of the students attended one of sixty-six HBCUs.

The bulk of my analysis will be based upon data from the BPS cohort because the level of detail available in this data set allows me to estimate more specifications of the model. For instance, data on financial aid, SAT scores, term-by-term enrollment history, and home state identifiers are not available in the public-use HSB data. Data from the larger sample of HSB cohorts will serve primarily to test the robustness of the base model estimates obtained from the smaller BPS sample.

Sample means for the BPS cohort are presented in Table 1. While the focus of this study is African-American college students, sample means for white college students are reported in column 1 in order to provide a broader context for comparison. Variable means for the total African-American student sample are presented in column 2, and for the sub-samples of TWI and HBCU students in columns 3 and 4 respectively.

Over 65 percent of the sample is female, reflecting higher college attendance rates for African-American females than for males. On average, TWI students came from families with higher income, and were more likely to live in a household with both parents.

In terms of academic preparation, students who opted to attend a TWI scored an average of seventy points higher on the SAT than their HBCU counterparts.[12] TWI students were also about twice as likely to report high school grades in the A to A- (100 to 90) range than were their HBCU counterparts.[13] These statistics seem to support the idea that HBCUs provide opportunities for a college education to African-American students whose academic background may limit their access to mainstream institutions, as HBCUs in general tend to have more flexible admission policies.

Overall, African-American students at both types of institutions appear very similar demographically; however, differences between white and African-American college students are more distinct. For example, the average family income of white college students was $25,000 higher than that of the African-American college students. This is reflected in the fact that white students were also more likely to come from two-parent households and to have college educated parents. In terms of pre-college academic indicators, the average SAT scores of white students were about 200 points higher than those of African-American students, and they were twice as likely to report an A to A- high school grade average than their African-American counterparts. However, despite family background and pre-college academic differences between white and African-American students, the differences in reported college GPA are not as large as one might expect.

African-American students at TWIs were twice as likely to be attending in-state public institutions as those at HBCUs. The data also reveal that on average HBCU students paid the lowest tuition rates (both in- and out-of-state), and that over two-thirds of all African-American students in the sample were recipients of some type of need-based scholarship or grant aid.

Table 1
Means of Explanatory Variables for Fall 1995
Standard Errors in Parentheses

	Whites	Total Blacks	Blacks	
Variables	Total (N = 2192)	Total (N = 469)	TWI (N = 323)	HBCU (N = 146)
Male	0.45	0.35	0.37	0.29
Family Income	$66,832	$41,495	$43,552	$36,943
	(56,453)	(51,477)	(58,144)	(31,859)
Father's Education				
less than high school	0.02	0.04	0.04	0.04
high school graduate	0.29	0.40	0.40	0.40
some college (less than bachelor's degree)	0.13	0.15	0.14	0.16
bachelor's degree or beyond	0.52	0.33	0.34	0.33
Single Parent/Broken Home	0.29	0.45	0.41	0.51
Mother's Education				
less than high school	0.01	0.03	0.03	0.02
high school graduate	0.36	0.41	0.43	0.38
some college (less than bachelor's degree)	0.16	0.20	0.20	0.21
bachelor's degree or beyond	0.43	0.34	0.32	0.39
Took the SAT	0.99	0.97	0.98	0.94
SAT score	996	792	813	741
	(198)	(187)	(186)	(181)
High School Grades Available	0.91	0.90	0.92	0.87
High School Grades				
A to A- (100–90)	0.43	0.20	0.24	0.12
A- to B (89–85)	0.31	0.36	0.35	0.40
B to B- (84–80)	0.10	0.16	0.18	0.11
B- to C (79–75)	0.05	0.14	0.11	0.21
C to C- (74–70)	0.01	0.03	0.03	0.03
C- to D- (69–60)	0.00	0.01	0.01	
College GPA Available	0.01	0.004	0.01	0.01
Cumulative 1995–96 College GPA				
3.75 and above	0.08	0.03	0.03	0.03
3.25–3.74	0.22	0.11	0.09	0.14
2.75–3.24	0.26	0.22	0.23	0.20
2.25–2.74	0.20	0.22	0.21	0.25

Table 1 (cont.)

Variables	Whites Total (N = 2192)	Total Blacks Total (N = 469)	Blacks TWI (N = 323)	Blacks HBCU (N = 146)
1.75–2.24	0.12	0.18	0.18	0.17
1.25–1.74	0.06	0.12	0.11	0.12
Below 1.24	0.05	0.12	0.15	0.08
Residence while enrolled 1995–96				
on campus	0.73	0.77	0.77	0.77
with parents	0.18	0.19	0.19	0.21
off campus	0.10	0.04	0.05	0.01
Public Institution	0.71	0.63	0.75	0.38
Student/Full-time Faculty Ratio	0.21	0.21	0.22	0.21
	(0.28)	(0.10)	(0.11)	(0.06)
Percentage of Black Faculty	0.03	0.21	0.04	0.60
	(0.03)	(0.27)	(0.03)	(0.10)
Percentage of Black Students	0.08	0.36	0.12	0.90
	(0.07)	(0.38)	(0.10)	(0.12)
Means of Financial Variables for Term 1[a]				
In State Student	0.75	0.72	0.80	0.53
In State Tuition (1995)	$6,144	$5,185	$5,390	$4,736
	(5,674)	(4,504)	(5,103)	(2,733)
Out of State Tuition (1995)	$9,711	$8,343	$9,052	$6,789
	(4,292)	(3,589)	(4,008)	(1,562)
Share Receiving Need-Based Grants	0.5	0.68	0.67	0.68
Amount of Need-Based Grants Awarded	$4,338	$4,081	$4,541	$3,081
	(4,155)	(3,697)	(4,048)	(2,529)
Share Receiving Non-Need-Based Grants	0.27	0.23	0.28	0.14
Amount of Non-Need-Based Grants Awarded	3,427	3,759	3,768	3,715
	(3,237)	(3,710)	(3,760)	(3,571)
State Labor Market				
State Unemployment Rate (1995)	5.43	5.53	5.58	5.43
	(1.02)	(1.02)	(0.98)	(1.10)
State Weekly Earnings in Mfg. Sector (1995)	$526	$503	$510	$493
	(79)	(73)	(76)	(64)

[a]Means for financial variables are based on non-zero values only.

According to Figure 1, differences in raw persistence rates, as represented by the survivor function,[14] are small. On average, white students had the highest rate of persistence, meaning they were least likely to stopout, and African-American students at HBCUs were most likely to stopout.

V. Results

Table 2 shows that the average probability of stopout for African-American students attending HBCUs is 1.2–1.4 percentage points higher than for African-American students attending TWIs. This difference, however, is not statistically different from zero. The estimates in Table 2, as well as all subsequent tables represent marginal effects calculated at the means of the independent variables.

Persistence Model with Exogenous School Type

Table 3 presents marginal effects for the semiparametric proportional hazard (SPH), panel data linear probability (PDLP) and probit models (PDP) under the assumption of exogenous school type. Holding family background and high school academic performance constant, those who attend an HBCU have only a 0.3 to 0.5 higher probability of stopping out. Though not statistically different from zero, the estimated effect is robust across each specification of the model.

Relative to all students who entered college for the fall of 1995, the probability of a stopout for those who were enrolled for the spring 1996

Figure 1
Persistence Rate (Survivor Function) by Race & School Type

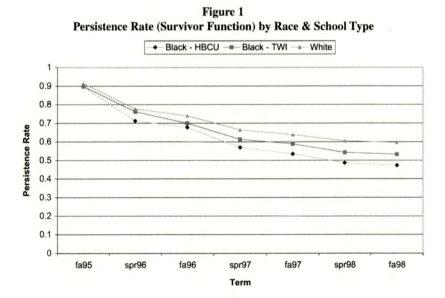

Table 2
Probability of First Stopout—Exogenous HBCU Attendance Only
(Marginal Effects)

	(1) Semiparametric PH Model	(2) Panel LP Model	(3) Panel Probit Model
HBCU	0.013	0.014	0.013
	(0.011)	(0.013)	(0.012)
Spring 1996	0.097	0.100	0.099
	(0.024)**	(0.020)**	(0.023)**
Fall 1996	0.004	0.003	0.004
	(0.018)	(0.017)	(0.019)
Spring 1997	0.069	0.067	0.069
	(0.024)**	(0.021)**	(0.023)**
Fall 1997	-0.025	-0.022	-0.026
	(0.017)	(0.016)	(0.017)
Spring 1998	0.015	0.014	0.015
	(0.021)	(0.019)	(0.021)
Fall 1998	-0.059	-0.047	-0.059
	(0.014)**	(0.013)**	(0.014)**
Person-term records	2,590	2,590	2,590
N	469	469	469
-2 log L	1,474.89		1,475.08
R-squared		0.03	

Robust standard errors in parentheses.
*Significant at 5%; **significant at 1%.
Full regression includes a constant term.

semester was 7.4 to 9.2 percentage points higher. There is also some evidence that the probability of a stopout at any point in time decreases the longer a student has been enrolled.

Family background also has significant effects on persistence. Students from single parent or broken homes were 2.6 to 3.5 percentage points more likely to stopout. The estimates further suggest that the probability of stopout for those whose fathers had at least a bachelor's degree was 3.6 to 4.9 percentage points lower than children of high school dropouts, implying that college educated African-American fathers significantly influence the decisions of their children to remain enrolled. This estimate was statistically significant at the 5% level. Holding all other characteristics constant, students in the lowest income category (less than $16,100) were 2.5 to 2.9 percentage points less likely to stop out in any given term than those with family income above $53,750.

Table 3
Probability of First Stopout—Exogenous HBCU Attendance
(Marginal Effects)

	(1) Semiparametric PH Model	(2) Panel LP Model	(3) Panel Probit Model
HBCU	0.005	0.005	0.003
	(0.010)	(0.014)	(0.012)
Spring 1996	0.074	0.092	0.083
	(0.020)**	(0.020)**	(0.021)**
Fall 1996	0.006	0.004	0.005
	(0.016)	(0.016)	(0.017)
Spring 1997	0.069	0.072	0.076
	(0.023)**	(0.021)**	(0.024)**
Fall 1997	−0.011	−0.008	−0.012
	(0.017)	(0.015)	(0.017)
Spring 1998	0.032	0.029	0.035
	(0.022)	(0.019)	(0.023)
Fall 1998	−0.040	−0.025	−0.042
	(0.015)**	(0.013)	(0.016)**
Male	0.006	0.005	0.007
	(0.010)	(0.013)	(0.011)
Family Income: 25th Percentile	−0.025	−0.037	−0.029
(<$16,100)	(0.012)*	(0.019)	(0.014)*
Family Income: 50th Percentile	−0.009	−0.012	−0.013
($16,100–$31,500)	(0.012)	(0.018)	(0.014)
Family Income: 75th Percentile	−0.021	−0.031	−0.024
($31,500–$53,750)	(0.012)	(0.016)	(0.014)
Father high school grad	−0.013	−0.028	−0.022
	(0.018)	(0.037)	(0.022)
Father has some college	−0.024	−0.052	−0.034
(no bachelor's degree)	(0.016)	(0.040)	(0.019)
Father has bachelor's degree or higher	−0.036	−0.064	−0.049
	(0.018)*	(0.039)	(0.022)*
Single Parent/Broken Home	0.026	0.035	0.032
	(0.011)*	(0.013)**	(0.012)**
Mother high school grad	−0.030	−0.048	−0.034
	(0.024)	(0.053)	(0.031)
Mom has some college (no bachelor's degree)	−0.004	−0.007	−0.002
	(0.026)	(0.054)	(0.033)
Mother has bachelor's degree or higher	−0.035	−0.049	−0.037
	(0.025)	(0.054)	(0.031)
SAT score/100	−0.010	−0.010	−0.011
	(0.003)**	(0.003)**	(0.003)**
Didn't take SAT or ACT	−0.008	0.023	0.003
	(0.035)	(0.070)	(0.047)
High School GPA: 84 to 75	0.043	0.057	0.047
	(0.014)**	(0.017)**	(0.016)**
High School GPA: 74 to 60	0.109	0.120	0.115
	(0.043)*	(0.047)*	(0.046)*
State weekly earnings in mfg. sector/1,000	−0.072	−0.076	−0.089
	(0.067)	(0.076)	(0.073)
State unemployment rate	0.008	0.010	0.009
	(0.005)	(0.006)	(0.005)
Person-term records	2,590	2,590	2,590
N	469	469	469
−2 log L	1,386.02		1,387.50
R-squared		0.06	

Robust standard errors in parentheses.
*Significant at 5%; **significant at 1%.
Full regression includes a constant term, and dummy variables for missing parental education, and missing high school GPA.

The probability of stopout is most strongly affected by academic preparation. Compared to students with a cumulative high school grade average of 85–100 (A to B), the probability of stopout for students with a 75–84 (B- to C) high school grade average is 4.3 to 5.7 percentage points higher. The difference is nearly twice that for students with less than a C high school grade average (10.9 to 12.0). A 200 point difference in the SAT scores of otherwise similar students is also associated with as much as a 2.2 percentage point difference in the probability of stopout. Overall, the estimates from the three models are qualitatively very similar.

Persistence Model With Tests for Unobserved Heterogeneity and Endogenous HBCU Attendance

In order to test whether the estimates are biased by unobserved heterogeneity, I model individual time-invariant random effects for each specification as well.[15] The estimates in Table 4 reveal that despite changes in the magnitude of some of the estimates, the estimated effect of HBCU attendance remains relatively unchanged and statistically insignificant. The sensitivity of the estimated effects of the term dummies is consistent with Wooldridge (2001) who argues that in practice duration dependence and unobserved heterogeneity cannot be separately identified in single spell hazard models. The random error variances for the SPH and PDP models are 3.18 and 0.78, respectively. The PDLP model estimated a zero random error variance.[16]

Next, I estimate a linear IV and nonlinear IV probit model[17] in order to isolate the effect of the exogenous component of attending an HBCU from other variables affecting both HBCU attendance and persistence. The instruments used to predict HBCU attendance were the number of HBCUs in the student's home state[18] as well as the quadratic and cubic forms of this variable.

The results of the stage one regression, found in Table 5, show that students who come from states with more HBCUs, as well as students from single parent or broken homes, those whose mothers are more highly educated, and those with lower SAT scores are more likely to attend HBCUs. I attribute the large positive effect of mothers who attended college (24.7 to 34.8) to some type of "legacy effect" in that many of the parents of these students would have been college students in the 1960s before integration became widespread. As a result, many of these mothers could have attended HBCUs and may encourage their children to do so as well.

Table 6A presents the probability of first stopout results using the predicted probability of HBCU attendance. After controlling for the endogeneity of HBCU attendance in this manner, the sign of the HBCU

Table 4
Probability of First Stopout—Exogenous HBCU Attendance and Random Effects
(Marginal Effects)

	(1) Semiparametric PH Model	(2) Panel LP Model	(3) Panel Probit Model
HBCU	0.000	0.005	0.002
	(0.011)	(0.013)	(0.015)
Spring 1996	0.094	0.092	0.107
	(0.025)**	(0.017)**	(0.028)**
Fall 1996	0.056	0.004	0.041
	(0.026)*	(0.018)	(0.025)
Spring 1997	0.179	0.072	0.163
	(0.051)**	(0.019)**	(0.041)**
Fall 1997	0.073	−0.008	0.051
	(0.041)	(0.020)	(0.034)
Spring 1998	0.171	0.029	0.141
	(0.064)**	(0.020)	(0.048)**
Fall 1998	0.031	−0.025	0.018
	(0.040)	(0.021)	(0.035)
Male	0.004	0.005	0.006
	(0.011)	(0.012)	(0.014)
Family Income: 25th Percentile	−0.029	−0.037	−0.034
(−$16,100)	(0.012)*	(0.019)*	(0.016)*
Family Income: 50th Percentile	−0.014	−0.012	−0.016
($16,100–$31,500)	(0.013)	(0.017)	(0.018)
Family Income: 75th Percentile	−0.021	−0.031	−0.027
($31,500–$53,750)	(0.012)	(0.016)	(0.016)
Father high school grad	−0.013	−0.028	−0.016
	(0.023)	(0.033)	(0.032)
Father has some college	−0.025	−0.052	−0.032
(no bachelor's degree)	(0.018)	(0.035)	(0.024)
Father has bachelor's degree or higher	−0.037	−0.064	−0.048
	(0.023)	(0.034)	(0.031)
Single Parent/Broken Home	0.031	0.035	0.039
	(0.014)*	(0.012)**	(0.017)*
Mother high school grad	−0.046	−0.048	−0.050
	(0.027)	(0.038)	(0.035)
Mom has some college (no bachelor's degree)	−0.020	−0.007	−0.016
	(0.023)	(0.039)	(0.034)
Mother has bachelor's degree or higher	−0.045	−0.049	−0.050
	(0.027)	(0.039)	(0.035)
SAT score/100	−0.013	−0.010	−0.015
	(0.003)**	(0.004)**	(0.004)**
Didn't take SAT or ACT	0.008	0.023	0.019
	(0.048)	(0.049)	(0.069)
High School GPA: 84 to 75	0.049	0.057	0.064
	(0.019)*	(0.014)**	(0.023)**
High School GPA: 74 to 60	0.114	0.120	0.152
	(0.083)	(0.035)**	(0.089)
State weekly earnings in mfg. sector/1,000	−0.050	−0.076	−0.048
	(0.062)	(0.077)	(0.094)
State unemployment rate	0.003	0.010	0.006
	(0.005)	(0.006)	(0.007)
Heterogeneity (Std. Dev.σ_u)	1.782	0.000	0.882
	(0.236)		(0.102)
Person-term records	2,590	2,590	2,590
N	469	469	469
−2 log L	1,340.80		1,357.36
R-squared		0.06	

Robust standard errors in parentheses.
*Significant at 5%; **significant at 1%.
Full regression includes a constant term, and dummy variables for missing parental education, and missing high school GPA.

coefficient becomes negative; however the estimate is still statistically insignificant. The marginal effects of other significant factors, including parent's marital status, father's education, high school grades and SAT score, are qualitatively similar to those presented in Tables 3 and 4. Given the similarity between the IV probit and linear IV estimates, the remainder of the analysis proceeds using the linear IV model, which is also computationally more efficient than the probit IV model for estimating interactions of HBCU attendance with other covariates.[19]

Next, I test for significant differences in the effect of HBCU attendance by test scores, gender, and family income. According to the estimates in columns (3)–(6) of Table 6A, I conclude that the effect of attending an HBCU does not differ statistically for students with below average SAT scores (less than 700), nor by gender or socioeconomic status. In the following section I test whether differences in institutional characteristics, financial aid, and social integration contribute to differences in persistence between HBCU and TWI students.

Persistence Model with Additional Controls for Institutional Characteristics & Financial Aid

Even with additional controls for institutional characteristics and financial aid, the overall effect of attending an HBCU remains small and relatively stable. As shown in column (1) of Table 6B, adding controls for tuition, whether the institution is public or private, and the student-faculty ratio[20] has a very negligible effect on the relative effect of HBCU attendance in the stopout equation.[21] Increasing the student-faculty ratio by a factor of ten increases the likelihood that a student stops out in any given term by 2.6 percentage points, suggesting that students with more opportunities for access to faculty are less likely to withdraw from school.

Next, I test alternative classifications of HBCUs. In column (2) I distinguish between public and private HBCUs, and in column (3) I distinguish between competitive and non-competitive HBCUs. "Competitive" HBCUs are those institutions classified as Research I and II, Baccalaureate I, and private not-for-profit Doctoral I and II universities.[22]

When the distinction between public and private HBCUs is made in column (2) African-American students who attend private HBCUs have a 1.2 percent lower probability of stopping out than those at private TWIs, those at public HBCUs are 0.4 percentage points more likely to stopout, and students at public TWIs are 3.6 percentage points less likely to stopout. However, there is still no statistical difference in persistence for those at HBCUs and TWIs, public or private. The likelihood of stopping

Table 5
Probability of HBCU Attendance
(Marginal Effects)

	Linear Probability
Male	−0.043
	(0.046)
Family Income: 25th Percentile (−$16,100)	0.004
	(0.075)
Family Income: 50th Percentile ($16,100–$31,500)	−0.099
	(0.069)
Family Income: 75th Percentile ($31,500–$53,750)	−0.043
	(0.064)
Father high school grad	−0.136
	(0.112)
Father has some college (no bachelor's degree)	−0.102
	(0.123)
Father has bachelor's degree or higher	−0.131
	(0.118)
Single Parent/Broken Home	0.116
	(0.046)*
Mother high school grad	0.156
	(0.084)
Mother has some college (no bachelor's degree)	0.247
	(0.091)**
Mother has bachelor's degree or higher	0.348
	(0.094)**
SAT score/100	−0.043
	(0.014)**
Didn't take SAT or ACT	0.043
	(0.191)
High School GPA: 84 to 75	0.020
	(0.060)
High School GPA: 74 to 60	−0.220
	(0.127)
State weekly earnings in mfg. sector/1,000	0.320
	(0.361)
State unemployment rate	0.027
	(0.023)
Number of HBCUs in home state	0.222
	(0.055)**
(Number of HBCUs in home state)^2	−0.052
	(0.015)**
(Number of HBCUs in home state)^3	0.003
	(0.001)**
Constant	0.062
	(0.344)
Person-spell records	2590
R-squared	0.18
P-value for test of joint significance of instruments	0.00

Robust standard errors in parentheses
*Significant at 5%; **significant at 1%.
Full regression includes a constant term, and dummy variables for missing parental education, and missing high school GPA.

out is roughly five percentage points higher for students attending a competitive HBCU compared to those attending non-competitive HBCUs, yet this difference also is not statistically significant.

In Table 6C, the effects of various individual- and institution-level controls for financial aid and social integration are presented. The inclusion of these additional variables has little effect on the estimated effect of HBCU attendance. The effect of financial aid on African-American college student persistence is measured using the amount of grant dollars a student received their freshman year. Grant dollars are used because they represent an unconditional discount to the cost of education that neither has to be repaid (like loans), nor earned in exchange for some service (like work-study or an assistantship). As indicated in column (1), the likelihood of a stopout decreases 0.8 and 1.6 percentage points per $2,000 increase in need-based and non-need-based grants respectively. The marginal effects of the aid variables are jointly significant and statistically equivalent.

Recognizing the endogeneity inherent in using individual grant dollars received, I also use the institution-level variable, average freshman grant dollars awarded, as an alternative measure. In column (3) the marginal effect of an additional $2,000 in average grant funds had no effect on the probability of stopping out. The loss of observations due to missing values for several institutions may have some effect on the magnitude and reliability of this estimate. The effect of attending an HBCU remained unchanged.

In column (2) I add individual-level controls for the student's first year place of residence as a measure of their potential to bond with other students and become socially integrated into the campus during the critical first year. Again, this variable is likely to be endogenous, so the percentage of students residing on campus is used in column (4) as an alternative institution-level control. Neither variable had a significant effect on stopout behavior.

Six-Year Graduation Rates

Finally, after observing no significant differences between HBCU and TWI students in the likelihood of experiencing a stopout in each semester within the first four years of college, I tested whether there were significant differences in the probability of attaining a bachelor's degree within six years. Using the IV approach, those at HBCUs were found to have a 16.7 percent higher probability of graduating in six years, but the effect was imprecisely estimated. These estimates are presented in column (1) of Table 7A.

Table 6A

Probability of First Stopout—IV Approach with Interaction of HBCU with Gender and Income

(Marginal Effects)

	(1) Probit	(2) Linear Probability	(3) Linear Probability	(4) Linear Probability	(5) Linear Probability	(6) Linear Probability
HBCU	-0.020	-0.025	0.027	-0.093	-0.289	-0.265
	(0.050)	(0.061)	(0.087)	(0.078)	(0.172)	(0.181)
Spring 1996	0.083	0.092	0.092	0.093	0.093	0.092
	(0.021)**	(0.020)**	(0.020)**	(0.020)**	(0.020)**	(0.020)**
Fall 1996	0.005	0.004	0.003	0.005	0.006	0.006
	(0.017)	(0.016)	(0.017)	(0.016)	(0.016)	(0.017)
Spring 1997	0.077	0.072	0.071	0.073	0.073	0.073
	(0.024)**	(0.021)**	(0.021)**	(0.021)**	(0.021)**	(0.021)**
Fall 1997	-0.012	-0.008	-0.010	-0.009	-0.007	-0.009
	(0.018)	(0.015)	(0.015)	(0.015)	(0.015)	(0.015)
Spring 1998	0.035	0.029	0.027	0.029	0.031	0.029
	(0.023)	(0.019)	(0.019)	(0.019)	(0.019)	(0.019)
Fall 1998	-0.042	-0.026	-0.028	-0.026	-0.023	-0.025
	(0.016)**	(0.013)	(0.013)*	(0.013)*	(0.014)	(0.014)
Male	0.006	0.003	0.003	-0.034	-0.039	-0.042
	(0.011)	(0.013)	(0.013)	(0.031)	(0.032)	(0.033)
HBCU · Male				0.129	0.142	0.169
				(0.097)	(0.097)	(0.105)
Family Income: 25th Percentile (<$16,100)	-0.029	-0.037	-0.032	-0.044	-0.111	-0.071
	(0.014)*	(0.019)	(0.020)	(0.021)*	(0.059)	(0.051)
Family Income: 50th Percentile ($16,100–$31,500)	-0.016	-0.015	-0.010	-0.023	-0.084	-0.060
	(0.015)	(0.018)	(0.018)	(0.020)	(0.061)	(0.053)
Family Income: 75th Percentile ($31,500–$53,750)	-0.026	-0.033	-0.027	-0.036	-0.130	-0.115
	(0.014)	(0.017)*	(0.016)	(0.018)*	(0.057)*	(0.054)*
HBCU · Family Income: 25th Percentile (<$16,100)					0.226	0.116
					(0.171)	(0.144)
HBCU · Family Income: 50th Percentile ($16,100–$31,500)					0.217	0.160
					(0.188)	(0.170)
HBCU · Family Income: 75th Percentile ($31,500–$53,750)					0.340	0.304
					(0.186)	(0.178)

Table 6A (cont.)

	(1)	(2)	(3)	(4)	(5)	(6)
Father high school grad	−0.027 (0.025)	−0.034 (0.040)	−0.019 (0.041)	−0.038 (0.041)	−0.034 (0.039)	−0.034 (0.042)
Father has some college (no bachelor's degree)	−0.037 (0.020)	−0.057 (0.042)	−0.042 (0.043)	−0.064 (0.044)	−0.065 (0.043)	−0.067 (0.047)
Father has bachelor's degree or higher	−0.053 (0.025)*	−0.069 (0.042)	−0.053 (0.042)	−0.072 (0.043)	−0.067 (0.042)	−0.068 (0.045)
Single Parent/Broken Home	0.035 (0.014)**	0.038 (0.014)**	0.033 (0.014)*	0.045 (0.043)	0.036 (0.042)	0.038 (0.045)
Mother high school grad	−0.028 (0.035)	−0.039 (0.057)	−0.043 (0.056)	−0.035 (0.060)	−0.047 (0.059)	−0.045 (0.060)
Mother has some college (no bachelor's degree)	0.007 (0.042)	0.005 (0.060)	−0.008 (0.058)	0.015 (0.063)	0.007 (0.062)	0.001 (0.062)
Mother has bachelor's degree or higher	−0.026 (0.042)	−0.035 (0.064)	−0.055 (0.060)	−0.024 (0.066)	−0.031 (0.063)	−0.040 (0.062)
SAT score/100	−0.012 (0.004)**	−0.012 (0.005)*		−0.015 (0.005)**	−0.016 (0.006)*	
SAT score <700			−0.030 (0.098)	0.013 (0.073)		0.023 (0.037)
HBCU · SAT score <700			0.038 (0.035)			0.084 (0.109)
Didn't take SAT or ACT	0.003 (0.048)	0.023 (0.070)		0.013 (0.073)	−0.018 (0.082)	
High School GPA: 84 to 75	0.048 (0.016)**	0.058 (0.017)**	0.062 (0.018)**	0.056 (0.018)**	0.056 (0.019)**	0.066 (0.019)**
High School GPA: 74 to 60	0.105 (0.049)*	0.113 (0.049)*	0.123 (0.050)*	0.107 (0.048)*	0.096 (0.051)	0.114 (0.049)*
State weekly earnings in mfg. sector/1,000	−0.100 (0.079)	−0.089 (0.080)	−0.077 (0.077)	−0.079 (0.080)	−0.051 (0.093)	−0.040 (0.091)
State unemployment rate	0.008 (0.005)	0.009 (0.006)	0.008 (0.006)	0.009 (0.006)	0.013 (0.007)	0.012 (0.007)
Person-term records	2,590	2,590	2,590	2,590	2,590	2,590
N	469	469	469	469	469	469
−2 log L	−4,192.72					
R-squared	0.06	0.06	0.06	0.05	0.02	0.02

Robust standard errors in parentheses.

*Significant at 5%; **significant at 1%.

Full regression includes a constant term, and dummy variables for missing parental education, and missing high school GPA.

The number of observed spell terms decreases across columns due to missing values for certain institutional characteristics.

Table 6B

Probability of First Stopout—IV Approach with Institutional Characteristics

(Marginal Effects)

	(1) Basic Model	(2) Various Classifications of HBCUs	(3) Various Classifications of HBCUs
HBCU	-0.014 (0.061)	-0.012 (0.077)	-0.026 (0.078)
Public HBCU		0.052 (0.074)	0.049 (0.074)
HBCU · Competitive			0.051 (0.139)
Spring 1996	0.094 (0.020)**	0.094 (0.020)**	0.094 (0.020)**
Fall 1996	0.005 (0.016)	0.006 (0.016)	0.006 (0.016)
Spring 1997	0.074 (0.021)**	0.075 (0.021)**	0.075 (0.021)**
Fall 1997	-0.006 (0.015)	-0.005 (0.015)	-0.005 (0.015)
Spring 1998	0.032 (0.019)	0.033 (0.019)	0.033 (0.019)
Fall 1998	-0.023 (0.013)	-0.023 (0.014)	-0.023 (0.014)
Male	0.005 (0.013)	0.002 (0.013)	0.005 (0.014)
Family Income: 25th Percentile (<$16,100)	-0.036 (0.020)	-0.040 (0.020)*	-0.038 (0.020)
Family Income: 50th Percentile ($16,100–$31,500)	-0.012 (0.019)	-0.012 (0.020)	-0.010 (0.020)
Family Income: 75th Percentile ($31,500–$53,750)	-0.032 (0.017)	-0.031 (0.017)	-0.030 (0.017)
Father high school grad	-0.033 (0.041)	-0.030 (0.040)	-0.033 (0.040)
Father has some college (no bachelor's degree)	-0.056 (0.042)	-0.053 (0.041)	-0.057 (0.042)
Father has bachelor's degree or higher	-0.065 (0.042)	-0.060 (0.041)	-0.065 (0.042)

Table 6B (cont.)

Single Parent/Broken Home	0.034	0.034	0.034
	(0.013)**	(0.013)**	(0.013)*
Mother high school grad	−0.039	−0.046	−0.042
	(0.058)	(0.056)	(0.057)
Mother has some college (no bachelor's degree)	0.002	−0.007	0.000
	(0.060)	(0.058)	(0.060)
Mother has bachelor's degree or higher	−0.041	−0.057	−0.051
	(0.064)	(0.060)	(0.060)
SAT score/100	−0.006	−0.004	−0.006
	(0.005)	(0.004)	(0.005)
Didn't take SAT or ACT	0.050	0.057	0.048
	(0.071)	(0.073)	(0.072)
High School GPA: 84 to 75	0.052	0.052	0.053
	(0.018)**	(0.018)**	(0.018)**
High School GPA: 74 to 60	0.109	0.117	0.115
	(0.048)*	(0.048)*	(0.047)*
State weekly earnings in mfg. sector/1,000	−0.064	−0.040	−0.053
	(0.083)	(0.085)	(0.097)
State unemployment rate	0.008	0.009	0.009
	(0.006)	(0.006)	(0.007)
Public	−0.028	−0.036	−0.029
	(0.047)	(0.072)	(0.082)
Tuition/1,000	−0.003	−0.005	−0.001
	(0.034)	(0.046)	(0.055)
Student-Faculty Ratio/10	0.026	0.027	0.029
	(0.012)*	(0.012)*	(0.013)*
Competitive			0.005
			(0.038)
Person-term records	2,562	2,562	2,562
N	467	467	467
R-squared	0.07	0.07	0.06

Robust standard errors in parentheses.

*Significant at 5%; **significant at 1%.

Full regression includes a constant term, and dummy variables for missing parental education, and missing high school GPA.

The number of observed spell terms decreases across columns due to missing values for certain institutional characteristics.

Table 6C
Probability of First Stopout—IV Approach with Financial Aid and Social Integration
(Marginal Effects)

	Individual-Level Controls		Institution-Level Controls[a]	
	(1)	**(2)**	**(3)**	**(4)**
HBCU	-0.017 (0.061)	-0.022 (0.060)	-0.035 (0.077)	0.065 (0.065)
Spring 1996	0.094*** (0.020)	0.099** (0.021)	0.083*** (0.023)	0.070** (0.022)
Fall 1996	0.005 (0.016)	0.006 (0.017)	-0.010 (0.018)	-0.006 (0.017)
Spring 1997	0.074** (0.021)	0.070** (0.022)	0.071*** (0.024)	0.067*** (0.023)
Fall 1997	-0.004 (0.015)	-0.004 (0.016)	0.002 (0.019)	-0.009 (0.017)
Spring 1998	0.034 (0.019)	0.034 (0.020)	0.028 (0.022)	0.028 (0.021)
Fall 1998	-0.022 (0.014)	-0.026 (0.014)	-0.022 (0.017)	-0.025 (0.015)
Male	0.010 (0.013)	0.011 (0.014)	-0.008 (0.016)	-0.003 (0.014)
Family Income: 25th Percentile (<$16,100)	-0.024 (0.021)	-0.017 (0.022)	-0.030 (0.024)	-0.028 (0.023)
Family Income: 50th Percentile ($16,100–$31,500)	-0.000 (0.019)	0.011 (0.020)	0.002 (0.022)	-0.005 (0.019)
Family Income: 75th Percentile ($31,500–$53,750)	-0.028 (0.018)	-0.022 (0.018)	-0.019 (0.020)	-0.021 (0.019)
Father high school grad	-0.026 (0.040)	-0.016 (0.040)	-0.005 (0.041)	0.011 (0.019)
Father has some college (no bachelor's degree)	-0.053 (0.042)	-0.047 (0.042)	-0.042 (0.044)	-0.020 (0.043)
Father has bachelor's degree or higher	-0.063 (0.042)	-0.058 (0.041)	-0.059 (0.043)	-0.037 (0.041)
Single Parent/Broken Home	0.035*** (0.013)	0.043*** (0.014)	0.037* (0.016)	0.031* (0.014)
Mother high school grad	-0.034 (0.058)	-0.029 (0.057)	-0.014 (0.055)	-0.035 (0.051)
Mother has some college (no bachelor's degree)	0.010 (0.060)	0.014 (0.060)	0.031 (0.059)	0.003 (0.053)
Mother has bachelor's degree or higher	-0.038 (0.063)	-0.027 (0.063)	-0.005 (0.066)	-0.039 (0.059)

Table 6C (cont.)

	(1)	(2)
SAT score/100	-0.003 (0.005)	-0.003 (0.005)
Didn't take SAT or ACT	0.067 (0.072)	0.101 (0.082)
High School GPA: 84 to 75	0.050 (0.018)***	0.050 (0.018)***
High School GPA: 74 to 60	0.108 (0.045)*	0.106 (0.049)*
State weekly earnings in mfg. sector/1,000	-0.101 (0.083)	-0.093 (0.092)
State unemployment rate	0.007 (0.006)	0.008 (0.007)
Public	-0.028 (0.047)	-0.027 (0.047)
Tuition/1,000	0.021 (0.032)	0.023 (0.032)
Student-Faculty Ratio/10	0.026 (0.012)*	0.020 (0.013)
Non-Need-Based Grant Dollars/1,000	-0.008 (0.002)***	
Need-Based Grant Dollars/1,000	-0.004 (0.002)*	
Total Grant Dollars (First Year)/1,000		-0.006 (0.002)**
Lives on campus		-0.024 (0.026)
Lives off campus(other than w/parents)		-0.021 (0.049)
Constant	0.134 (0.138)	0.136 (0.141)
Person-term records	2,562	2,427
N	467	447
R-squared	0.07	0.08
Test for equivalence of financial aid marginal effects:		
$F_{(1,466)}$	2.99	
p-value	0.08	

	(3)	(4)
SAT score/100	-0.005 (0.005)	-0.004 (0.005)
Didn't take SAT or ACT	0.128 (0.096)	0.091 (0.084)
High School GPA: 84 to 75	0.057 (0.020)***	0.049 (0.019)*
High School GPA: 74 to 60	0.046 (0.050)	0.095 (0.087)
State weekly earnings in mfg. sector/1,000	-0.004 (0.100)	-0.049 (0.096)
State unemployment rate	0.008 (0.008)	0.008 (0.007)
Public	-0.051 (0.068)	0.018 (0.053)
Tuition/1,000	-0.021 (0.046)	0.029 (0.038)
Student-Faculty Ratio/10	0.021 (0.013)	0.028 (0.013)*
Average Freshman Grant Dollars/1,000	-0.000 (0.002)	
Percentage of students living on campus		0.054 (0.032)
Constant	0.099 (0.163)	-0.016 (0.142)
Person-term records	1,972	2,025
N	358	356
R-squared	0.06	0.05

Robust standard errors in parentheses.

*Significant at 5%; **significant at 1%.

[a]Average freshman grant dollars and the percentage of students living on campus were obtained from Barron's Profiles of American Colleges.

Full regression includes a constant term, and dummy variables for missing parental education, and missing high school GPA.

The number of observed spell terms decreases across columns due to missing values for certain institutional characteristics.

In columns (2)–(5) I repeat the exercise of interacting HBCU atten-dance with SAT score, gender, and family income. Just as there were no gender differences in stopout behavior, there are also no differences in the likelihood of graduating within six years between males and females at HBCUs and TWIs. Students who scored 700 or lower on the SAT were no more likely to complete a degree within six years at an HBCU than at a TWI. However, the estimates in column (4) suggest that graduation outcomes do vary by income for African-American students at TWIs. Students in the lowest income quartile, as well as those in the second high-est income quartile are more likely to graduate than those in the highest income quartile by at least 35 percentage points.

Academic ability seems to be the strongest determinant of college completion. For example, students who had a B to C (75 to 84) high school grade average were as much as 23.6 percentage points less likely to graduate within six years than those with an A or B (85 to 100) high school grade average. Similarly, the probability of graduating within six years increases by 6.5–6.8 percentage points per 100 point difference in SAT score.

When the distinctions between public, private, and competitive HBCUs are made in columns (2)–(3) of Table 7B, none of the marginal effects for these various classifications of HBCUs have statistically significant effects on the probability of attaining a bachelor's degree within six years.

In Table 7C I control for financial aid, social and academic environ-ment in the graduation equation using individual- and institution-level variables, and obtain results similar to those obtained from the stopout equation.

VI. Extension of Analysis with High School & Beyond Data

The BPS sample includes a total of 165 four-year institutions with only 15 (7 private and 8 public) of the total 105 HBCUs represented. By combining data from the sophomore and senior cohorts of High School and Beyond (HSB) I was able to obtain a sample of 816 students who began college in 1980 or 1982. This sample includes a total of 364 four-year institutions, and 66 HBCUs are represented.

Since HSB public use files do not provide the detailed information on enrollment history, college characteristics, SAT scores, state identi-fiers, and financial aid that would enable me to replicate the IV analysis with this data set, I am only able to estimate the total effect of HBCU attendance (assumed exogenous) on persistence and graduation prob-abilities using the pre-college variables available in both data sets. I create a term by term enrollment history for each of the students in the HSB sample using available data on the month and year when a student began and ended their enrollment at each school attended. Beginning with all students who first enrolled in a four-year postsecondary institution in either August or September (beginning of fall semester) of 1980 or 1982, I created a dichotomous enrollment variable which was coded as a 0 for each term up until the date they reported ending enrollment at that school, at which point the variable was assigned a value of 1 indicating a stopout.

Table 8A presents a comparison of estimates from the BPS and HSB samples for the probability of a first stopout. Assuming exogenous HBCU attendance, and controlling for family background and high school grades, HBCU students in the BPS cohort were 1.2–1.4 percentage points more likely to stop out than their counterparts at TWIs, compared to HBCU students in the HSB cohorts who acutally have a 0.5 to 0.8 percent lower probability of stopping out each term than their counterparts at TWIs. The effect of HBCU attendance is statistically insignificant for each sample individually, as well as for the pooled sample.

Family background, and high school grades are significant factors in determining the probability of a stop out for both the BPS and HSB cohorts. Estimates from the pooled sample suggest that students from single parent or broken homes were on average 2.1 to 2.8 percentage points more likely to stopout than those from two-parent households, and the effect of having less than a C average made a student 4.8 to 5.5 percentage points more likely to stopout. In the HSB sample, students from families with an annual income of $20,000 or more were 3.2 to 5.0 percentage points less likely to stopout than students from families earning less than $7,000 per year.

Table 8B presents a similar comparison of estimates from the BPS and HSB samples for the probability of completing a bachelor's degree within six years, assuming exogenous HBCU attendance. Due to the length of panels available from each cohort in the HSB data, I was only able to estimate six-year graduation equations for those who began college in 1980. For this cohort of students the probability of attaining a bachelor's degree in six years was 13.0 to 14.5 percentage points *higher* for HBCU students. These estimates are significant at the 5% and 1% levels, respectively. For those beginning college in 1995, the probability of completing a bachelor's degree within six years was 7.2 to 7.7 percentage points *lower* for HBCU students than for TWI students, but these estimates were not statistically significant. Those who attended college

Table 7A
Probability of Degree Completion Within Six Years—Probit, Linear Probability and IV Approach with Interaction of HBCU with Gender and Income
(Marginal Effects)

	(1) IV Model	(2)	(3) IV Model with HBCU Interactions	(4)	(5)
HBCU	0.167 (0.175)	−0.069 (0.340)	0.220 (0.220)	0.883 (0.543)	0.472 (0.590)
Male	−0.037 (0.048)	−0.039 (0.048)	0.012 (0.097)	0.016 (0.102)	−0.005 (0.098)
Male · HBCU			−0.170 (0.279)	−0.165 (0.276)	−0.115 (0.283)
Family Income: 25th Percentile (<$16,100)	0.111 (0.074)	0.091 (0.075)	0.118 (0.075)	0.351 (0.174)*	0.211 (0.150)
Family Income: 50th Percentile ($16,100–$31,500)	0.068 (0.072)	0.050 (0.073)	0.072 (0.073)	0.236 (0.173)	0.137 (0.152)
Family Income: 75th Percentile ($31,500–$53,750)	0.064 (0.065)	0.052 (0.065)	0.065 (0.065)	0.383 (0.174)*	0.274 (0.169)
HBCU · Family Income: 25th Percentile (<$16,100)				−0.833 (0.547)	−0.426 (0.445)
HBCU · Family Income: 50th Percentile ($16,100–$31,500)				−0.639 (0.595)	−0.337 (0.516)
HBCU · Family Income: 75th Percentile ($31,500–$53,750)				−1.137 (0.589)	−0.786 (0.555)
Father high school grad	0.095 (0.122)	0.054 (0.126)	0.096 (0.123)	0.098 (0.111)	0.075 (0.131)
Father has some college (no bachelor's degree)	0.185 (0.133)	0.138 (0.139)	0.184 (0.133)	0.198 (0.127)	0.172 (0.145)
Father has bachelor's degree or higher	0.203 (0.128)	0.168 (0.132)	0.205 (0.129)	0.188 (0.127)	0.185 (0.142)

Table 7A (cont.)

	(1)	(2)	(3)	(4)	(5)
Single Parent/Broken Home	-0.080	-0.060	-0.085	-0.051	-0.054
	(0.053)	(0.053)	(0.055)	(0.059)	(0.058)
Mother high school grad	0.079	0.082	0.086	0.087	0.086
	(0.138)	(0.138)	(0.138)	(0.135)	(0.144)
Mother has some college (no bachelor's degree)	-0.050	-0.010	-0.045	-0.055	-0.021
	(0.146)	(0.144)	(0.146)	(0.144)	(0.149)
Mother has bachelor's degree or higher	0.099	0.164	0.103	0.090	0.141
	(0.151)	(0.148)	(0.151)	(0.149)	(0.153)
SAT score/100	0.064		0.065	0.068	
	(0.017)**		(0.018)**	(0.020)**	
SAT score <700		-0.197			-0.176
		(0.122)			(0.115)
HBCU · SAT <700		0.180			0.042
		(0.377)			(0.361)
Didn't take SAT or ACT	0.127		0.139	0.216	
	(0.184)		(0.186)	(0.195)	
High School GPA: 84 to 75	-0.193	-0.228	-0.193	-0.200	-0.236
	(0.055)**	(0.055)**	(0.055)**	(0.058)**	(0.056)**
High School GPA: 74 to 60	-0.216	-0.258	-0.207	-0.167	-0.221
	(0.125)*	(0.125)*	(0.128)	(0.116)	(0.132)
State weekly earnings in mfg. sector/1,000	0.409	0.316	0.388	0.305	0.283
	(0.344)	(0.338)	(0.342)	(0.350)	(0.351)
State unemployment rate	-0.010	0.000	-0.011	-0.015	-0.005
	(0.023)	(0.024)	(0.023)	(0.024)	(0.025)
N	469	469	469	469	469
R-squared	0.14	0.14	0.13	0.04	0.09
-2 log L					

Robust standard errors in parentheses.
*significant at 5%; **significant at 1%.
Full regression includes a constant term, and dummy variables for missing parental education, and missing high school GPA.

Table 7B

Probability of Degree Completion Within Six Years—IV Approach with Institutional Characteristics

(Marginal Effects)

	(1) Basic Model	(2) Various classifications of HBCUs	(3) Various classifications of HBCUs
HBCU	0.214	−0.243	−0.112
	(0.181)	(0.278)	(0.271)
HBCU · Public		0.336	0.266
		(0.284)	(0.278)
HBCU · Competitive			−0.343
			(0.524)
Male	−0.056	−0.073	−0.081
	(0.048)	(0.049)	(0.055)
Family Income: 25th Percentile (<$16,100)	0.104	0.087	0.088
	(0.074)	(0.075)	(0.077)
Family Income: 50th Percentile ($16,100–$31,500)	0.071	0.019	0.020
	(0.073)	(0.076)	(0.080)
Family Income: 75th Percentile ($31,500–$53,750)	0.069	0.046	0.041
	(0.066)	(0.066)	(0.067)
Father high school grad	0.103	0.067	0.065
	(0.122)	(0.121)	(0.123)
Father has some college (no bachelor's degree)	0.193	0.162	0.148
	(0.133)	(0.132)	(0.134)
Father has bachelor's degree or higher	0.206	0.181	0.169
	(0.127)	(0.126)	(0.127)
Single Parent/Broken Home	−0.078	−0.054	−0.060
	(0.051)	(0.051)	(0.052)
Mother high school grad	0.101	0.131	0.089
	(0.138)	(0.136)	(0.146)

Table 7B (cont.)

	(1)	(2)	(3)
Mother has some college (no bachelor's degree)	−0.019	0.030	−0.020
	(0.145)	(0.144)	(0.055)
Mother has bachelor's degree or higher	0.116	0.176	0.135
	(0.149)	(0.145)	(0.151)
SAT score/100	0.044	0.042	0.038
	(0.018)*	(0.017)*	(0.019)*
Didn't take SAT or ACT	0.039	0.075	0.049
	(0.191)	(0.194)	(0.197)
High School GPA: 84 to 75	−0.182	−0.176	−0.167
	(0.055)**	(0.054)**	(0.055)**
High School GPA: 74 to 60	−0.207	−0.198	−0.189
	(0.123)	(0.122)	(0.124)
State weekly earnings in mfg. sector/1,000	0.199	0.220	0.345
	(0.343)	(0.344)	(0.381)
State unemployment rate	−0.003	−0.001	−0.004
	(0.023)	(0.023)	(0.023)
Public	0.213	−0.181	−0.204
	(0.144)	(0.258)	(0.290)
Competitive			0.172
			(0.129)
Tuition/1,000	0.020	−0.009	−0.014
	(0.013)	(0.020)	(0.023)
Student-Faculty Ratio/10	−0.040	−0.075	−0.056
	(0.033)	(0.033)*	(0.035)
N	466	466	466
R-squared	0.15	0.16	0.15

Robust standard errors in parentheses.
*Significant at 5%; **significant at 1%.
Full regression includes a constant term, and dummy variables for missing parental education, and missing high school GPA.

Table 7C

Probability of Degree Completion Within Six Years—IV Approach with Financial Aid and Social Integration

(Marginal Effects)

	Individual-Level Controls		Institution-Level Controls[a]	
	(1)	(2)	(3)	(4)
HBCU	0.252	0.263	0.222	0.010
	(0.182)	(0.183)	(0.214)	(0.205)
Male	−0.075	−0.068	−0.005	−0.044
	(0.047)	(0.048)	(0.057)	(0.055)
Family Income: 25th Percentile (<$16,100)	0.029	0.018	0.010	0.045
	(0.082)	(0.079)	(0.086)	(0.084)
Family Income: 50th Percentile ($16,100–$31,500)	0.006	−0.018	0.010	0.023
	(0.078)	(0.075)	(0.082)	(0.081)
Family Income: 75th Percentile ($31,500–$53,750)	0.048	0.033	−0.007	0.030
	(0.067)	(0.066)	(0.075)	(0.075)
Father high school grad	0.075	0.031	−0.018	−0.010
	(0.121)	(0.122)	(0.133)	(0.140)
Father has some college (no bachelor's degree)	0.174	0.140	0.149	0.116
	(0.132)	(0.132)	(0.147)	(0.156)
Father has bachelor's degree or higher	0.188	0.156	0.177	0.168
	(0.126)	(0.126)	(0.141)	(0.146)
Single Parent/Broken Home	−0.078	−0.083	−0.082	−0.057
	(0.050)	(0.051)	(0.058)	(0.057)
Mother high school grad	0.059	0.042	0.020	0.053
	(0.138)	(0.138)	(0.150)	(0.156)
Mother has some college (no bachelor's degree)	−0.063	−0.089	−0.129	−0.042
	(0.145)	(0.145)	(0.160)	(0.163)
Mother has bachelor's degree or higher	0.090	0.053	0.033	0.064
	(0.148)	(0.149)	(0.169)	(0.170)
SAT score/100	0.035	0.035	0.017	0.022
	(0.017)*	(0.017)*	(0.019)	(0.020)

Table 7C (cont.)

	(1)	(2)	(3)	(4)
Didn't take SAT or ACT	−0.027 (0.189)	−0.024 (0.190)	−0.139 (0.218)	−0.096 (0.232)
High School GPA: 84 to 75	−0.173 (0.054)**	−0.169 (0.054)**	−0.195 (0.062)**	−0.213 (0.063)**
High School GPA: 74 to 60	−0.190 (0.122)	−0.205 (0.123)	−0.051 (0.161)	−0.135 (0.189)
State weekly earnings in mfg. sector/1,000	0.372 (0.345)	0.411 (0.345)	−0.146 (0.388)	0.342 (0.398)
State unemployment rate	0.001 (0.023)	−0.006 (0.023)	0.005 (0.026)	−0.006 (0.026)
Public	0.223 (0.143)	0.207 (0.143)	0.278 (0.203)	0.126 (0.174)
Tuition/1,000	0.008 (0.013)	0.008 (0.013)	0.024 (0.018)	0.010 (0.016)
Student-Faculty Ratio/10	−0.036 (0.033)	−0.015 (0.034)	−0.048 (0.038)	−0.086 (0.039)*
First Year Non-Need-Based Grant Dollars/1,000	0.035 (0.010)**			
First Year Need-Based Grant Dollars/1,000	0.022 (0.009)*			
Total First Year Grant Dollars/1,000		0.026 (0.008)**		
Average Freshman Grant Dollars/1,000			0.010 (0.008)	
Lives on campus		0.131 (0.064)*		
Percentage of Student Body Residing on Campus				−0.109 (0.118)
Lives off campus(other than w/ parents)		0.235 (0.118)*		
N	466	465	357	355
R-squared	0.17	0.17	0.17	0.18

Robust standard errors in parentheses.

*Significant at 5%; **significant at 1%.

[a]Institution level controls were obtained from Barron's Profiles of American Colleges.

Full regression includes a constant term, and dummy variables for missing parental education, and missing high school GPA.

The number of observed spell terms decreases across columns due to missing values for certain institutional characteristics.

Table 8A
Comparison of Probability of First Stopout for BPS and HSB Cohorts
(*Marginal Effects*)

	BPS: 1995			HSB: 1980, 1982			Pooled Sample		
	(1) Semiparametric PH Model	(2) Linear Probability Model	(3) Probit Model	(4) Semiparametric PH Model	(5) Linear Probability Model	(6) Probit Model	(7) Semiparametric PH Model	(8) Linear Probability Model	(9) Probit Model
HBCU	0.012 (0.011)	0.014 (0.014)	0.013 (0.012)	-0.006 (0.009)	-0.008 (0.011)	-0.005 (0.010)	-0.006 (0.009)	-0.008 (0.011)	-0.005 (0.010)
Spring Year 1	0.079 (0.021)**	0.093 (0.020)**	0.085 (0.022)**	0.234 (0.029)**	0.194 (0.016)**	0.226 (0.022)**	0.236 (0.031)**	0.194 (0.016)**	0.227 (0.023)**
Fall Year 2	0.005 (0.017)	0.004 (0.017)	0.002 (0.017)	0.096 (0.024)**	0.065 (0.013)**	0.091 (0.020)**	0.096 (0.024)**	0.065 (0.013)**	0.091 (0.021)**
Spring Year 2	0.069 (0.023)**	0.071 (0.021)**	0.073 (0.023)**	0.038 (0.020)	0.024 (0.012)*	0.037 (0.019)*	0.038 (0.020)	0.024 (0.012)*	0.037 (0.019)**
Fall Year 3	-0.014 (0.017)	-0.012 (0.015)	-0.017 (0.017)	0.013 (0.019)	0.010 (0.011)	0.015 (0.018)	0.013 (0.019)	0.010 (0.011)	0.015 (0.018)
Spring Year 3	0.028 (0.022)	0.026 (0.019)	0.028 (0.022)	0.093 (0.026)**	0.061 (0.015)**	0.090 (0.023)**	0.093 (0.027)**	0.061 (0.015)**	0.090 (0.023)**
Fall Year 4	-0.045 (0.015)**	-0.031 (0.013)*	-0.047 (0.015)**	0.004 (0.019)	0.004 (0.011)	0.005 (0.018)	0.004 (0.019)	0.004 (0.011)	0.005 (0.018)
Male	0.008 (0.010)	0.006 (0.013)	0.008 (0.011)	-0.005 (0.007)	-0.007 (0.009)	-0.005 (0.008)	-0.005 (0.007)	-0.007 (0.009)	-0.005 (0.008)
Family Income: $7,000–$11,999	0.009 (0.016)	0.015 (0.023)	0.014 (0.019)	-0.016 (0.011)	-0.027 (0.021)	-0.022 (0.013)	-0.016 (0.011)	-0.027 (0.021)	-0.022 (0.013)
Family Income: $12,000–$15,999	0.024 (0.022)	0.031 (0.026)	0.023 (0.019)	-0.016 (0.011)	-0.026 (0.021)	-0.021 (0.014)	-0.016 (0.011)	-0.026 (0.021)	-0.021 (0.013)
Family Income: $16,000–$19,999	-0.010 (0.017)	-0.009 (0.022)	-0.013 (0.024)	-0.019 (0.012)	-0.033 (0.023)	-0.027 (0.014)	-0.019 (0.011)	-0.033 (0.023)	-0.027 (0.013)
Family Income: $20,000–$24,999	-0.010 (0.017)	-0.011 (0.025)	-0.006 (0.019)	-0.032 (0.010)**	-0.050 (0.021)*	-0.038 (0.012)**	-0.032 (0.012)**	-0.050 (0.021)*	-0.037 (0.014)*
Family Income: $25,000–$37,999	0.003 (0.016)	0.008 (0.020)	0.005 (0.021)	-0.030 (0.011)**	-0.048 (0.023)**	-0.037 (0.013)**	-0.031 (0.012)**	-0.048 (0.023)**	-0.038 (0.012)**
Family Income: $38,000 +	0.015 (0.020)	0.024 (0.023)	0.019 (0.023)	-0.019 (0.015)	-0.032 (0.027)	-0.024 (0.017)	-0.019 (0.016)	-0.032 (0.027)	-0.025 (0.018)
Father high school grad	-0.010 (0.020)	-0.023 (0.040)	-0.019 (0.024)	0.013 (0.011)	0.014 (0.013)	0.015 (0.013)	0.012 (0.010)	0.014 (0.013)	0.015 (0.012)
Father has some college (no bachelor's degree)	-0.023 (0.018)	-0.046 (0.042)	-0.032 (0.021)	0.002 (0.012)	0.002 (0.015)	0.001 (0.014)	0.002 (0.012)	0.002 (0.015)	0.001 (0.014)

Table 8A (cont.)

	BPS: 1995			HSB: 1980, 1982			Pooled Sample		
	(1) Semiparametric PH Model	(2) Linear Probability Model	(3) Probit Model	(4) Semiparametric PH Model	(5) Linear Probability Model	(6) Probit Model	(7) Semiparametric PH Model	(8) Linear Probability Model	(9) Probit Model
Father has bachelor's degree or higher	-0.037 (0.020)	-0.059 (0.041)	-0.050 (0.024)*	0.004 (0.013)	0.003 (0.015)	0.001 (0.014)	0.004 (0.013)	0.003 (0.015)	0.001 (0.014)
Single Parent/Broken Home	0.021 (0.011)*	0.029 (0.013)*	0.025 (0.012)*	0.022 (0.008)**	0.028 (0.011)**	0.025 (0.009)**	0.021 (0.008)**	0.028 (0.011)**	0.025 (0.009)**
Mother high school grad	-0.031 (0.025)	-0.048 (0.054)	-0.036 (0.032)	-0.002 (0.009)	-0.004 (0.013)	-0.003 (0.011)	-0.002 (0.009)	-0.004 (0.013)	-0.003 (0.011)
Mom has some college (no bachelor's degree)	-0.011 (0.025)	-0.020 (0.055)	-0.014 (0.032)	-0.007 (0.009)	-0.011 (0.013)	-0.011 (0.011)	-0.007 (0.009)	-0.011 (0.013)	-0.011 (0.011)
Mother has bachelor's degree or higher	-0.044 (0.026)	-0.064 (0.055)	-0.048 (0.032)	-0.023 (0.009)	-0.029 (0.013)	-0.024 (0.011)	-0.024 (0.009)	-0.029 (0.013)	-0.025 (0.011)
High School GPA: 84 to 75	0.065 (0.015)**	0.073 (0.016)**	0.067 (0.016)**	0.031 (0.010)**	0.038 (0.014)*	0.038 (0.011)**	0.033 (0.010)*	0.038 (0.014)*	0.039 (0.012)*
High School GPA: 74 to 60	0.146 (0.052)**	0.136 (0.047)**	0.148 (0.051)**	0.047 (0.008)**	0.050 (0.010)**	0.054 (0.009)**	0.048 (0.018)**	0.050 (0.017)**	0.055 (0.019)**
State weekly earnings in mfg. sector/1,000	-0.032 (0.131)	-0.059 (0.152)	-0.049 (0.143)	0.235 (0.097)*	0.281 (0.125)*	0.268 (0.109)*	0.235 (0.097)*	0.281 (0.125)*	0.269 (0.110)*
State unemployment rate	0.007 (0.005)	0.007 (0.006)	0.007 (0.005)	-0.001 (0.002)	-0.000 (0.002)	-0.001 (0.002)	-0.001 (0.002)	-0.000 (0.002)	-0.001 (0.002)
BPS							0.085 (0.087)	0.101 (0.089)	0.112 (0.094)
Senior Cohort				-0.011 (0.008)	-0.012 (0.009)	-0.014 (0.009)	-0.011 (0.007)	-0.012 (0.009)	-0.013 (0.008)
BPS · HBCU							0.020 (0.017)	0.022 (0.018)	0.019 (0.018)
BPS · Fall Year 2							-0.044 (0.017)	-0.101 (0.018)	-0.052 (0.018)
BPS · Spring Year 2							-0.042 (0.009)**	-0.062 (0.021)**	-0.048 (0.010)**
BPS · Fall Year 3							0.023 (0.026)	0.046 (0.024)	0.029 (0.027)
BPS · Spring Year 3							-0.023 (0.018)	-0.022 (0.019)	-0.028 (0.018)
BPS · Fall Year 4							-0.030 (0.013)*	-0.035 (0.024)	-0.034 (0.024)
BPS · Spring Year 4							-0.044 (0.014)**	-0.035 (0.017)*	-0.047 (0.015)**

Table 8A (cont.)

	(1)	(2)	(3)	(4)	(5)	(6)	(7)	(8)	(9)
BPS · Male							0.013 (0.014)	0.013 (0.016)	0.014 (0.015)
BPS · Family Income: $7,000–$11,999							0.030 (0.027)	0.042 (0.031)	0.045 (0.032)
BPS · Family Income: $12,000–$15,999							0.050 (0.036)	0.057 (0.034)	0.055 (0.039)
BPS · Family Income: $16,000–$19,999							0.011 (0.028)	0.024 (0.032)	0.018 (0.033)
BPS · Family Income: $20,000–$24,999							0.034 (0.036)	0.039 (0.032)	0.047 (0.040)
BPS · Family Income: $25,000–$37,999							0.052 (0.038)	0.056 (0.031)	0.064 (0.041)
BPS · Family Income: $38,000 +							0.045 (0.042)	0.056 (0.035)	0.056 (0.045)
BPS · Father high school grad							-0.019 (0.018)	-0.037 (0.042)	-0.029 (0.021)
BPS · Father has some college (no bachelor's degree)							-0.024 (0.018)	-0.048 (0.044)	-0.032 (0.021)
BPS · Father has bachelor's degree or higher							-0.035 (0.017)*	-0.063 (0.044)	-0.044 (0.019)*
BPS · Single Parent/Broken Home							-0.000 (0.013)	0.001 (0.017)	-0.000 (0.014)
BPS · Mother high school grad							-0.026 (0.021)	-0.044 (0.055)	-0.031 (0.027)
BPS · Mom has some college (no bachelor's degree)							-0.004 (0.028)	-0.009 (0.056)	-0.004 (0.035)
BPS · Mother has bachelor's degree or higher							-0.019 (0.025)	-0.035 (0.056)	-0.022 (0.031)
BPS · High School GPA: 84 to 75							0.025 (0.017)	0.035 (0.019)	0.022 (0.018)
BPS · High School GPA: 74 to 60							0.059 (0.040)	0.086 (0.050)	0.064 (0.044)
BPS · State weekly earnings in mfg. sector/1,000							-0.267 (0.162)	-0.340 (0.196)	-0.318 (0.180)
BPS · State unemployment rate							0.008 (0.005)	0.008 (0.006)	0.007 (0.006)
Person-term records	2,590	2,590	2,590	4,502	4,502	4,502	7,092	7,092	7,092
N	469	469	469	816	816	816	1,285	1,285	1,285
−2 log L	1,400.84		1,403.23	2,424.95		2,423.40	3,825.80		3,826.63
R-squared		0.06			0.08			0.07	

Standard errors in parentheses.
*Significant at 5%; **significant at 1%.

Full regression includes a constant term, and dummy variables for missing parental education, and missing high school GPA.

Table 8B
Comparison of Probability of Graduation within Six Years for BPS and HSB Cohorts
(Marginal Effects)

	BPS: 1995		HSB: 1980		Pooled Sample	
	(1) Probit Model	(2) LP Model	(3) Probit Model	(4) LP Model	(5) Probit Model	(6) LP Model
HBCU	-0.077 (0.053)	-0.072 (0.050)	0.145 (0.055)**	0.130 (0.051)*	0.164 (0.061)**	0.130 (0.052)*
Male	-0.061 (0.051)	-0.055 (0.048)	-0.045 (0.043)	-0.050 (0.041)	-0.067 (0.052)	-0.050 (0.045)
Family Income: $7,000–$11,999	0.012 (0.082)	0.007 (0.075)	0.047 (0.082)	0.060 (0.069)	0.078 (0.094)	0.060 (0.076)
Family Income: $12,000–$15,999	-0.091 (0.091)	-0.076 (0.084)	0.031 (0.083)	0.045 (0.070)	0.056 (0.097)	0.045 (0.077)
Family Income: $16,000–$19,999	0.009 (0.098)	0.015 (0.092)	0.113 (0.105)	0.113 (0.083)	0.150 (0.114)	0.113 (0.089)
Family Income: $20,000–$24,999	0.025 (0.100)	0.020 (0.094)	0.051 (0.090)	0.064 (0.076)	0.080 (0.105)	0.064 (0.084)
Family Income: $25,000–$37,999	-0.068 (0.082)	-0.056 (0.078)	0.143 (0.121)	0.126 (0.096)	0.149 (0.134)	0.126 (0.107)
Family Income: $38,000 +	-0.039 (0.095)	-0.028 (0.086)	0.081 (0.121)	0.078 (0.103)	0.110 (0.141)	0.078 (0.114)
Father high school grad	0.102 (0.132)	0.079 (0.109)	-0.020 (0.063)	-0.041 (0.062)	-0.043 (0.073)	-0.041 (0.064)
Father has some college (no bachelor's degree)	0.216 (0.139)	0.181 (0.122)	-0.027 (0.074)	-0.039 (0.073)	-0.038 (0.088)	-0.039 (0.078)
Father has bachelor's degree or higher	0.238 (0.135)	0.205 (0.116)	0.169 (0.090)	0.161 (0.081)*	0.185 (0.092)*	0.161 (0.079)*
BPS · Single Parent/Broken Home	-0.055 (0.055)	-0.048 (0.051)	-0.074 (0.048)	-0.056 (0.047)	-0.086 (0.056)	-0.056 (0.049)

Table 8B (cont.)

	(1)	(2)	(3)	(4)	(5)	(6)
Mother high school grad	0.135 (0.148)	0.118 (0.123)	0.114 (0.065)	0.113 (0.055)*	0.154 (0.071)*	0.113 (0.059)
Mom has some college (no bachelor's degree)	0.051 (0.157)	0.042 (0.130)	0.106 (0.073)	0.094 (0.063)	0.132 (0.082)	0.094 (0.067)
Mother has bachelor's degree or higher	0.244 (0.151)	0.216 (0.131)	0.089 (0.078)	0.094 (0.069)	0.119 (0.087)	0.094 (0.072)
High School GPA: 84 to 75	−0.285 (0.048)**	−0.274 (0.050)**	−0.172 (0.044)**	−0.155 (0.045)**	−0.184 (0.050)**	−0.155 (0.047)**
High School GPA: 74 to 60	−0.325 (0.073)**	−0.343 (0.097)**	−0.215 (0.041)**	−0.233 (0.061)**	−0.253 (0.053)**	−0.233 (0.071)**
State weekly earnings in mfg. sector/1,000	0.337 (0.641)	0.277 (0.588)	−1.273 (0.604)*	−1.270 (0.584)*	−1.578 (0.725)*	−1.270 (0.623)*
State unemployment rate	−0.003 (0.024)	−0.003 (0.022)	0.013 (0.018)	0.012 (0.016)	0.016 (0.023)	0.012 (0.019)
BPS					−0.234 (0.325)	−0.178 (0.298)
BPS · HBCU					−0.207 (0.058)**	−0.202 (0.070)**
BPS · Male					0.010 (0.073)	−0.005 (0.064)
BPS · Family Income: $7,000-$11,999					−0.063 (0.110)	−0.053 (0.104)
BPS · Family Income: $12,000-$15,999					−0.130 (0.108)	−0.121 (0.114)
BPS · Family Income: $16,000-$19,999					−0.125 (0.116)	−0.098 (0.123)
BPS · Family Income: $20,000-$24,999					−0.053 (0.126)	−0.044 (0.119)
BPS · Family Income: $25,000-$37,999					−0.184 (0.111)	−0.182 (0.130)
BPS · Family Income: $38,000 +					−0.132 (0.132)	−0.106 (0.140)
BPS · Father high school grad					0.143 (0.159)	0.121 (0.132)
BPS · Father has some college (no bachelor's degree)					0.254 (0.176)	0.220 (0.148)

Table 8B (cont.)

	BPS: 1995		HSB: 1980		Pooled Sample	
	(1) Probit Model	(2) LP Model	(3) Probit Model	(4) LP Model	(5) Probit Model	(6) LP Model
BPS · Father has bachelor's degree or higher					0.045 (0.167)	0.044 (0.144)
BPS · Single Parent/Broken Home					0.036 (0.078)	0.007 (0.068)
BPS · Mother high school grad					-0.025 (0.159)	0.004 (0.143)
BPS · Mom has some college (no bachelor's degree)					-0.077 (0.156)	-0.051 (0.150)
BPS · Mother has bachelor's degree or higher					0.117 (0.182)	0.122 (0.153)
BPS · High School GPA: 84 to 75					-0.088 (0.069)	-0.119 (0.067)
BPS · High School GPA: 74 to 60					-0.056 (0.151)	-0.110 (0.134)
BPS · State weekly earnings in mfg. sector/1,000					1.892 (0.947)*	1.547 (0.842)
BPS · State unemployment rate					-0.018 (0.033)	-0.015 (0.029)
N	469	469	468	468	937	937
-2 log L	577.6199		493.52		1062.78	
R-squared		0.14		0.13		0.16

Standard errors in parentheses.

*Significant at 5%; **significant at 1%.

Full regression includes a constant term, and dummy variables for missing parental education, and missing high school GPA.

during the 1990s were about 21 percentage points less likely than those who attended during the 1980s to complete a degree within six years, indicating that the average time to degree completion has increased over time. This difference was statistically significant at the 1% level.

High school grades and father's education also had significant effects on the likelihood of graduating within six years that were consistent with the effects these variables had on stopout behavior. According to estimates from the pooled sample, having less than a C average (grade average of 74 to 60) in high school resulted in a 23.3 to 25.3 percent lower probability of graduating within six years. Having a father with a bachelor's degree or more also increased one's likelihood of graduating within six years by 16.1 to 18.5 percentage points.

VII. Conclusion

The results of this analysis suggest that African-American students who attend HBCUs are statistically no more likely to experience an interruption in their college enrollment (a stopout) than their counterparts at TWIs. This result was robust across various specifications of the model and across different cohorts of students, as all marginal effects of this variable were found to be small and statistically insignificant. Rather, the major factors influencing college persistence in fact seem to come from academic performance and family background. Not surprisingly, those who performed well academically, as reflected by their high school grades and SAT scores, were consistently less likely to stopout than other students. High school grades were found to be significant determinants of a six-year degree attainment as well. These results suggest that a student's performance in the higher education arena is intricately linked to his or her ability to develop the skills necessary to compete and meet the demands of college before they arrive.

A more unanticipated result of this analysis however was the fact that students from single parent or broken home backgrounds—meaning parents were either divorced, separated or never married—were 3 to 4 percentage points more likely to stopout than students from two-parent homes. The result suggests there is a significant relationship between college outcomes and sociological factors, such as the students' home environment.

In comparing the 1980s cohort of students with the 1990s cohort of students I found that there were neither within- nor between-cohort differences in the stopout behavior of HBCU and TWI students. However, there were between-cohort differences in graduation outcomes. The overall effect of attending an HBCU on the probability of completing a bachelor's degree within six years was lower for those who began college in 1995 compared to those who began college in 1980, and the 1980 cohort of HBCU students were as much as 16 percentage points more likely to receive a bachelor's degree within six years than those attending TWIs. This was the only case where the estimated effect of HBCU attendance was statiscally different from zero.

Ultimately, the question is what, if anything, does the absence of a distinct HBCU effect really mean? On one hand, if a student is just as likely to persist and complete a degree at an HBCU as a TWI, then it is more economical to attend an HBCU at a fraction of the cost of an education at a comparable TWI. On the other hand, although degree attainment is the primary reason why colleges and universities exist, the observation of this outcome alone gives no consideration to the quality of education, or the personal satisfaction and pride derived from the educational experience. It is also difficult to identify the specific underlying reasons why students choose to leave college, which may vary from discontentment with the institution, to disciplinary sanctions, academic incompatibility, or change of interest. I would argue that each of these factors are relevant to varying degrees although they may not be reflected in overall differences in persistence or graduation rates. Also, since the students in this particular sample are very similar, it seems reasonable that we would not observe large differences in college outcomes.

Though this paper fills some of the holes in the HBCU and persistence literatures, this analysis is not without its own limitation. First, the small sample size may be hampering the ability to produce statistically significant estimates of the HBCU effect. Second, the model in this paper presents a simplified school choice between an HBCU or TWI. Given the vast array of institutional characteristics even within these two groups, the choice of a college goes far beyond this broad characterization. A logical next step in this line of research would be to control for the choice of a specific college in the persistence and graduation equations. Finally, in light of these results, an investigation of post-baccalaureate outcomes would also provide further insight.

Notes

1. Source: U.S. Census Bureau (Census of Population).
2. Source: Congressman James E. Clyburn. 2004. "HBCUs: Institutions for Past, Present & Future." *Capitol Column.*
3. Manski and Wise (1983) also use NLS-72 data to estimate their model of college choice.

4.   In order to maintain the comparability of her study to that of Rothstein and Ehrenberg, Constantine estimates a reduced form wage equation for four-year college attendees only.

5.   Constantine controls for B.A. attainment as a dummy variable equal to 1 if the respondent had a B.A. degree or more as of 1979, and 0 otherwise.

6.   There is an emerging literature estimating the effect of financial aid on persistence behavior, though not specifically for African-American students at HBCUs. A review of this literature can be found in Wilson (2006).

7.   Discrete time hazard models can also be estimated using logistic regression analysis. The clolog and logit links are extremely similar for event probabilities less that 50-percent.

8.   A stopout is not synonymous with a dropout. However, only twenty-one percent of students in the sample later return to the school where they began their post-secondary education (within the four years being observed) after experiencing the first stopout.

9.   Although data for this cohort of BPS are actually collected through the 2001 spring semester, the tuition data are missing for fall 1999 and spring 2000 (terms 9 and 10). Therefore, I am only able to estimate the full model using pre- fall 1999 observations.

10. These are students whose parents reported on their financial aid application that they were either divorced, separated, or never married.

11. While this is a small sample size, the nature of the population being analyzed inevitably limits the number of observations available from nationally representative samples. Ehrenberg & Rothstein (1994) only had a sample size of 638, with 298 coming from HBCUs.

12. I assume students without a reported SAT score did not take the exam. For estimation purposes, the missing values are recoded as zeros, and a dummy variable is created to indicate whether the student took the SAT. The means reported in Table 1, however, are based on the non-zero values only.

13. Both the high school and college GPA are self-reported by the student. The high school GPA is based on the student's reported GPA on his or her most recent SAT questionnaire. Those with a missing their SAT score were also missing their high school GPA, so I created a "missing" dummy variable for those individuals. The college GPA for the first year was based on institutional records when available, but was supplemented by self-reported grades for year one as well as for each subsequent follow-up interview.

14. The survivor function measures the joint probability that stopout did not occur in any of the previous terms.

15. A full description of the random effects specification for each of the models estimated in this paper is available in Wilson (2006).

16. The **xtreg** command used to estimate the random effects linear model typically reports zero heterogeneity standard deviations when there is limited variation in the values of the dependent variables (in this case they're just 0 or 1). Therefore, the nonlinear models are more likely to detect unobserved heterogeneity with a binary dependent variable.

17. The **ivprobit** command is used in STATA to estimate a probit model with endogenous regressors. However, only the second stage is estimated using a probit model. The first stage is still estimated by a linear probability model.

18. I also attempted to use distance to the nearest HBCU as an instrument. Distance can be calculated using zip codes; however, this data was missing for more than one-third of the sample.

19. Attempts to estimate the probit IV model with interaction terms were unsuccessful as the maximization process failed to converge.
20. The student-teacher ratio was estimated by dividing the 12-month undergraduate unduplicated head count by the number of full-time faculty, as reported in IPEDS.
21. Tuition and student-teacher ratios are allowed to vary annually.
22. The selectivity index included in the BPS database classifies institutions as "very selective" if the 25th percentile of SAT scores of incoming freshman exceeded 1,000. "Selective institutions are Research I and II, Baccalaureate I, and private not-for-profit Doctoral I and II universities that did not meet the "very selective" criteria. Since none of the HBCUs in the database met the criteria for "very selective," I combined the "very selective" and "selective" categories into a single category labeled competitive for the purpose of my analysis. I opted to label them as competitive and non-competitive because these labels seemed more intuitive in light of the fact that the criteria used to classify institutions identifies them more in terms of their ability to compete for similar types of students. Three HBCUs in the sample met the competitive criteria.

References

Constantine, Jill M. (1995). The Effect of Attending Historically Black Colleges and Universities on Future Wages of Black Students. *Industrial and Labor Relations Review,* 48(3), 531–546.

Ehrenberg, Ronald G. and Donna S. Rothstein. (1994). "Do Historically Black Institutions of Higher Education Confer Unique Advantages on Black Students? An Initial Analysis." In Ronald G. Ehrenberg, ed., *Choices and Consequences: Contemporary Policy Issues in Education.* Ithaca, NY: ILR Press.

Manski, Charles F. and David A. Wise. (1983). *College Choice in America.* Cambridge, MA: Harvard University Press.

Meyer, Bruce. (1986). "Semi-parametric Estimation of Hazard Models." Department of Economics, MIT.

Morse, Lawrence, Ryoichi Sakano, and Gregory N. Price. (1996). Black Colleges and Universities as Projects: How Do They Rank Relative To White Public Colleges and Universities? *The Review of Black Political Economy,* 24(4), 65-79.

Wilson, Valerie R. (2006). Mind over a Matter of Money: Two Essays on College Persistence and Graduation Outcomes of Low-Income and African-American College Students. PhD Dissertation, University of North Carolina, Chapel Hill.

Faculty Research Productivity: Institutional and Personal Determinants of Faculty Publications

Charles L. Betsey

A good deal has been written about faculty productivity, usually measured by the number of publications in refereed journals, books, and/or the number of citations of those publications by discipline, by type of educational institution, and at various stages of the life cycle. A number of generalizations can be made that are applicable across a wide range of studies: 1) a small share of scholars account for the great majority of publications; 2) publication productivity differs across disciplines and types of institutions; 3) personal characteristics such as gender and race matter; 4) institutional characteristics matter; and 5) publication productivity varies over the life cycle.

According to a U.S. Department of Education report, there were about 75,000 undergraduate students and 3,200 graduate students attending Historically Black Colleges and Universities (HBCUs) in 1953–54 prior to the *Brown v. Board* decision. Black colleges awarded nearly 12,000 bachelor's degrees and first-professional degrees and 1,300 master's degrees. In the aftermath of the decision, black enrollment grew at both HBCUs and Historically White Colleges and Universities (HWCUs). Indeed, a 1961 study showed that only 17 percent of public higher education institutions in the South had admitted Black students. By 1965, HWCUs enrolled about one-quarter of Black students in the South and this increased to 40 percent by 1970. Enrollment in HBCUs continued to increase throughout the 1970s, peaking at 222,000 students in 1980. Some of the decline in Black enrollments at some HBCUs was counterbalanced by increased enrollment of students who were white and of other races. White students were concentrated in graduate and first-professional programs, and more often enrolled part-time.

Challenges Facing HBCUs

Several types of challenges confront HBCUs: Administrative and staff challenges including funding; student challenges including competition for the best and brightest students who now have widely different choices than even a few decades ago; and faculty challenges, including competition from HWCUs to attract and retain faculty talent.

Who are HBCU faculty; how do they compare with faculty at non-HBCU institutions in demographic terms; what can we say generally about their training and their productivity? Finally, what does the picture we sketch about these various aspects of HBCUs and HBCU faculty portend for the future?

HBCU Faculty

What do we know about the characteristics of HBCU faculty? Who are they, where are they, how have they changed over time, how do they compare with non-HBCU faculty?

Brief History of HBCUs

According to Drewry and Doermann, "a typical teacher in a freedmen school during the decade following the Civil War was a well-educated, white, middle-class, Protestant woman from New England" (p. 53). The number of black educators was small, and since the organization of most private colleges and universities serving black students was under the control of religious and missionary organizations that were principally white, whites constituted the majority of faculty and administrators at black schools into the first decade of the 20th century. According to one report, by 1915 blacks constituted 71 percent of the faculty at private institutions, with the percentage being significantly higher (91 percent) at those established by three black religious denominations, African Methodist Episcopal (AME), African Methodist Episcopal Zion, and Colored Methodist. A 1927 survey conducted by the federal government claimed that the number of black faculty in independent and Northern denominational colleges was increasing but provided no data. The same report claimed that public and black denominational colleges were staffed exclusively with black faculty.[1]

The Great Depression resulted in serious hardships for black colleges but also some opportunities. Apparently as a result of the loss of jobs, significant numbers of young blacks stayed in secondary school in 1932 compared to 1929 (14% of 15–19 year olds vs. 10%). This contributed to a rising number of black high school graduates, which in turn led to a decreasing emphasis on preparatory instruction in black colleges. According to the Office of Education, the proportion of students enrolled in preparatory education at black colleges fell from 24 percent to 17 percent of total enrollment between 1931 and 1936.[2] While blacks could increasingly receive baccalaureate education, most were limited, especially in the South, in terms of access to graduate education. Six black colleges offered graduate instruction in some fields in 1936; all were private institutions. States that maintained racially separate educational institutions sometimes made provisions for black residents to attend graduate or professional schools by providing scholarships for black residents to attend school out-of-state. Others added programs to the public colleges and universities; while still others made no provisions for blacks who wanted to obtain graduate or professional school training. In its 1938 decision in *Gaines*, the Supreme Court required all states to make provision for graduate education of blacks by either providing them access to the same institutions that whites attended or by establishing the same programs at black colleges, thus, destroying the validity of out-of-state scholarships as a mechanism for excluding blacks from professional schools.[3] In fact, when such programs were in effect, available funding usually limited the number of blacks who could obtain graduate and first-professional degrees under them.[4] In subsequent decisions in *McLaurin*, the landmark May 1954 *Brown* decision, and the *Brown II* decision in May 1955, the Supreme Court declared unconstitutional state Jim Crow provisions for graduate and professional education of blacks, outlawed segregation in public education altogether, and required timely dismantling of federal, state, and local laws that permitted or required segregation in public education.

In the aftermath of the *Brown* decision some public HBCUs closed or were merged with predominantly white institutions. Others began to enroll significant numbers of white students. Even as there was a trend in the 1970s of high-achieving black students to attend traditionally white colleges in larger numbers, the vast majority of black college students attended HBCUs, and an even higher percentage of black college graduates received their educations at HBCUs.[5] Despite this, for most HBCUs it could not be business as usual. Overall declines in black college attendance and declines in the share of high-achieving black students attending HBCUs led many schools to adapt their curricular offerings, programs, and instructional schemes. Drewry and Doermann credit Spelman College for being among the first to recognize the need for curricular innovation and other changes that would continue to attract high-achieving black students. Drewry and Doermann also credit faculty development efforts at Spelman and other HBCUs with the successful adaptation that many have undergone to help themselves remain viable. And Allen and Jewell identify what they refer to as "a select set of historically black colleges and universities" (including Spelman, Morehouse College, Xavier University, Hampton University, Howard University, and Florida A&M University), that have been able to maintain strong academic programs, build endowments, and compete for the top black students.[6]

Faculty Composition

In several dimensions the profile of HBCU faculty indicates a more diverse workforce than exists elsewhere in academe: race/ethnicity, gender, and country of origin. One area of possible concern is the age distribution at HBCUs compared to HWCUs. If HBCU faculty are significantly older than other faculty and the production of new minority faculty is lagging, there may be a growing faculty shortage at the same time that the baby boom echo generation is approaching college age. This presents some challenges as well as some opportunities for HBCUs. According to the IPEDS survey during fall 1999, women constituted 37.2 percent of the full-time instructional faculty nationwide and black non-Hispanic faculty were 4.9 percent of the total. Our analysis of data from the NSOPF survey indicates that black non-Hispanic faculty were 61 percent of full-time instructional faculty at HBCUs and 3.8 percent of HWCU faculty. These data indicate that women faculty constituted about 35.5 percent of HBCU faculty and about 36.2 percent of HWCU faculty. A significantly larger share of HBCU faculty were born outside of the United States than was true for HWCUs. In 1999, about three-fourths of full-time instructional HBCU faculty were US-born compared to more than four-fifths at HWCUs. Similarly, although roughly equal proportions of HBCU and HWCU faculty were US citizens (91.6 percent and 93.0 percent), HBCU faculty were twice as likely as HWCU faculty to be naturalized citizens, 16.8 percent versus 8.1 percent.

In 1999, faculty at HBCUs were significantly older than their counterparts at HWCUs. While the median age of full-time instructional faculty nationwide was about 49.30 years,[7] the median age of faculty at HBCUs was 50.56 and for HWCUs it was 49.25, a difference statistically significant the .001 level. The age distributions differed in interesting ways. As might be expected, given the differences in life expectancies between African-Americans and whites, HWCUs had a larger share of faculty over the age of 70, 2.1 percent vs. 1.7 percent. But the share of faculty over 65 was significantly larger for HBCUs than HWCUs. On the other hand, HWCUs had a significantly larger share of young faculty than did HBCUs; 3.5 percent of HWCU faculty were under age 30 compared to only 1.2 percent of HBCU faculty.

The highest degree attained and highest degree fields differ considerably between HBCU and HWCU faculties. HBCU faculty are about 47 percent more likely to hold a doctoral degree than HWCU faculty members (58.7 percent vs. 40 percent). At the same time, HWCU faculty are more than 4 times as likely to hold a first professional degree (e.g., JD, MD, etc.) than HBCU faculty who are largely concentrated in institutions offering undergraduate and master's level degree programs. While in the past HBCU faculty were disproportionately trained in education, that appears not to be the case at present. About 15.9 percent of HBCU faculty received their highest degrees in teacher or other education fields, compared with 15.0 percent of HWCU faculty. HWCU faculty are more likely than HBCU faculty to have their highest degrees in engineering (3.5 percent vs. 4.2 percent), fine arts (7.0 percent vs. 4.6 percent), or first-professional health sciences (6.8 percent vs. 1.9 percent).

Faculty Research Productivity

One measure of faculty productivity is the number of publications and presentations produced by individual faculty. Previous research has shown that a small number of faculty account for a disproportionately large share of publications in refereed journals, and that productivity is related to age and discipline.[8] The number of research products published or presented during a career ranges from zero to over 700 among HBCU faculty, and from zero to 1200 for HWCU faculty in our sample. The mean number of items published or presented over their careers is 42.3 among HBCU faculty and 57.6 for HWCU faculty, while the median number of items published or presented is 20 among HBCU faculty and 15 for HWCU faculty. Data for other measures of research productivity appear in Table 1 and indicate that while the mean number of publications and presentations is higher for HWCU faculty, the median is equal or higher for HBCU faculty. The substantial differences between the mean and median measures of research output indicate the wide dispersion and skewed distribution of research output across various faculty groups.

From reviewing the data in Tables 1 and 2 it is apparent that the measure of faculty productivity used makes a difference in how productivity is assessed. What determines the level of faculty productivity and do

TABLE 1
Average Faculty Age and Productivity

	Total Faculty	HBCU Faculty	HWCU Faculty	Female Faculty	Male Faculty	Black Faculty	White Faculty
Age Mean	48.73	51.00	48.69	46.94	49.99	48.51	49.10
S.D.	10.54	9.72	10.54	10.03	10.70	10.31	10.54
Median	49.00	51.00	49.00	47.00	50.00	48.00	49.00
Output1 Mean	4.57	4.36	4.58	2.85	5.78	3.55	4.47
S.D	10.07	9.61	10.08	7.08	11.57	8.25	9.87
Median	0.00	1.00	0.00	0.00	1.00	0.00	0.00
Output2 Mean	13.45	12.14	13.47	9.87	15.96	12.60	13.22
S.D.	29.59	25.25	29.66	23.36	33.04	27.79	28.96
Median	0.00	4.00	4.00	2.00	5.00	3.00	4.00
Output3 Mean	15.28	13.87	15.31	11.17	18.17	14.50	15.03
S.D.	32.62	27.71	32.70	25.46	36.55	30.27	31.84
Median	4.00	5.00	4.00	3.00	5.00	3.00	4.00
Career Mean	57.28	42.29	57.55	36.01	72.21	39.16	50.02
S.D.	118.97	77.45	119.55	88.44	134.38	86.04	103.52
Median	15.00	20.00	15.00	8.00	24.00	10.00	16.00

Source: Author's calculations from 1999 National Study of Postsecondary Faculty.

the determinants of productivity differ across institutional settings and demographic subgroups of faculty?

To answer these questions a series of regression models of the following form were estimated:

Productivity $= f$ (Personal, Institutional, Other) $+ e$

- Where, Productivity is a series of composite variables indicating the numbers of articles published in refereed journals, book chapters, books, presentations, copyrights, and patents acquired in the past two years, or alternately over one's career;
- Personal characteristics variables include age, gender, race and ethnicity, rank, discipline, the number of years since attaining the highest degree, tenure status, and other variables;
- Institutional characteristics include the 1994 Carnegie classification of the school, geographic region, unionization, whether or not the school is an HBCU;
- Other characteristics include the proportion of time spent on research, teaching, service, professional development, and other activities, and other variables.

Models were estimated for the entire sample and for various subsamples using OLS regression. The dependent variables measuring research productivity are censored since they have a lower limit of zero. Therefore, the models were also estimated with Stata using Tobit

Table 2
Variable Means and Standard Deviations

Variable	Obs	Mean	Std. Dev.	Min	Max
hbcu	12401	.0345133	.182551	0	1
black	12401	.0763648	.2655916	0	1
white	12401	.8458995	.3610596	0	1
asian	12401	.0726554	.2595805	0	1
hispanic	12401	.0549956	.2279808	0	1
amerind	12401	.0069349	.0829903	0	1
age	12401	49.01839	9.688053	23	82
agesq	12401	2496.653	958.9266	529	6724
female	12401	.4243206	.4942594	0	1
married	12401	.732199	.4428312	0	1
carneg1	12401	.3420692	.4744218	0	1
carneg2	12401	.1029756	.3039392	0	1
carneg3	12401	.2046609	.4034699	0	1
carneg4	12401	.0300782	.1708095	0	1
carneg5	12401	.0274171	.1633022	0	1
carneg6	12401	.0398355	.1955805	0	1
carneg7	12401	.0033868	.0581001	0	1
carneg8	12401	.1816789	.3855952	0	1
carneg9	12401	.0562051	.2303267	0	1
totlprod	12401	67.7672	117.5982	0	1200
pctteach	12401	.5445158	.290633	0	1
pctresearch	12401	.1590565	.2075476	0	1
pctservice	12401	.0702048	.1444994	0	1
pctprofgro~h	12401	.0456689	.0734643	0	1
pctadmin	12401	.1453592	.2044669	0	1
pctconsultg	12401	.0352794	.0978252	0	1
professor	12401	.2875575	.4526419	0	1
assocprof	12401	.2382872	.4260529	0	1
asstprof	12401	.2367551	.4251079	0	1
instructor	12401	.1307153	.3371023	0	1
lecturer	12401	.0253205	.1571031	0	1
adjunct	12401	.0068543	.0825097	0	1
output1	12401	6.239416	11.36759	0	122
output2	12401	17.29998	31.53606	0	351
output3	12401	19.59439	34.99292	0	417
dependents	12401	1.296186	1.350481	0	5
agric	12401	.022982	.1498521	0	1
business	12401	.0659624	.2482264	0	1
educ	12401	.0758003	.2646891	0	1

Table 2 (cont.)

engin	12401	.0427385	.2022751	0	1
finearts	12401	.0532215	.224484	0	1
health	12401	.1556326	.3625213	0	1
humanities	12401	.1409564	.3479906	0	1
natsci	12401	.1870817	.3899928	0	1
socsci	12401	.1059592	.3077978	0	1
othdisp	12401	.1207161	.3258102	0	1
federalfunds	12401	.1586969	.3654079	0	1
instfunds	12401	.1886138	.3912173	0	1
foundfunds	12401	.1048303	.3063469	0	1
busfunds	12401	.0592694	.2361378	0	1
otherfunds	12401	.0083864	.0911963	0	1
othunivfunds	12401	.002016	.044856	0	1
s_lgovtfunds	12401	.0682203	.2521337	0	1
union	12401	.2153052	.4110505	0	1
foreignborn	12401	.1492622	.3563611	0	1

Variable Definitions:

HBCU	= 1 if student population at least 51 percent Black and Carnegie classification is category 1 through 9, 0 otherwise;
Black	= 1 if faculty race is Black or African-American, 0 otherwise;
White	= 1 if faculty race is White, 0 otherwise;
Asian	= 1 if faculty race is Asian, Native Hawaiian, or Pacific Islander, 0 otherwise;
Hispanic	= 1 if faculty ethnicity is Hispanic, 0 otherwise;
Amerind	= 1 if faculty race is American Indian or Alaska Native, 0 other wise;
Age	= actual age in 1999;
Agesq	= actual age squared;
Female	= 1 if gender is female, 0 otherwise;
Married	= 1 if marital status is married, 0 otherwise;
Carneg1	= 1 if Carnegie classification is Doctoral/Research University-Extensive, 0 otherwise;
Carneg2	= 1 if Carnegie classification is Doctoral/Research University-Intensive, 0 otherwise;
Carneg3	= 1 if Carnegie classification is Masters College or University I, 0 otherwise;
Carneg4	= 1 if Carnegie classification is Masters College or University II, 0 otherwise;
Carneg5	= 1 if Carnegie classification is Baccalaureate College-Liberal Arts, 0 otherwise;
Carneg6	= 1 if Carnegie classification is Baccalaureate College-General, 0 otherwise;

Carneg7	= 1 if Carnegie classification is Baccalaureate/Associates College, 0 otherwise;
Carneg8	= 1 if Carnegie classification is Associates College, 0 otherwise;
Carneg9	= 1 if Carnegie classification is Specialized Institutions (including Schools of Theology, Medicine, Engineering, Business, Arts, and Law), 0 otherwise;
Totlprod	= Career number of sole or jointly authored articles, books, monographs, presentations, copyrights, and patents produced;
Pctteach	= Percent of time spent teaching undergraduate and graduate students during Fall 1998;
Pctresearch	= Percent of time spent on research and scholarship during Fall 1998;
Pctservice	= Percent of time spent on various service activities during Fall 1998;
Pctprofgrth	= Percent of time spent engaged in activities to remain current in the field during Fall 1998;
Pctadmin	= Percent of time spent on departmental or institution-wide meetings or committee work during Fall 1998;
Pctconsultg	= Percent of time spent on outside consulting during Fall 1998;
Professor	= 1 if Rank is Full Professor, 0 otherwise;
Assocprof	= 1 if Rank is Associate Professor, 0 otherwise;
Asstprof	= 1 if Rank is Assistant Professor, 0 otherwise;
Instructor	= 1 if Rank is Instructor, 0 otherwise;
Lecturer	= 1 if Rank is Lecturer, 0 otherwise;
Adjunct	= 1 if Rank is Adjunct, 0 otherwise;
Output1	= Number of sole or jointly authored articles in refereed professional or trade journals, creative works published in juried media, book reviews, chapters in edited volumes, books, monographs, technical reports, patents, or software during the past two years;
Output2	= Output1 and sole or jointly authored presentations at conferences or workshops, exhibitions, or performances in the fine or applied arts during the past two years;
Output3	= Output2 and sole or jointly authored articles in Nonrefereed professional or trade journals, creative works published in nonjuried media or in-house newsletters during the past two years;
Mideast	= 1 if Region is Middle Atlantic states, 0 otherwise;
Southeast	= 1 if Region is Southeastern states, 0 otherwise;
Southwest	= 1 if Region is Southwestern states, 0 otherwise;
Dependents	= Number of dependents;
Agric	= 1 if academic discipline is Agriculture and related fields, 0 otherwise;
Business	= 1 if academic discipline is Business and related fields, 0 otherwise;
Educ	= 1 if academic discipline is Education and related fields, 0 otherwise;
Engin	= 1 if academic discipline is Engineering and related fields, 0 otherwise;
Finearts	= 1 if academic discipline is Fine Arts and related fields, 0 otherwise;

Health	= 1 if academic discipline is Health Sciences and related fields, 0 otherwise;
Humanities	= 1 if academic discipline is Languages and Literatures and related fields, 0 otherwise;
Natsci	= 1 if academic discipline is Biological and Physical Sciences, 0 otherwise;
Socsci	= 1 if academic discipline is Social Sciences and History, 0 otherwise;
Othdisp	= 1 if academic discipline is not one previously listed, 0 otherwise;
Federalfunds	= 1 if research or creative work funded by federal grants, contracts, or institutional awards in Fall 1998, 0 otherwise;
Instfunds	= 1 if research or creative work funded by institution funds in Fall 1998, 0 otherwise;
Foundfunds	= 1 if research or creative work funded by foundation or other nonprofit organization funds in Fall 1998, 0 otherwise;
Busfunds	= 1 if research or creative work funded by for-profit private sector business or industry funds in Fall 1998, 0 otherwise;
Othfunds	= 1 if research or creative work funded by unspecified other funds in Fall 1998, 0 otherwise;
Othunivfunds	= 1 if other university funds used for professional activities, e.g., travel, release time from teaching, sabbatical leave, 0 otherwise;
S_lgovtfunds	= 1 if research or creative work funded by state or local government funds in Fall 1998, 0 otherwise;
Union	= 1 if eligible to join and a member of a union that is the legally recognized representative of the faculty at the institution, 0 otherwise;
Foreignborn	= 1 if country of birth is not USA, 0 otherwise.

regression.[9] Many of the results of the Tobit regressions were similar to the OLS results, but others differed considerably. The Tobit results are reported in Appendix tables.

Some previous studies of faculty productivity have found that women and African-Americans had lower records of productivity compared to men and whites, while Hispanics and Asians had greater productivity. Bellas and Toutkoushian, who used NCES data similar to ours, found that being married and having dependents were each positively related to research output, as was being employed at an institution with doctoral programs.[10] They also found faculty rank to be a significant predictor of research output, with Professors and Associate Professors producing more than Assistant Professors, and Lecturers and Instructors producing less. In addition, their study found that measures of faculty time spent teaching or engaged in service activities, were both negatively related to research output.[11] One important limitation of the Bellas-Toutkoushian study is their use of OLS regression to estimate faculty output. As indicated earlier, OLS regression where the dependent variable is censored results in biased and inconsistent estimates.

Results for the Total Sample

Our results for the total sample of full-time faculty are given in the Appendix tables. They suggest that other things equal, women faculty are somewhat less productive than male faculty when measured in terms of our narrowest indicator of faculty output, but the difference is not statistically significant. Other measures of output in the past two years show no significant differences by gender. However, career productivity is significantly lower for female faculty than that of their male counterparts: other things equal, women have 13.4 fewer products over their careers than comparable male faculty members.

Marital status has no significant impact on various types of research produced in the past two years, but being married is negatively related to career output, a difference that is significant at the 10 percent level; while having dependents is positively and significantly related to productivity. Race and ethnicity are not significant predictors of research output within the past two years, but African Americans have significantly lower career output, the difference significant at the 10 percent level. We introduced a variable indicating whether the individual was foreign or U.S.-born, regardless of citizenship status. Being foreign-born was significantly related to increased research productivity both within the past two years and over a career. The difference was significant at the .001 level. The foreign-born variable may be picking up the effect that other researchers observed with ethnic and race dummies for Hispanic and Asian.[12]

We find no significant effects of age on faculty publications of refereed journal articles or books within the past two years. However, there is a significant curvilinear relationship between age and productivity in the past two years when output is measured in broader terms. The effect of age on broader measures of productivity within the past two years is significant at the 10 percent level, and maximum productivity is indicated slightly above age 54.[13]

Despite the complementarities that we often acknowledge exist between research and teaching, particularly graduate-level teaching, most of the empirical literature [e.g., Bellas and Toutkoushian; Nettles and Perna (1995)] indicates that there is competition between research output and time spent teaching. Our results support those earlier findings, and indicate that, other things equal, there is a significant negative effect of increased time spent on teaching and research output, however it is measured.

Other uses of time are ambiguous in their impact on research productivity, except time spent on consulting activity. It has a surprisingly consistent positive impact on research productivity across each of the various measures of output. While consulting activity may be thought to compete with research, it actually appears to be complementary, resulting in increased levels of research output in the short-term as well as in terms of career faculty productivity. Since we cannot distinguish types of clients we cannot determine whether it is the nature of the consultancy, the client, or the consultant that accounts for this positive relationship between time spent consulting and research output.

Faculty rank has the expected effects on research output. Full professors produce significantly more research in the short term (two years) and over their careers than do those of more junior rank. Associate professors produce significantly less research than full professors but more than Assistant Professors (the excluded category). Finally, Lecturers and Instructors produce less research than Assistant Professors, but the magnitudes and significance of the difference vary with the measure of output chosen.

Regional location dummy variables for the Mideast (Middle Atlantic) and Southeast were significant and negative compared to the omitted New England and Western categories.

Contrary to our expectations, the dummy variable for HBCUs was consistently *positive* and significant in two of the four measures of faculty productivity; the broadest measure of output in the past two years and career productivity. This is a surprising result given the substantial differences apparent in the univariate measures of faculty productivity for HBCU and HWCU faculty in the Appendix tables. It suggests that after controlling for other variables related to faculty productivity such as personal characteristics, time spent on teaching and consulting, location, and other factors, HBCU faculty are actually somewhat more productive than their HWCU counterparts. Differences between HBCU and HWCU faculty are explored further below.

Dummy variables for discipline are usually significant and indicate wide variation in the level of research productivity in the short- and long-term. Our findings are consistent with earlier research that showed many fewer articles published in the natural sciences than in other disciplines, for example, health, social sciences, and humanities.[14]

Levin and Stephan hypothesized that receipt of federal research support would be a determinant of academic scientists' research productivity. Although they do not report these specific results, they indicate that their findings were consistent with their expectations.[15] Our results demonstrate that source of research funding is significantly related to faculty research productivity for the entire sample. Federal support is strongly related to research productivity and its importance is greater the broader the definition of output used. Non-federal sources of research support are also generally associated with increased research productivity, except state and local government funding which sometimes enters the equations with a negative sign but is never statistically significant. Of course, we cannot ignore the possible simultaneity inherent in the receipt of research support and productivity: those who are most productive will be able to attract more support which in turn will aid their efforts to be productive. Nonetheless, the findings relative to source of support as a factor in faculty research productivity are noteworthy.[16]

Other things being equal, being foreign-born is positively related to increased faculty productivity, both within the past two years and over one's career. We have no ready explanation for this finding, which is consistent across various model specifications. One possible explanation is related to self-selection of productive foreign-born faculty into U.S. universities. We are not aware of any previous research that investigates the relationship between place of birth or citizenship and faculty productivity. Indeed, the research on race, ethnicity, and gender correlates of faculty productivity is sparse. This result bears further scrutiny.[17]

Years since achieving tenure never enters the equations for the total sample significantly, although the variable has a nominally negative effect on research output that would indicate a sort of "retirement in place" effect. Being a member of a union has a consistently significant negative effect on faculty productivity, other things equal. The literature on faculty unions suggests that their presence may reduce the rewards administrators are able to use to recognize individual faculty achievement. This may result in diminished incentives for faculty to produce research. An alternative explanation is that union membership is endogenous and related to personal or institutional characteristics. As with some other variables, the effect of union membership is significant and the magnitude of its impact is greater the broader the outcome measure. This result also bears further investigation.[18]

Carnegie Classification Variables

Introducing Carnegie classification variables appreciably changes the results for the total sample in only a few areas. Most notably, perhaps, once Carnegie classification indicators are included the HBCU variable becomes insignificant in each equation predicting faculty productivity. Apparently, in earlier equations the HBCU variable may have acted as a proxy for institutional characteristics such as size, teaching load, resources, teaching orientation, and the like that the Carnegie classifications are able to distinguish. Interaction terms between HBCU and the various Carnegie classification variables were all insignificant.[19]

Agesa, Granger, and Price have noted that the majority of HBCUs are classified as Masters (Comprehensive) Colleges and Universities I or below, and are thus primarily teaching institutions.[20] Our analysis uses a definition of HBCUs that is based on characteristics of the student population, and thus includes a broader group of institutions than that studied by Agesa, Granger, and Price.

Other Regression Results

Tobit regression models of faculty research productivity were estimated separately for HBCU and HWCU faculty, male and female faculty, and black and white faculty. The results for publications in the past two years and career productivity appear in the Appendix and are briefly summarized below.

HBCU-HWCU Faculty Differences

Among HBCU faculty, publications in the past two years are significantly related to faculty rank (Professor), region (Southeast), discipline (Social Sciences), and source of funding (federal or institutional funds); all have a positive impact on productivity. Career productivity for HBCU faculty is negatively related to marital status, and positively related to Hispanic origin (with an implausibly large positive effect), faculty rank (Professor), discipline (Fine Arts and Humanities), and source of funding (federal and institutional funds). Some of our results for all HBCU faculty mirror those of Agesa, Granger, and Price for HBCU economics faculty. Specifically, they found that while non-HBCU economics faculty tended to have a steady stream of publications over their careers, research productivity among HBCU economics faculty was strongly associated with having the rank of Full Professor and/or having greater years of experience.

Agesa, Granger, and Price, suggest that institutional differences in incentives and expectations between HBCUs and non-HBCUs account for the finding. They argue that HBCUs may place more emphasis on teaching generally than their HWCU counterparts, and that only with the acquisition of advanced standing (rank and years of experience) are HBCU faculty able to engage more in research activities.[21] A complementary explanation is that HBCUs may not be as likely to provide the mentorship and resources (including time away from teaching) that result in research and publications even if there is an avowed value placed on scholarship.

Not surprisingly, the results for HWCU faculty mirror those for the total sample with significant impacts of the time allocation variables, rank, Carnegie classification, discipline, source of research funding, years since attaining tenure, and whether foreign-born. Career productivity among HWCU faculty is negatively related to gender (female), time spent teaching, or union membership, and positively related to time spent in service activities or consulting, faculty rank (Professor), region (Southeast), Carnegie classification, source of funding, and foreign-born.

Female-Male Faculty Differences

Among female faculty members having dependents was positively associated with publications during the past two years. Time allocation, i.e., the percent of time spent teaching, or in professional growth activities both negatively impact women faculty's short-term research productivity. Faculty rank (Professor or Associate Professor) is positively related to research output, as are (generally) the Carnegie classification of the institution in which the woman teaches, her discipline, and the source of research funding (federal or institutional funds). Being foreign-born is also positively associated with increased short-term research productivity among women faculty.

Short-term male faculty research productivity is also positively associated with having dependents. The percent of time spent teaching negatively affects male faculty research output in the past two years; while time spent consulting has a positive impact. In the short-term, being a Professor is the only rank that matters for predicting research output among male faculty, while being in other than the reference Carnegie classification of institution, when it matters, negatively affects research productivity. Source of research funding typically matters more for predicting male faculty productivity than that of women. And years since attaining tenure has a negative effect on faculty productivity, while being foreign-born has a positive impact.

Women's career research productivity appears to be strongly associated with age in the manner observed in the results for the total sample, contrasting sharply with the findings for male career productivity. While there is no significant effect of age in the model predicting male faculty career productivity, the results for females are statistically significant at the 1 percent level and imply productivity peaking around 57 years of age. The different gender patterns of age effects on career productivity bear further investigation.

Other factors that affect women's career productivity include time spent teaching (negatively), faculty rank (Professor), Carnegie classification, discipline, and source of research funding. Other things equal, among women faculty time since attaining tenure is positively associated with greater career research productivity. Finally, foreign-born women faculty have greater career productivity than their native-born counterparts.

We have noted the significant difference in the effect that age has in predicting male and female career research productivity. Besides this finding there are perhaps more similarities in the predictors of male and female career productivity than differences. A notable exception is the effect of union membership. While union status has no impact on women's research productivity it has a significant negative impact on men's. This finding appears to be at variance with a substantial literature on union impact on productivity in education and elsewhere and suggests the need for further investigation. The most likely explanation is that self-selection is at work. That is, faculty who are more likely to join faculty unions may be more likely to have personal or institutional characteristics associated with lower productivity.

Black-White Faculty Differences

A small number of variables are significant predictors of black faculty research productivity in the short-term. Having dependents is positively related to increased faculty productivity, as is having the rank of full professor. Black faculty at community colleges have significantly lower short-term research output than their counterparts at specialized institutions. Receipt of foundation funding, time since achieving tenure, and being foreign-born all have significant positive impacts on black faculty research output in the short-term. Results for short-term productivity of white faculty closely follow those for the total sample, including significant effects of time spent teaching, faculty rank, Carnegie classification, discipline, source of research funding, and being foreign-born. For white faculty, years since attaining tenure has a negative effect on short-term research productivity. Recently tenured faculty are more likely to have produced research in the preceding two years, other things equal.

A somewhat larger though still minimal number of variables is significant in predicting career productivity among black faculty. None of the personal characteristics variables is significant (gender, marital status, dependents, age). Time spent teaching has a large significant negative impact on career research productivity of black faculty. Faculty rank has a positive impact on productivity (Professor and Instructor), but other things equal, Carnegie classification of the institution does not matter. Some of the disciplinary dummies are significantly related to career output, as is receipt of federal research funding. Finally, the impact of being foreign-born has the expected positive impact on career productivity of black faculty, while surprisingly time since receipt of tenure has a positive impact. That is, among black faculty greater career output is associated with longer time in tenured status. This may be related to the institutional characteristics of colleges and universities where large numbers of black faculty are employed (i.e., HBCUs), if, for example, they are more likely to impose heavier teaching loads on junior than senior faculty. This result also bears further investigation.

Among white faculty, the determinants of career productivity generally follow those for the total sample. Other things equal, gender and place of birth are the only personal characteristics significantly associated with career output. Women faculty members have significantly lower career output than their white male counterparts, and foreign-born whites have significantly higher career output than native-born whites. Other things equal, we find no age-related variation in career research output among white faculty. This result runs counter to our expectations, and the findings for various faculty subgroups. Time spent teaching lowers career research production while time spent consulting or in service activities appears to increase research output. Faculty rank matters for white faculty in the expected manner, but only faculty employed at Doctoral/Research-Extensive universities have significantly greater career research output than those in the reference group. Discipline matters, as does source of funding. Again we find that union membership is significantly negatively related to faculty research productivity; in this case the career research productivity of white faculty. Our previous caveats notwithstanding, this result certainly bears further investigation.

Conclusion

Previous studies of faculty research productivity have often focused on the determinants of research output within a discipline or a limited number of disciplines, or within certain categories of institutions. Those studies have often, but not always, been constrained in the conclusions that could be drawn because of small sample sizes. Our analysis involves the use of a national probability sample of college and university faculty collected by the National Center for Education Statistics and attempts to identify the determinants of faculty research productivity and to determine whether there are systematic differences in the determinants across types of institutions and demographic subgroups of faculty.

Our analysis shows that, other things equal, if no other institutional factors are considered, HBCU faculty in fact have *greater* research productivity in the short- and long-run than their non-HBCU counterparts. However, when account is taken of the size, level of instruction, and other factors implicit in the Carnegie classifications, there are no significant differences between HBCU and HWCU faculty in terms of their short- or long-run research output.

In addition, there are significant differences in the determinants of faculty productivity by gender. Other things equal, women's career research productivity is significantly related to age, while men's is not. Our results indicate that women's productivity exhibits a clear life-cycle pattern increasing steeply at the early ages and reaching a peak around age fifty-seven. By contrast, male faculty productivity is relatively constant throughout. Among male faculty a noteworthy finding is the apparent strong negative association of union membership and research productivity. This result suggests the presence of self-selection bias that further research should take into account.

Finally, our models perform poorly in predicting research productivity among Black faculty. Among the significant factors found are having dependents, faculty rank, discipline, source of research funding, and foreign birth. On the other hand, the predictors of research productivity for white faculty are generally the same as for the total sample and for HWCUs. As expected, we find that time spent in teaching lowers research productivity among white faculty, but there is no significant pattern of age and productivity among White faculty, other things equal. The negative association of union membership and research productivity among White faculty suggests the possibility of self-selection of union members in the sample.

Earlier in the paper we noted the significant difference in the average age of HBCU and HWCU faculty. The looming retirement of large
numbers of African-American faculty at HBCUs may result in those
institutions becoming less diverse, less the homes for African-American
faculty development and nurturing. If faculty interested in teaching at
HBCUs are not being produced, or if such faculty cannot be retained, the
fate of HBCUs and students interested in attending them are problematic.
The findings of the current study regarding faculty productivity suggest
that the characteristics of individual faculty interact with institutional
characteristics to determine faculty research productivity. HBCUs, like
other teaching-oriented colleges and universities, have lower faculty
research productivity in significant part because of the emphasis they
place on their teaching mission.[22]

APPENDIX TABLES
Total Sample Results Productivity In The Past Two Years

Tobit estimates

Number of obs	= 6414
LR chi^2 (44)	= 2125.35
Prob > chi^2	= 0.0000
Pseudo R^2	= 0.0514

Log likelihood = −19601.45

output1	Coef.	Std. Err.	t	P > |t|	[95% Conf. Interval]	
female	−.6090158	.4914059	−1.24	0.215	−1.572337	.3543052
married	.4617347	.5333862	0.87	0.387	−.5838817	1.507351
dependents	.6032019	.1707943	3.53	0.000	.2683876	.9380163
black	−.7985571	.9677209	−0.83	0.409	−2.695616	1.098502
asian	−.5821406	.9225751	−0.63	0.528	−2.390698	1.226417
hispanic	.7678425	1.006217	0.76	0.445	−1.204682	2.740367
age	.3469328	.2510422	1.38	0.167	−.1451944	.83906
agesq	−.0029199	.0023407	−1.25	0.212	−.0075085	.0016687
pctteach	−4.970435	.9326848	−5.33	0.000	−6.798811	−3.142059
pctservice	−3.110538	2.01385	−1.54	0.122	−7.058361	.8372859
pctprofgro−h	−4.955096	3.031612	−1.63	0.102	−10.89807	.987883
pctconsultg	5.231273	2.448169	2.14	0.033	.4320388	10.03051
professor	6.127698	.8023131	7.64	0.000	4.554894	7.700501
assocprof	1.669081	.8099391	2.06	0.039	.0813276	3.256834
instructor	−.9901919	1.43569	−0.69	0.490	−3.804627	1.824243
lecturer	−11.60134	5.401532	−2.15	0.032	−22.19016	−1.01252
mideast	.0083953	.0149857	0.56	0.575	−.0209816	.0377723
southeast	.0137181	.0227083	0.60	0.546	−.0307978	.058234
carneg1	1.510142	1.020665	1.48	0.139	−.4907047	3.510988
carneg2	−1.599748	1.146059	−1.40	0.163	−3.846409	.6469122
carneg3	−5.432291	1.078139	−5.04	0.000	−7.545806	−3.318777
carneg4	−7.94937	1.683476	−4.72	0.000	−11.24955	−4.649191
carneg5	−4.488196	1.552848	−2.89	0.004	−7.532301	−1.444092
carneg6	−10.43129	1.543526	−6.76	0.000	−13.45712	−7.405464
carneg7	−14.51527	4.175129	−3.48	0.001	−22.69993	−6.330615
carneg8	−14.60352	1.228844	−11.88	0.000	−17.01247	−12.19457
agric	−.7891454	1.436137	−0.55	0.583	−3.604456	2.026166
educ	3.338058	1.089664	3.06	0.002	1.20195	5.474166
engin	3.862716	1.16536	3.31	0.001	1.578218	6.147215
finearts	−2.492407	1.18325	−2.11	0.035	−4.811975	−.1728383
health	2.995135	.9962217	3.01	0.003	1.042206	4.948065
humanities	5.084175	.9253128	5.49	0.000	3.270251	6.8981
natsci	1.186498	.894792	1.33	0.185	−.5675952	2.940592
socsci	4.311838	.9408873	4.58	0.000	2.467382	6.156293
othdisp	1.287903	.9689892	1.33	0.184	−.6116422	3.187447
federalfunds	5.913478	.5922195	9.99	0.000	4.752528	7.074427
instfunds	1.741635	.5143391	3.39	0.001	.7333573	2.749913
foundfunds	3.644287	.6562423	5.55	0.000	2.357831	4.930742
busfunds	2.17497	.8306456	2.62	0.009	.5466249	3.803314
othunivfunds	−.5926311	4.459728	−0.13	0.894	−9.335198	8.149936
s_lgovtfunds	−.5479416	.7844797	−0.70	0.485	−2.085786	.9899025
tenuryrs	−.0790981	.0322662	−2.45	0.014	−.1423507	−.0158454
foreignborn	4.146207	.6367797	6.51	0.000	2.897905	5.39451
union	−.1445483	.519798	−0.28	0.781	−1.163527	.8744306
_cons	−7.619869	6.842056	−1.11	0.265	−21.0326	5.792862
_se	15.07141	.1634516			(Ancillary parameter)	

Obs. summary:	1943	left-censored observations at output1 ≤ 0
	4471	uncensored observations

Total Sample Results Career Productivity

Tobit estimates

Number of obs = 6414
LR chi^2 (44) = 2173.82
Prob > chi^2 = 0.0000
Pseudo R^2 = 0.0288

Log likelihood = −36644.679

totlprod	Coef.	Std. Err.	t	P > |t|	[95% Conf. Interval]	
female	−13.47947	3.830417	−3.52	0.000	−20.98837	−5.970562
married	−7.182078	4.144222	−1.73	0.083	−15.30615	.9419905
dependents	2.213045	1.348665	1.64	0.101	−.4307922	4.856882
black	−12.93626	7.544912	−1.71	0.086	−27.72683	1.854302
asian	−7.783052	7.385893	−1.05	0.292	−22.26189	6.695785
hispanic	−7.566038	7.974008	−0.95	0.343	−23.19778	8.0657
age	2.262672	1.942672	1.16	0.244	−1.545619	6.070963
agesq	−.0086799	.0181213	−0.48	0.632	−.0442038	.026844
pctteach	−34.70323	7.339755	−4.73	0.000	−49.09162	−20.31484
pctservice	43.1382	15.97043	2.70	0.007	11.83078	74.44562
pctprofgro~h	−21.57456	23.46376	−0.92	0.358	−67.57143	24.42231
pctconsultg	97.00143	19.29691	5.03	0.000	59.173	134.8299
professor	38.02084	5.981387	6.36	0.000	26.29531	49.74637
assocprof	−8.312234	6.042536	−1.38	0.169	−20.15764	3.533169
instructor	−12.22182	9.968532	−1.23	0.220	−31.7635	7.319854
lecturer	−42.16016	35.01378	−1.20	0.229	−110.799	26.47863
mideast	−.24433	.116479	−2.10	0.036	−.472668	−.015992
southeast	.3248865	.1712034	1.90	0.058	−.0107298	.6605028
carneg1	22.06402	8.26571	2.67	0.008	5.860447	38.26759
carneg2	−4.750538	9.260887	−0.51	0.608	−22.90499	13.40392
carneg3	−31.3753	8.662688	−3.62	0.000	−48.35708	−14.39351
carneg4	−37.5164	13.01067	−2.89	0.004	−63.12169	−12.1111
carneg5	−26.00537	12.35627	−2.10	0.035	−50.22782	−1.782924
carneg6	−49.90037	11.86289	−4.21	0.000	−73.15563	−26.64511
carneg7	−56.60871	28.08351	−2.02	0.044	−111.6618	−1.555595
carneg8	−81.78677	9.551349	−8.56	0.000	−100.5106	−63.06292
agric	60.49346	11.32146	5.34	0.000	38.29958	82.68734
educ	45.00068	8.482636	5.31	0.000	28.37186	61.6295
engin	9.025793	9.252428	0.98	0.329	−9.112079	27.16367
finearts	82.27461	8.88106	9.26	0.000	64.86475	99.68448
health	46.44084	7.744391	6.00	0.000	31.25923	61.62246
humanities	23.40412	7.171204	3.26	0.001	9.346151	37.4621
natsci	8.958976	6.921793	1.29	0.196	−4.610068	22.52802
socsci	19.98933	7.346018	2.72	0.007	5.588664	34.39
othdisp	12.20531	7.467781	1.63	0.102	−2.43405	26.84468
federalfunds	54.265	4.831603	11.23	0.000	44.79343	63.73657
instfunds	8.892149	4.13769	2.15	0.032	.7808854	17.00341
foundfunds	31.02844	5.367757	5.78	0.000	20.50583	41.55105
busfunds	44.58391	6.811046	6.55	0.000	31.23197	57.93585
othunivfunds	4.006865	35.06118	0.11	0.909	−64.72484	72.73857
s_lgovtfunds	−3.576611	6.361547	−0.56	0.574	−16.04738	8.894162
tenuryrs	.2591257	.2504543	1.03	0.301	−.231849	.7501004
foreignborn	16.96525	5.11358	3.32	0.001	6.94091	26.98958
union	−7.9125	4.023898	−1.97	0.049	−15.80069	−.0243066
_cons	−30.68361	53.03681	−0.58	0.563	−134.6536	73.28638
_se	124.9904	1.167561			(Ancillary parameter)	

Obs. summary: 616   left-censored observations at totlprod ≤ 0
                   5798   uncensored observations

HBCU Results Productivity in the Past Two Years

Tobit estimates

Number of obs = 428
LR chi^2 (29) = 121.28
Prob > chi^2 = 0.0000

Log likelihood = −1042.7582

Pseudo R^2 = 0.0550

output1	Coef.	Std. Err.	t	P > |t|	[95% Conf. Interval]	
black	−4.029371	1.586813	−2.54	0.011	−7.14893	−.9098119
asian	−6.746203	3.00686	−2.24	0.025	−12.65747	−.8349354
hispanic	−10.73818	4.972638	−2.16	0.031	−20.51402	−.9623316
age	−.0661877	.6029299	−0.11	0.913	−1.251504	1.119129
agesq	.000675	.0057899	0.12	0.907	−.0107076	.0120576
pctteach	−3.363458	3.079297	−1.09	0.275	−9.417131	2.690216
pctservice	5.438496	6.728715	0.81	0.419	−7.789669	18.66666
pctprofgro~h	−4.238234	7.846752	−0.54	0.589	−19.66438	11.18791
pctconsultg	−1.515302	5.429856	−0.28	0.780	−12.19	9.159401
professor	6.699269	2.113817	3.17	0.002	2.543659	10.85488
assocprof	3.133334	1.893721	1.65	0.099	−.5895835	6.856251
instructor	−6.82894	2.493649	−2.74	0.006	−11.73127	−1.926607
lecturer	−8.368748	4.643576	−1.80	0.072	−17.49768	.760184
mideast	.0729939	.0721467	1.01	0.312	−.0688414	.2148291
southeast	.7940104	.3393638	2.34	0.020	.1268459	1.461175
dependents	.9577099	.4969252	1.93	0.055	−.019209	1.934629
agric	2.077924	4.321636	0.48	0.631	−6.418098	10.57395
educ	−1.912109	3.014276	−0.63	0.526	−7.837957	4.013739
engin	3.815484	4.470484	0.85	0.394	−4.973163	12.60413
finearts	3.940756	3.221815	1.22	0.222	−2.393097	10.27461
health	2.918443	3.049376	0.96	0.339	−3.076408	8.913294
humanities	−.2050355	2.700226	−0.08	0.940	−5.513485	5.103413
natsci	3.016593	2.522344	1.20	0.232	−1.942151	7.975337
socsci	6.792844	3.000739	2.26	0.024	.8936093	12.69208
othdisp	−1.81579	2.679372	−0.68	0.498	−7.08324	3.451661
federalfunds	4.680224	1.75119	2.67	0.008	1.237512	8.122936
foreignborn	4.526442	1.878602	2.41	0.016	.833247	8.219636
union	−.5394774	2.248816	−0.24	0.811	−4.960487	3.881532
tenured	1.072388	1.744026	0.61	0.539	−2.35624	4.501017
_cons	−6.757342	17.38662	−0.39	0.698	−40.93818	27.42349
_se	11.7888	.5595337			(Ancillary parameter)	

Obs. summary: 186   left-censored observations at output1 ≤ 0
                 242   uncensored observations

HWCU Results Productivity in the Past Two Years

Tobit estimates

Number of obs = 11973
LR chi^2 (29) = 3061.82
Prob > chi^2 = 0.0000

Log likelihood = −33493.745

Pseudo R^2 = 0.0437

output1	Coef.	Std. Err.	t	P > |t|	[95% Conf. Interval]	
black	−.9767198	.6494541	−1.50	0.133	−2.249756	.2963158
asian	.3228214	.5980067	0.54	0.589	−.8493689	1.495012
hispanic	.9470516	.6447945	1.47	0.142	−.3168504	2.210954
age	−.0289391	.1266511	−0.23	0.819	−.2771958	.2193176
agesq	−.0001984	.0012688	−0.16	0.876	−.0026855	.0022886
pctteach	−8.85283	.5870214	−15.08	0.000	−10.00349	−7.702173
pctservice	−3.237426	1.104289	−2.93	0.003	−5.402012	−1.07284
pctprofgro~h	−16.99472	2.106048	−8.07	0.000	−21.12292	−12.86652
pctconsultg	−.708864	1.532426	−0.46	0.644	−3.712669	2.294941
professor	7.246407	.48371	14.98	0.000	6.298257	8.194557
assocprof	3.190095	.4490046	7.10	0.000	2.309973	4.070217
instructor	−6.872402	.5396429	−12.74	0.000	−7.93019	−5.814615
lecturer	−3.956691	.9931472	−3.98	0.000	−5.903421	−2.009961
mideast	−.084629	.0156288	−5.41	0.000	−.1152639	−.053994
southeast	−.0522969	.014615	−3.58	0.000	−.0809446	−.0236492
dependents	.3775442	.1069662	3.53	0.000	.167873	.5872154
agric	2.785756	1.016914	2.74	0.006	.79244	4.779073
educ	3.267389	.6948322	4.70	0.000	1.905405	4.629373
engin	5.31363	.8114656	6.55	0.000	3.723026	6.904235
finearts	.5993196	.7943349	0.75	0.451	−.957706	2.156345
health	4.374734	.5985044	7.31	0.000	3.201568	5.547899
humanities	5.183572	.6049134	8.57	0.000	3.997844	6.369301
natsci	2.102688	.5798259	3.63	0.000	.9661348	3.239241
socsci	4.56418	.6288165	7.26	0.000	3.331598	5.796763
othdisp	2.138018	.6272202	3.41	0.001	.9085646	3.367472
federalfunds	8.22029	.3978653	20.66	0.000	7.44041	9.000171
foreignborn	4.014968	.4454987	9.01	0.000	3.141718	4.888218
union	−2.202497	.3567026	−6.17	0.000	−2.901692	−1.503302
tenured	.7206396	.4057592	1.78	0.076	−.0747144	1.515994
_cons	3.115926	3.096343	1.01	0.314	−2.95341	9.185262
_se	13.92745	.1172042		(Ancillary parameter)		

Obs. summary: 4364   left-censored observations at output1 ≤ 0
                  7609   uncensored observations

HBCU Results Career Productivity

Tobit estimates

Number of obs = 186
LR chi^2 (39) = 68.15
Prob > chi^2 = 0.0026
Log likelihood = −984.10212

Pseudo R^2 = 0.0335

totlprod	Coef.	Std. Err.	t	P > |t|	[95% Conf. Interval]	
female	−9.079175	13.16508	−0.69	0.492	−35.09644	16.93809
married	−26.44978	14.06927	−1.88	0.062	−54.25393	1.354383
dependents	5.764712	5.10338	1.13	0.260	−4.320759	15.85018
black	1.440815	15.69422	0.09	0.927	−29.57463	32.45626
asian	−2.759855	26.37377	−0.10	0.917	−54.88058	49.36087
hispanic	208.8699	57.86303	3.61	0.000	94.5191	323.2208
age	7.619855	8.591527	0.89	0.377	−9.359008	24.59872
agesq	−.0588601	.0756944	−0.78	0.438	−.2084499	.0907298
pctteach	−13.99717	24.8967	−0.56	0.575	−63.19886	35.20452
pctservice	−5.352639	64.17818	−0.08	0.934	−132.1837	121.4784
pctprofgro~h	20.10965	66.39651	0.30	0.762	−111.1053	151.3246
pctconsultg	−30.90965	53.88753	−0.57	0.567	−137.404	75.58468
professor	34.93552	18.16983	1.92	0.056	−.9723024	70.84333
assocprof	16.90948	18.11155	0.93	0.352	−18.88317	52.70212
instructor	7.84283	77.36473	0.10	0.919	−145.0479	160.7336
lecturer	−17.70378	64.75398	−0.27	0.785	−145.6727	110.2652
mideast	.1045694	.6954698	0.15	0.881	−1.269841	1.47898
southeast	2.498603	3.359233	0.74	0.458	−4.140025	9.137232
carneg1	−22.4827	21.86439	−1.03	0.306	−65.69183	20.72643
carneg2	−4.287368	21.81094	−0.20	0.844	−47.39087	38.81614
carneg3	−25.87059	17.34053	−1.49	0.138	−60.13953	8.39834
carneg6	−34.86988	22.09559	−1.58	0.117	−78.53592	8.79617
agric	−25.05164	39.18653	−0.64	0.524	−102.4934	52.39009
educ	10.94385	26.66716	0.41	0.682	−41.75668	63.64437
engin	26.15586	40.60726	0.64	0.521	−54.09356	106.4053
finearts	63.16663	26.80143	2.36	0.020	10.20074	116.1325
health	29.36083	32.11035	0.91	0.362	−34.09671	92.81837
humanities	39.18913	23.76985	1.65	0.101	−7.785627	86.16389
natsci	33.27642	22.92023	1.45	0.149	−12.01931	78.57215
socsci	23.14641	26.34088	0.88	0.381	−28.90932	75.20213
othdisp	24.99877	24.14649	1.04	0.302	−22.72033	72.71787
federalfunds	67.50509	17.34343	3.89	0.000	33.23043	101.7798
instfunds	28.74699	15.00091	1.92	0.057	−.8983128	58.3923
foundfunds	−17.08877	20.76379	−0.82	0.412	−58.12287	23.94533
busfunds	7.650442	30.60926	0.25	0.803	−52.84059	68.14148
s_lgovtfunds	4.906217	21.97477	0.22	0.824	−38.52106	48.33349
tenuryrs	−.351031	.848353	−0.41	0.680	−2.027574	1.325512
foreignborn	28.41428	18.20717	1.56	0.121	−7.567341	64.3959
union	7.496237	19.72211	0.38	0.704	−31.47925	46.47173
_cons	−223.9371	246.52	−0.91	0.365	−711.1181	263.2438
_se	71.39721	3.894009		(Ancillary parameter)		

Obs. summary:	15	left-censored observations at totlprod ≤ 0
	171	uncensored observations

HWCU Results Career Productivity

Tobit estimates

Number of obs = 6228
LR chi^2 (44) = 2132.23
Prob > chi^2 = 0.0000

Log likelihood = −35608.203

Pseudo R^2 = 0.0291

totlprod	Coef.	Std. Err.	t	P > |t|	[95% Conf. Interval]	
female	−13.64005	3.927239	−3.47	0.001	−21.33881	−5.941299
married	−6.749683	4.247798	−1.59	0.112	−15.07684	1.577478
dependents	2.142882	1.381441	1.55	0.121	−.5652226	4.850987
black	−11.55728	8.208663	−1.41	0.159	−27.64912	4.53455
asian	−7.61149	7.580708	−1.00	0.315	−22.47231	7.249334
hispanic	−8.141507	8.082065	−1.01	0.314	−23.98516	7.702152
age	1.923399	1.988066	0.97	0.333	−1.973901	5.820698
agesq	−.0053439	.0185835	−0.29	0.774	−.0417741	.0310862
pctteach	−35.34245	7.525237	−4.70	0.000	−50.09453	−20.59037
pctservice	42.38101	16.29634	2.60	0.009	10.43452	74.3275
pctprofgro~h	−24.18604	24.28268	−1.00	0.319	−71.78853	23.41646
pctconsultg	104.0859	19.94733	5.22	0.000	64.98221	143.1896
professor	37.56361	6.173111	6.09	0.000	25.46217	49.66505
assocprof	−9.226109	6.242334	−1.48	0.139	−21.46325	3.011035
instructor	−13.04685	10.11035	−1.29	0.197	−32.86666	6.77295
lecturer	−46.78177	37.54884	−1.25	0.213	−120.3905	26.82701
mideast	−.2811698	.1967719	−1.43	0.153	−.6669111	.1045714
southeast	.3213177	.1728032	1.86	0.063	−.0174367	.6600722
carneg1	22.39662	8.342338	2.68	0.007	6.042742	38.75051
carneg2	−4.26515	9.378855	−0.45	0.649	−22.65097	14.12067
carneg3	−31.31514	8.761415	−3.57	0.000	−48.49056	−14.13972
carneg4	−45.5745	13.96815	−3.26	0.001	−72.95693	−18.19207
carneg5	−25.97448	12.47003	−2.08	0.037	−50.42008	−1.528882
carneg6	−51.0621	12.46388	−4.10	0.000	−75.49564	−26.62855
carneg7	−56.44686	28.31287	−1.99	0.046	−111.9499	−.9437996
carneg8	−81.43739	9.674426	−8.42	0.000	−100.4026	−62.47215
agric	62.47974	11.62764	5.37	0.000	39.68553	85.27396
educ	47.00933	8.712955	5.40	0.000	29.92891	64.08975
engin	8.172337	9.435341	0.87	0.386	−10.32421	26.66889
finearts	83.30524	9.139988	9.11	0.000	65.38768	101.2228
health	46.11629	7.915932	5.83	0.000	30.59831	61.63427
humanities	23.29732	7.356976	3.17	0.002	8.875087	37.71955
natsci	7.794756	7.099037	1.10	0.272	−6.121823	21.71134
socsci	19.50902	7.522198	2.59	0.010	4.762892	34.25514
othdisp	11.46545	7.666851	1.50	0.135	−3.564242	26.49514
federalfunds	54.66244	4.968465	11.00	0.000	44.92252	64.40236
instfunds	8.761141	4.238181	2.07	0.039	.4528325	17.06945
foundfunds	31.4545	5.489	5.73	0.000	20.69415	42.21485
busfunds	45.87302	6.941625	6.61	0.000	32.26502	59.48102
othunivfunds	4.052043	35.34139	0.11	0.909	−65.22936	73.33345
s_lgovtfunds	−5.03188	6.528392	−0.77	0.441	−17.8298	7.766038
tenuryrs	.2727327	.2572539	1.06	0.289	−.2315743	.7770397
foreignborn	15.88429	5.254714	3.02	0.003	5.583228	26.18536
union	−8.38177	4.10288	−2.04	0.041	−16.42484	−.3386981
_cons	−21.21122	54.1444	−0.39	0.695	−127.3531	84.93062
_se	125.9462	1.194283			(Ancillary parameter)	

Obs. summary: 601   left-censored observations at totlprod ≤ 0
                5627   uncensored observations

Female Results Productivity in the Past Two Years

Tobit estimates

Number of obs = 2197
LR chi^2 (44) = 756.87
Prob > chi^2 = 0.0000
Pseudo R^2 = 0.0606

Log likelihood = −5863.0738

output1	Coef.	Std. Err.	t	P > |t|	[95% Conf. Interval]	
married	.8705694	.6456988	1.35	0.178	−.3956889	2.136828
dependents	.8718242	.2698293	3.23	0.001	.3426711	1.400977
black	−.3198937	1.28559	−0.25	0.804	−2.84102	2.201233
asian	−2.022051	1.518961	−1.33	0.183	−5.000835	.9567331
hispanic	−.1170437	1.536851	−0.08	0.939	−3.130911	2.896823
age	.2768057	.3584406	0.77	0.440	−.4261202	.9797316
agesq	−.0017315	.0033973	−0.51	0.610	−.0083938	.0049308
pctteach	−6.742571	1.320453	−5.11	0.000	−9.332068	−4.153074
pctservice	−3.632172	2.933163	−1.24	0.216	−9.3843	2.119955
pctprofgro−h	−9.840791	3.921931	−2.51	0.012	−17.53196	−2.149625
pctconsultg	−2.480248	3.286601	−0.75	0.451	−8.92549	3.964994
professor	5.313083	.988196	5.38	0.000	3.375165	7.251001
assocprof	2.760009	.9600625	2.87	0.004	.8772625	4.642755
instructor	−.096502	1.657778	−0.06	0.954	−3.347514	3.15451
lecturer	−8.947907	5.193629	−1.72	0.085	−19.13296	1.237145
mideast	−.0061681	.0320137	−0.19	0.847	−.0689492	.056613
southeast	.0001181	.0307816	0.00	0.997	−.0602467	.060483
hbcu	−.0222742	3.044289	−0.01	0.994	−5.992328	5.94778
carneg1	.5524765	1.707841	0.32	0.746	−2.796712	3.901665
carneg2	−.5305496	1.868236	−0.28	0.776	−4.194284	3.133185
carneg3	−5.228489	1.735374	−3.01	0.003	−8.631672	−1.825305
carneg4	−6.451935	2.5241	−2.56	0.011	−11.40186	−1.502007
carneg5	−4.115427	2.356666	−1.75	0.081	−8.737006	.5061514
carneg6	−9.02633	2.260452	−3.99	0.000	−13.45923	−4.593434
carneg7	−15.97164	5.157108	−3.10	0.002	−26.08507	−5.858209
carneg8	−12.68974	1.837762	−6.90	0.000	−16.29371	−9.085765
agric	.7627543	2.492185	0.31	0.760	−4.124585	5.650094
educ	4.25835	1.381927	3.08	0.002	1.5483	6.968401
engin	1.77126	3.058232	0.58	0.563	−4.226137	7.768657
finearts	−.8547747	1.654986	−0.52	0.606	−4.100313	2.390764
health	2.694505	1.289949	2.09	0.037	.1648305	5.22418
humanities	4.484005	1.262765	3.55	0.000	2.007638	6.960371
natsci	2.187235	1.371532	1.59	0.111	−.5024312	4.8769
socsci	5.303764	1.364507	3.89	0.000	2.627876	7.979652
othdisp	2.064376	1.345399	1.53	0.125	−.5740407	4.702792
federalfunds	3.876134	.9402617	4.12	0.000	2.032218	5.720049
instfunds	1.684125	.72406	2.33	0.020	.264195	3.104055
foundfunds	1.225024	.9731231	1.26	0.208	−.683335	3.133383
busfunds	2.102268	1.54283	1.36	0.173	−.9233231	5.12786
othunivfunds	4.392418	4.467721	0.98	0.326	−4.36908	13.15392
s_lgovtfunds	−.8537821	1.235702	−0.69	0.490	−3.277076	1.569512
tenuryrs	−.0579553	.049076	−1.18	0.238	−.1541966	.0382859
foreignborn	3.803482	1.031083	3.69	0.000	1.781459	5.825505
union	−.3832836	.6830047	−0.56	0.575	−1.722701	.956134
_cons	−6.014609	9.729132	−0.62	0.537	−25.09408	13.06486
_se	12.19982	.2396444		(Ancillary parameter)		

Obs. summary:	814	left-censored observations at output1 ≤ 0
	1383	uncensored observations

Male Results Productivity in the Past Two Years

Tobit estimates

Number of obs = 4217
LR chi^2 (44) = 1308.12
Prob > chi^2 = 0.0000

Log likelihood = −13652.129

Pseudo R^2 = 0.0457

output1	Coef.	Std. Err.	t	P > |t|	[95% Conf. Interval]	
married	.3330398	.7866196	0.42	0.672	−1.209154	1.875233
dependents	.512171	.2151519	2.38	0.017	.0903588	.9339833
black	−.9919848	1.325206	−0.75	0.454	−3.590094	1.606124
asian	−.0374931	1.138909	−0.03	0.974	−2.270362	2.195376
hispanic	1.042473	1.278687	0.82	0.415	−1.464434	3.549379
age	.3217481	.3306114	0.97	0.331	−.3264265	.9699226
agesq	−.0029923	.0030545	−0.98	0.327	−.0089807	.0029961
pctteach	−3.995761	1.22284	−3.27	0.001	−6.393179	−1.598342
pctservice	−2.907957	2.616412	−1.11	0.266	−8.037519	2.221605
pctprofgro~h	−2.335236	4.189489	−0.56	0.577	−10.54887	5.878393
pctconsultg	9.765748	3.300778	2.96	0.003	3.294465	16.23703
professor	6.002622	1.161882	5.17	0.000	3.724715	8.28053
assocprof	.5021715	1.197735	0.42	0.675	−1.846027	2.850369
instructor	−1.87435	2.160976	−0.87	0.386	−6.111013	2.362313
lecturer	−15.62304	11.34615	−1.38	0.169	−37.86753	6.621461
mideast	.0141378	.0362434	0.39	0.696	−.0569187	.0851942
southeast	.0162577	.0304172	0.53	0.593	−.0433762	.0758916
hbcu	.0155133	3.263253	0.00	0.996	−6.3822	6.413226
carneg1	1.820049	1.256114	1.45	0.147	−.642603	4.2827
carneg2	−2.038544	1.427932	−1.43	0.153	−4.838052	.760964
carneg3	−5.528113	1.358218	−4.07	0.000	−8.190944	−2.865281
carneg4	−8.710937	2.179472	−4.00	0.000	−12.98386	−4.438011
carneg5	−4.761824	1.992487	−2.39	0.017	−8.668161	−.8554878
carneg6	−11.01561	2.031257	−5.42	0.000	−14.99795	−7.033263
carneg7	−11.80951	6.04605	−1.95	0.051	−23.66299	.0439664
carneg8	−15.19832	1.639621	−9.27	0.000	−18.41285	−11.98379
agric	−1.052485	1.76402	−0.60	0.551	−4.510903	2.405933
educ	2.395059	1.579773	1.52	0.130	−.7021381	5.492255
engin	3.652737	1.388338	2.63	0.009	.9308558	6.374619
finearts	−3.38929	1.559165	−2.17	0.030	−6.446083	−.3324968
health	3.311294	1.408656	2.35	0.019	.5495783	6.073009
humanities	5.385881	1.240081	4.34	0.000	2.954661	7.8171
natsci	.8040279	1.142429	0.70	0.482	−1.435742	3.043798
socsci	3.837168	1.219605	3.15	0.002	1.446093	6.228243
othdisp	.9201865	1.285014	0.72	0.474	−1.599125	3.439498
federalfunds	6.671647	.7409721	9.00	0.000	5.218947	8.124347
instfunds	1.717524	.6751614	2.54	0.011	.3938483	3.0412
foundfunds	4.793919	.8422814	5.69	0.000	3.142599	6.445239
busfunds	1.836849	.9949849	1.85	0.065	−.1138511	3.78755
othunivfunds	−13.11964	8.755486	−1.50	0.134	−30.28506	4.045772
s_lgovtfunds	−.5169472	.9824806	−0.53	0.599	−2.443133	1.409238
tenuryrs	−.0817903	.0414297	−1.97	0.048	−.1630147	−.000566
foreignborn	4.26633	.7907806	5.40	0.000	2.715979	5.816681
union	−.0092305	.7115264	−0.01	0.990	−1.404201	1.38574
_cons	−6.485214	9.072478	−0.71	0.475	−24.2721	11.30168
_se	16.09349	.2095885			(Ancillary parameter)	

Obs. summary: 1129 left-censored observations at output1 ≤ 0
3088 uncensored observations

Female Results Career Productivity

Tobit estimates

Log likelihood = −11690.185

Number of obs = 2197
LR chi^2 (43) = 688.95
Prob > chi^2 = 0.0000
Pseudo R^2 = 0.0286

totlprod	Coef.	Std. Err.	t	P > |t|	[95% Conf. Interval]	
married	−2.026891	4.827416	−0.42	0.675	−11.49377	7.43999
dependents	−.2897043	2.035574	−0.14	0.887	−4.2816	3.702191
black	−13.91054	9.661991	−1.44	0.150	−32.85834	5.037266
asian	−16.3595	11.44054	−1.43	0.153	−38.79515	6.076158
hispanic	−5.973253	11.48696	−0.52	0.603	−28.49994	16.55343
age	7.762239	2.640921	2.94	0.003	2.583219	12.94126
agesq	−.068631	.0251052	−2.73	0.006	−.1178639	−.0193981
pctteach	−25.07477	10.00641	−2.51	0.012	−44.698	−5.451544
pctservice	9.64385	22.057	0.44	0.662	−33.61138	52.89909
pctprofgro~h	−46.67192	29.53409	−1.58	0.114	−104.5902	11.24638
pctconsultg	31.13136	24.79582	1.26	0.209	−17.49488	79.75759
professor	43.12706	7.111068	6.06	0.000	29.18178	57.07233
assocprof	14.85305	6.890728	2.16	0.031	1.339877	28.36622
instructor	1.829234	11.05102	0.17	0.869	−19.84254	23.50101
lecturer	−27.35854	33.70233	−0.81	0.417	−93.45104	38.73396
mideast	−.2049287	.1588269	−1.29	0.197	−.5163987	.1065413
southeast	−.2390013	.2230382	−1.07	0.284	−.6763939	.1983912
carneg1	−8.659864	13.29167	−0.65	0.515	−34.7257	17.40598
carneg2	−16.38346	14.53294	−1.13	0.260	−44.88351	12.11658
carneg3	−38.38127	13.44028	−2.86	0.004	−64.73855	−12.024
carneg4	−49.8378	18.86322	−2.64	0.008	−86.82982	−12.84577
carneg5	−45.43387	18.17332	−2.50	0.012	−81.07296	−9.794783
carneg6	−65.00265	16.92988	−3.84	0.000	−98.20325	−31.80204
carneg7	−103.8379	33.38349	−3.11	0.002	−169.3052	−38.37069
carneg8	−87.93072	13.8846	−6.33	0.000	−115.1593	−60.7021
agric	32.17767	18.798	1.71	0.087	−4.686454	69.04179
educ	50.99956	10.21036	4.99	0.000	30.97636	71.02275
engin	47.70111	23.59691	2.02	0.043	1.426006	93.97621
finearts	89.31669	11.88163	7.52	0.000	66.01603	112.6173
health	21.54037	9.390315	2.29	0.022	3.125341	39.95539
humanities	23.5333	9.257262	2.54	0.011	5.379195	41.6874
natsci	10.01013	9.964824	1.00	0.315	−9.531546	29.55181
socsci	16.90461	10.16736	1.66	0.097	−3.034248	36.84346
othdisp	28.60855	9.811582	2.92	0.004	9.367393	47.84971
federalfunds	44.75521	7.397231	6.05	0.000	30.24875	59.26167
instfunds	2.670194	5.596675	0.48	0.633	−8.305255	13.64564
foundfunds	18.59445	7.62919	2.44	0.015	3.633107	33.5558
busfunds	17.26793	12.14523	1.42	0.155	−6.549667	41.08552
othunivfunds	14.18564	35.30503	0.40	0.688	−55.04985	83.42112
s_lgovtfunds	12.23634	9.464898	1.29	0.196	−6.32495	30.79763
tenuryrs	.7188117	.3608583	1.99	0.047	.0111447	1.426479
foreignborn	19.21103	7.923032	2.42	0.015	3.673438	34.74861
union	−2.763276	5.072649	−0.54	0.586	−12.71108	7.184524
_cons	−158.7607	71.63118	−2.22	0.027	−299.2342	−18.28725
_se	98.20154	1.597103			(Ancillary parameter)	

Obs. summary:	281	left-censored observations at totlprod ≤ 0
	1916	uncensored observations

Male Results Career Productivity

Tobit estimates

Number of obs = 4217
LR chi^2 (43) = 1441.94
Prob > chi^2 = 0.0000

Log likelihood = −24769.853

Pseudo R^2 = 0.0283

totlprod	Coef.	Std. Err.	t	P > |t|	[95% Conf. Interval]	
married	−9.592187	6.204491	−1.55	0.122	−21.75629	2.571919
dependents	3.26865	1.720023	1.90	0.057	−.1035117	6.640811
black	−9.678894	10.38886	−0.93	0.352	−30.0466	10.68881
asian	−4.011354	9.255875	−0.43	0.665	−22.1578	14.13509
hispanic	−9.196281	10.30509	−0.89	0.372	−29.39975	11.00719
age	.0921518	2.610537	0.04	0.972	−5.025891	5.210195
agesq	.0152788	.024082	0.63	0.526	−.0319348	.0624923
pctteach	−36.69863	9.726688	−3.77	0.000	−55.76811	−17.62914
pctservice	49.05206	21.19301	2.31	0.021	7.50247	90.60165
pctprofgro~h	4.686945	32.55655	0.14	0.886	−59.14123	68.51512
pctconsultg	144.8718	26.35859	5.50	0.000	93.1949	196.5487
professor	27.31847	8.781688	3.11	0.002	10.10169	44.53526
assocprof	−26.85742	9.074914	−2.96	0.003	−44.64908	−9.065755
instructor	−23.83953	15.30549	−1.56	0.119	−53.84645	6.167385
lecturer	−65.78578	67.58748	−0.97	0.330	−198.2932	66.72166
mideast	−.2532797	.1538555	−1.65	0.100	−.5549184	.0483589
southeast	.6674489	.2331858	2.86	0.004	.2102805	1.124617
carneg1	36.62988	10.27128	3.57	0.000	16.49271	56.76705
carneg2	4.722615	11.64515	0.41	0.685	−18.10807	27.5533
carneg3	−24.74174	11.00533	−2.25	0.025	−46.31804	−3.165429
carneg4	−27.02185	16.87308	−1.60	0.109	−60.10207	6.058373
carneg5	−14.26754	15.92439	−0.90	0.370	−45.48781	16.95274
carneg6	−36.79551	15.64494	−2.35	0.019	−67.46792	−6.123091
carneg7	−17.6747	41.76491	−0.42	0.672	−99.55615	64.20676
carneg8	−77.28632	12.76642	−6.05	0.000	−102.3153	−52.25734
agric	70.98628	14.09863	5.03	0.000	43.34547	98.6271
educ	34.9097	12.52722	2.79	0.005	10.34968	59.46971
engin	7.663839	11.13215	0.69	0.491	−14.1611	29.48878
finearts	78.55131	11.87208	6.62	0.000	55.27571	101.8269
health	73.5028	11.3221	6.49	0.000	51.30545	95.70016
humanities	23.3613	9.805107	2.38	0.017	4.13807	42.58453
natsci	10.68127	9.024013	1.18	0.237	−7.010602	28.37314
socsci	24.16747	9.680623	2.50	0.013	5.188297	43.14665
othdisp	3.856925	10.10817	0.38	0.703	−15.96047	23.67432
federalfunds	57.05127	6.088131	9.37	0.000	45.11529	68.98725
instfunds	11.19375	5.491108	2.04	0.042	.4282527	21.95924
foundfunds	36.64328	6.960027	5.26	0.000	22.99792	50.28864
busfunds	45.55716	8.227421	5.54	0.000	29.42703	61.68729
othunivfunds	−22.45418	61.1804	−0.37	0.714	−142.4003	97.49199
s_lgovtfunds	−10.70915	8.095207	−1.32	0.186	−26.58007	5.161765
tenuryrs	.0759034	.3268299	0.23	0.816	−.5648572	.716664
foreignborn	16.01787	6.412274	2.50	0.013	3.446394	28.58934
union	−12.14892	5.582492	−2.18	0.030	−23.09358	−1.204267
_cons	13.40377	71.82942	0.19	0.852	−127.4201	154.2277
_se	134.3002	1.532666			(Ancillary parameter)	

Obs. summary: 335   left-censored observations at totlprod ≤ 0
                 3882   uncensored observations

Black Faculty Productivity In Past Two Years

Tobit estimates

Number of obs = 416
LR chi^2 (40) = 178.19
Prob > chi^2 = 0.0000
Pseudo R^2 = 0.0763

Log likelihood = −1079.1487

output1	Coef.	Std. Err.	t	P > |t|	[95% Conf. Interval]	
female	−.3773905	1.536413	−0.25	0.806	−3.398429	2.643648
married	−2.359599	1.573309	−1.50	0.135	−5.453186	.7339884
dependents	1.125456	.5585071	2.02	0.045	.0272677	2.223645
age	−.3792457	.8175801	−0.46	0.643	−1.986848	1.228356
agesq	.0024143	.0076851	0.31	0.754	−.012697	.0175255
pctteach	−3.848166	3.12971	−1.23	0.220	−10.00209	2.305761
pctservice	−.9671293	7.673369	−0.13	0.900	−16.05522	14.12096
pctprofgro~h	6.615688	10.21303	0.65	0.518	−13.46612	26.6975
pctconsultg	−.5136372	8.127324	−0.06	0.950	−16.49434	15.46706
professor	7.671191	2.245324	3.42	0.001	3.256226	12.08616
assocprof	2.148669	2.175588	0.99	0.324	−2.129175	6.426512
instructor	1.257087	3.995868	0.31	0.753	−6.599961	9.114135
lecturer	−13.62494	10.13968	−1.34	0.180	−33.56252	6.312635
mideast	−.0292328	.0239951	−1.22	0.224	−.0764142	.0179485
southeast	−.0141434	.0914539	−0.15	0.877	−.1939686	.1656819
carneg1	1.352457	4.427846	0.31	0.760	−7.353987	10.0589
carneg2	−1.252653	4.730726	−0.26	0.791	−10.55465	8.049341
carneg3	−6.260254	4.504496	−1.39	0.165	−15.11741	2.596905
carneg4	−3.075652	5.303316	−0.58	0.562	−13.50353	7.352224
carneg5	−1.831339	6.453764	−0.28	0.777	−14.52133	10.85865
carneg6	−6.800117	5.192731	−1.31	0.191	−17.01055	3.410315
carneg7	−85.906	.	.	.	.	.
carneg8	−17.79101	4.809651	−3.70	0.000	−27.2482	−8.333828
agric	2.613864	5.900271	0.44	0.658	−8.987799	14.21553
educ	−3.906226	3.222538	−1.21	0.226	−10.24268	2.430229
engin	−6.219427	4.438966	−1.40	0.162	−14.94774	2.508882
finearts	−3.321743	3.324585	−1.00	0.318	−9.858852	3.215367
health	.0321216	3.538554	0.01	0.993	−6.925714	6.989957
humanities	−.5524838	3.141614	−0.18	0.860	−6.729819	5.624851
natsci	−4.379542	3.17132	−1.38	0.168	−10.61529	1.856203
socsci	1.40306	2.97614	0.47	0.638	−4.448904	7.255025
othdisp	−4.568556	3.055456	−1.50	0.136	−10.57648	1.439367
federalfunds	3.228382	2.192363	1.47	0.142	−1.082446	7.53921
instfunds	.4188939	1.836933	0.23	0.820	−3.193055	4.030843
foundfunds	3.982871	2.247771	1.77	0.077	−.4369047	8.402648
busfunds	−2.308606	4.033739	−0.57	0.567	−10.24012	5.622908
s_lgovtfunds	.8572272	2.700467	0.32	0.751	−4.452683	6.167138
tenuryrs	.2240072	.1117515	2.00	0.046	.0042711	.4437434
foreignborn	4.813627	1.883026	2.56	0.011	1.111046	8.516209
union	2.535284	1.619939	1.57	0.118	−.6499911	5.720559
_cons	17.41118	22.07995	0.79	0.431	−26.00447	60.82682
_se	11.87494	.5427047			(Ancillary parameter)	

Obs. summary:	160	left-censored observations at output1 ≤ 0
	256	uncensored observations

Black Faculty Career Productivity

Tobit estimates

Number of obs = 416
LR chi^2 (40)   = 119.22
Prob > chi^2 = 0.0000

Log likelihood = −2154.7828

Pseudo R^2 = 0.0269

totlprod	Coef.	Std. Err.	t	P > |t|	[95% Conf. Interval]	
female	−5.625083	13.67004	−0.41	0.681	−32.50439	21.25422
married	−14.23958	13.94207	−1.02	0.308	−41.65377	13.17462
dependents	2.700072	5.030955	0.54	0.592	−7.19226	12.5924
age	2.391708	7.131519	0.34	0.738	−11.63095	16.41437
agesq	−.0285589	.0670356	−0.43	0.670	−.1603706	.1032528
pctteach	−52.11647	27.34225	−1.91	0.057	−105.8794	1.646422
pctservice	−13.14809	68.12488	−0.19	0.847	−147.1016	120.8054
pctprofgro–h	39.36229	90.88747	0.43	0.665	−139.3491	218.0737
pctconsultg	−46.24368	70.69892	−0.65	0.513	−185.2585	92.77113
professor	43.93946	19.54117	2.25	0.025	5.515783	82.36313
assocprof	20.67854	18.72955	1.10	0.270	−16.14924	57.50632
instructor	52.17059	30.82299	1.69	0.091	−8.436452	112.7776
lecturer	11.39779	58.47303	0.19	0.846	−103.5773	126.3729
mideast	−.3324487	.2134955	−1.56	0.120	−.7522435	.0873461
southeast	.4127093	.7697804	0.54	0.592	−1.100905	1.926323
carneg1	62.9284	42.21368	1.49	0.137	−20.07607	145.9329
carneg2	73.92385	44.93367	1.65	0.101	−14.42891	162.2766
carneg3	40.00224	42.73299	0.94	0.350	−44.02336	124.0278
carneg4	68.54443	49.46096	1.39	0.167	−28.71031	165.7992
carneg5	40.44821	60.58364	0.67	0.505	−78.677	159.5734
carneg6	36.46827	48.52351	0.75	0.453	−58.94317	131.8797
carneg7	1.278485	96.52179	0.01	0.989	−188.5117	191.0686
carneg8	−49.37817	44.52896	−1.11	0.268	−136.9352	38.17882
agric	−35.86639	55.22534	−0.65	0.516	−144.4556	72.72283
educ	19.52816	27.94889	0.70	0.485	−35.42755	74.48388
engin	18.98084	40.3253	0.47	0.638	−60.31052	98.27219
finearts	104.6715	29.32129	3.57	0.000	47.0172	162.3257
health	12.10539	31.63876	0.38	0.702	−50.10568	74.31647
humanities	53.71269	27.63697	1.94	0.053	−.629687	108.0551
natsci	22.32368	27.2659	0.82	0.413	−31.28908	75.93645
socsci	9.950587	26.5943	0.37	0.708	−42.3416	62.24278
othdisp	9.864491	26.57674	0.37	0.711	−42.39317	62.12215
federalfunds	50.24828	20.24515	2.48	0.014	10.44039	90.05617
instfunds	−3.626391	16.98675	−0.21	0.831	−37.02732	29.77454
foundfunds	17.22278	20.90534	0.82	0.411	−23.88325	58.32882
busfunds	−1.326593	36.48062	−0.04	0.971	−73.05818	70.40499
s_lgovtfunds	−20.34156	24.56049	−0.83	0.408	−68.63468	27.95157
tenuryrs	2.53746	.9680008	2.62	0.009	.6340866	4.440833
foreignborn	40.98821	16.99758	2.41	0.016	7.565985	74.41044
union	18.44973	14.15758	1.30	0.193	−9.388234	46.28769
_cons	−76.32162	193.4907	−0.39	0.693	−456.781	304.1378
_se	113.5238	4.388446			(Ancillary parameter)	

Obs. summary: 73   left-censored observations at totlprod ≤ 0
343   uncensored observations

White Faculty Productivity In Past Two Years

Tobit estimates

Number of obs = 5556
LR chi^2 (41)   = 1802.50
Prob > chi^2 = 0.0000

Log likelihood = −16933.135

Pseudo R^2 = 0.0505

output1	Coef.	Std. Err.	t	P > |t|	[95% Conf. Interval]	
female	−.6465936	.5256835	−1.23	0.219	−1.67714	.3839532
married	.5012153	.5733963	0.87	0.382	−.6228675	1.625298
dependents	.5895606	.1847825	3.19	0.001	.2273141	.951807
age	.3890261	.2721255	1.43	0.153	−.1444472	.9224994
agesq	−.0033036	.0025306	−1.31	0.192	−.0082647	.0016574
pctteach	−4.850002	.9984438	−4.86	0.000	−6.807345	−2.892659
pctservice	−2.575171	2.166004	−1.19	0.235	−6.821392	1.671051
pctprofgro~h	−6.942137	3.263094	−2.13	0.033	−13.33909	−.5451869
pctconsultg	5.66093	2.597922	2.18	0.029	.5679793	10.75388
professor	5.953603	.8642085	6.89	0.000	4.259414	7.647792
assocprof	1.620143	.8760427	1.85	0.064	−.0972465	3.337532
instructor	−1.142137	1.554685	−0.73	0.463	−4.189932	1.905657
lecturer	−8.376198	6.704545	−1.25	0.212	−21.51975	4.767355
mideast	.0232035	.0223622	1.04	0.299	−.0206351	.0670421
southeast	.0191923	.0234086	0.82	0.412	−.0266978	.0650823
carneg1	1.900403	1.069923	1.78	0.076	−.1970681	3.997875
carneg2	−1.376229	1.207292	−1.14	0.254	−3.742996	.9905389
carneg3	−5.058754	1.129566	−4.48	0.000	−7.273149	−2.844358
carneg4	−8.9593	1.839467	−4.87	0.000	−12.56538	−5.353219
carneg5	−4.206003	1.622968	−2.59	0.010	−7.38766	−1.024346
carneg6	−10.70405	1.67079	−6.41	0.000	−13.97946	−7.428647
carneg7	−13.44247	4.259841	−3.16	0.002	−21.79344	−5.091502
carneg8	−14.13309	1.294291	−10.92	0.000	−16.67041	−11.59577
agric	−1.01644	1.524227	−0.67	0.505	−4.004525	1.971646
educ	4.070363	1.183585	3.44	0.001	1.750069	6.390657
engin	3.293691	1.315265	2.50	0.012	.7152538	5.872129
finearts	−2.717725	1.288302	−2.11	0.035	−5.243304	−.1921464
health	2.956854	1.072643	2.76	0.006	.8540501	5.059658
humanities	5.46031	.9956337	5.48	0.000	3.508476	7.412145
natsci	1.478627	.9802618	1.51	0.132	−.4430724	3.400327
socsci	4.418263	1.024343	4.31	0.000	2.410148	6.426379
othdisp	1.700831	1.045271	1.63	0.104	−.3483119	3.749974
federalfunds	5.716643	.6432387	8.89	0.000	4.455641	6.977644
instfunds	1.894656	.5513402	3.44	0.001	.8138115	2.9755
foundfunds	3.800686	.7098634	5.35	0.000	2.409074	5.192299
busfunds	2.743741	.8979438	3.06	0.002	.9834172	4.504065
othunivfunds	2.214694	4.607808	0.48	0.631	−6.818427	11.24781
s_lgovtfunds	−.7773977	.8558559	−0.91	0.364	−2.455213	.9004172
tenuryrs	−.0857808	.0342576	−2.50	0.012	−.1529392	−.0186225
foreignborn	4.015821	.688697	5.83	0.000	2.665703	5.365938
union	−.142412	.559443	−0.25	0.799	−1.239141	.9543169
_cons	−9.221284	7.437842	−1.24	0.215	−23.80239	5.359818
_se	15.04135	.1756328			(Ancillary parameter)	

Obs. summary: 1695   left-censored observations at output1 ≤ 0
                  3861   uncensored observations

White Faculty Career Productivity

Tobit estimates

Number of obs = 5556
LR chi^2 (41) = 1891.46
Prob > chi^2 = 0.0000

Log likelihood = −31879.752

Pseudo R^2 = 0.0288

totlprod	Coef.	Std. Err.	t	P > |t|	[95% Conf. Interval]	
female	−13.50269	4.124478	−3.27	0.001	−21.58829	−5.417085
married	−6.878337	4.483376	−1.53	0.125	−15.66732	1.910849
dependents	1.715348	1.466471	1.17	0.242	−1.159514	4.59021
age	2.484666	2.113676	1.18	0.240	−1.658973	6.628304
agesq	−.010237	.0196654	−0.52	0.603	−.048789	.028315
pctteach	−33.37096	7.915228	−4.22	0.000	−48.88793	−17.85399
pctservice	46.64696	17.3791	2.68	0.007	12.57707	80.71685
pctprofgro–h	−24.16313	25.24337	−0.96	0.339	−73.65008	25.32382
pctconsultg	105.0155	20.62116	5.09	0.000	64.5899	145.4411
professor	35.88123	6.460171	5.55	0.000	23.21675	48.54571
assocprof	−10.8582	6.556644	−1.66	0.098	−23.71181	1.995404
instructor	−21.01398	10.85509	−1.94	0.053	−42.29422	.2662689
lecturer	−90.5358	51.58617	−1.76	0.079	−191.665	10.59344
mideast	−.2971867	.1730591	−1.72	0.086	−.6364507	.0420774
southeast	.3247493	.1768752	1.84	0.066	−.0219958	.6714944
carneg1	20.26722	8.711889	2.33	0.020	3.18848	37.34596
carneg2	−4.473675	9.808347	−0.46	0.648	−23.7019	14.75455
carneg3	−33.81965	9.121708	−3.71	0.000	−51.70179	−15.9375
carneg4	−45.50365	14.14367	−3.22	0.001	−73.23081	−17.77649
carneg5	−25.26966	12.969	−1.95	0.051	−50.694	.1546824
carneg6	−55.09389	12.79772	−4.30	0.000	−80.18247	−30.00531
carneg7	−63.90235	29.61378	−2.16	0.031	−121.957	−5.847669
carneg8	−81.01084	10.10397	−8.02	0.000	−100.8186	−61.20307
agric	65.8294	12.0676	5.46	0.000	42.17214	89.48666
educ	49.28674	9.282053	5.31	0.000	31.09026	67.48323
engin	3.637868	10.46405	0.35	0.728	−16.8758	24.15154
finearts	80.25478	9.678489	8.29	0.000	61.28113	99.22843
health	45.68566	8.365293	5.46	0.000	29.28639	62.08494
humanities	21.90346	7.747862	2.83	0.005	6.714592	37.09232
natsci	7.152598	7.608559	0.94	0.347	−7.763176	22.06837
socsci	19.29998	8.030874	2.40	0.016	3.556302	35.04366
othdisp	10.27124	8.106322	1.27	0.205	−5.62035	26.16283
federalfunds	54.79877	5.284539	10.37	0.000	44.43899	65.15855
instfunds	9.300302	4.460019	2.09	0.037	.5569065	18.0437
foundfunds	35.09351	5.846816	6.00	0.000	23.63144	46.55557
busfunds	44.77204	7.410451	6.04	0.000	30.24463	59.29944
othunivfunds	28.8429	36.55838	0.79	0.430	−42.82594	100.5117
s_lgovtfunds	−3.13835	6.993017	−0.45	0.654	−16.84742	10.57072
tenuryrs	.1078068	.267572	0.40	0.687	−.4167398	.6323535
foreignborn	11.39171	5.593292	2.04	0.042	.4266515	22.35677
union	−8.744404	4.357724	−2.01	0.045	−17.28726	−.2015467
_cons	−31.95974	57.86859	−0.55	0.581	−145.405	81.48552
_se	125.5998	1.257894			(Ancillary parameter)	

Obs. summary: 514   left-censored observations at totlprod ≤ 0
                  5042   uncensored observations

Notes

1.   Survey of Negro Colleges and Universities, reported in Susan T. Hill, *The Traditionally Black Institutions of Higher Education, 1960 to 1982*, Washington, DC: U.S. Department of Education, 1984, p. 9.
2.   Statistics of the Education of Negroes, 1933–34 and 1935–36, reported in *The Traditionally Black Institutions of Higher Education*, p. 11.
3.   *Missouri ex Rel. Gaines* v. *Canada*, 305 U.S. 337 (1938).
4.   Our late colleague Dr. Phyllis Wallace related the story of how the State of Maryland paid for her to attend New York University: "There was a provision in the regulations that blacks who chose not to attend the predominantly black college in the state would be subsidized to attend the college of their choice out of state if they majored in a course not offered by the black institution. Thus, for my last three years as an undergraduate student at New York University I received a Maryland scholarship because economics was not offered to blacks within the state," unpublished remarks by Phyllis A. Wallace at the Westerfield Awards Luncheon in Washington, DC on December 29, 1981. Dr. Wallace received her baccalaureate degree from NYU and went on to receive her PhD from Yale in 1954.

   The decision in the Fordice case and others only recently required states to avoid duplicative programs for black and white students at separate state-funded institutions.
5.   *The Traditionally Black Institutions of Higher Education*, p. 14.
6.   Walter R. Allen and Joseph O. Jewell, "A Backward Glance Forward: Past, Present, and Future Perspectives on Historically Black Colleges and Universities," *The Review of Higher Education*, 25:3 (2002), 241–261.
7.   Based on 1992 data from the Digest of Education Statistics the overall median age of full-time instructional faculty was 48.20.
8.   Elizabeth G. Creamer, *Assessing Faculty Publication Productivity: Issues of Equity*, ASHE-ERIC Higher Education Report, 26:2 (1998), Washington, DC.
9.   G.S. Maddala, *Limited Dependent and Qualitative Variables in Econometrics*, Cambridge University Press, 1983.
10. Marcia L. Bellas and Robert K. Toutkoushian, "Faculty Time Allocations and Research Productivity: Gender, Race and Family Effects," *The Review of Higher Education*, 22:4 (1999), 367–390.
11. *Op. Cit.*
12. Further research will investigate the possible interactive effect of being foreign-born and Asian or Hispanic. As discussed, there is a significant positive effect of being foreign-born on both the short-term and career productivity of white faculty.
13. The effect of age is significant at the 5 percent level or below for some productivity measures when dummy variables for the Carnegie classifications are included in the model.
14. Creamer, *op. cit.*, reviews the literature on publication rates by field.
15. Sharon G. Levin and Paula E. Stephan, "Research Productivity Over the Life Cycle: Evidence for Academic Scientists," *American Economic Review*, 81:1 (1991), 114–132.
16. One hypothesis for the consistent positive finding for federal funding is the importance of agencies such as the National Science Foundation, National Institutes of Health, and others, whose funding often results in publishable research and/or conference presentations.
17. See Jacqueline Agesa, Maury Granger, and Gregory Price, "Swimming Upstream?: The Relative Research Productivity of Economists at Black Colleges," *Review of*

Black Political Economy, 29:3 (2002), 63-84; Elizabeth Corley, Meghna Sabharwal, "Foreign-born academic scientists and engineers: producing more and getting less than their U.S.-born peers?," *Research in Higher Education*, 48:8 (2007), 909-940.

18. Several previous studies have examined the effect of unionism on faculty productivity; see for example, Mark Meador and Stephen J.K. Walters, "Union Productivity: Evidence from Academe," *Journal of Labor Research*, 15:4 (1994), 373-386; Richard B. Freeman, "Unionism Comes to the Public Sector," *Journal of Economic Literature*, 24: 1 (1986), 41-86; Christos Doucouliagos and Patrice Larouche, "What do Unions do to Productivity?," *Industrial Relations*, 42:4 (2003), 650-691.

19. Thomas J.Kane and Cecelia E. Rouse, "The Community College: Educating Students at the Margin Between College and Work," *Journal of Economic Perspectives*, 13:1 (1999), 63-84.

20. Agesa, Granger, and Price, *op. cit.*

21. Howard Bodenhorn, "Economic Scholarship at Elite Liberal Arts Colleges: A Citation Analysis with Ranking," *Journal of Economic Education*, 34:4 (2003) 341-359.

22. Bodenhorn has shown that there are exceptions to this rule in the case of elite liberal arts colleges that emphasize both teaching and research; H. Bodenhorn, "Economic Scholarship at Elite Liberal Arts Colleges: A Citation Analysis with Rankings," *Journal of Economic Education*, Fall 2003, pp. 341–359.

Cases Cited

1. *Brown v. Board of Education of Topeka*, 347 U.S. 483 (1954).
2. *Brown v. Board of Education*, 349 U. S. 294 (1955).
3. *McLaurin v. Oklahoma State Regents*, 339 U.S. 637 (1950).
4. *Missouri ex Rel. Gaines v. Canada*, 305 U.S. 337 (1938).
5. *U.S. v. Fordice*, 112 S. Ct 2727 (1992).

Would Increased National Science Foundation Research Support to Economists at Historically Black Colleges and Universities Increase Their Research Productivity?

Gregory N. Price

I. Introduction

Economics faculty research productivity is an important social good. The basic and applied research efforts of economics faculty add to the stock of knowledge, and either directly or indirectly engender progress. This is not only the case for economics faculty at research universities. Bodenhorn (1997) shows that increasingly, the economics faculty of non-research universities are expected to do research, and account for a nontrivial proportion of the stock of economics research published in refereed journals. An exception appears to be the case with respect to Historically Black Colleges and Universities (HBCUs). Agesa, Granger, and Price (2000) find that being at a non-research HBCU has the effect of lowering individual economist research productivity as measured by publications in refereed economics journals.

The consequences of HBCUs having a negative effect on the research productivity of economists are potentially important. First, both Hartley and Robinson (1997) and Agesa, Granger, and Price (1998, 2000) find that the number of a baccalaureate institution's graduates who ultimately go on to earn a doctorate in economics is positively correlated with the research productivity of economics faculty. This suggests that the research productivity of economists is important for the future supply of economic scientists. Given the historical underrepresentation of minorities—especially black Americans—among the ranks of Ph.D. economists, this suggests that the research productivity of economists at HBCUs is an important catalyst for the pipeline of minority economists originating from HBCUs.[1]

The research productivity of economics faculty at HBCUs is also important for tenure.[2] If an economics faculty member is not a productive researcher, the likelihood of tenure is compromised at those HBCUs where the promotion and reward system places a premium on faculty research—especially publications in refereed journals. To the extent that tenure track professors have an incentive to do safe and uncontroversial research so as to maximize their tenure probabilities, it is conceivable that tenured status encourages more innovative research efforts, or it at least extends the period over which the faculty member can contribute to the stock of knowledge.

Given the implied link between HBCU economics faculty research productivity, tenure, and the impact it has on the future supply of economists, an understanding of what influences the research productivity of economists at HBCUs could cast insight upon what policy interventions are possible, if any, that would increase both the tenure probabilities and future supply of minority economists. Stephan (1996, p. 1217) has argued that "another factor that affects research productivity and varies by cohort is access to the resources that affect research." One factor that could matter for the individual research productivity of economists is having National Science Foundation (NSF) research support. While Arora and Gambardella (1996) found that NSF basic research support in economics increases the research productivity for relatively young principal investigators, nothing is known as to whether these effects have disparate impacts with respect to race and ethnicity.

This paper explores the possibly causal link between NSF funding for research in economics, and the research productivity of minority and non-minority economists. We also consider the implications it has for the research productivity of black economists at HBCUs. If the correlates of minority and non-minority faculty research productivity are distinguishable (Creamer, 1998), these differences could translate into research productivity differentials. NSF research support is of course not the only determinant of faculty research productivity, as factors such as age, compensation, student quality, and quality of doctoral training all seem to matter (Agesa, Granger and Price, 2000). However, given that the NSF is the only source of funding for basic scientific research that translates ultimately into influential publications in refereed economics journals, the central focus of this paper is to determine the importance of NSF funding.

NSF research support for economists is likely to be important for many reasons. NSF funding can be viewed as conferring upon the recipient a prestige that attracts other resources to subsidize research. Many published articles in the top economics journals acknowledge NSF funding. An author who successfully publishes research that was subsidized with NSF funding could presumably leverage this experience so as to command other resources, both within his institution, and without, to subsidize future research efforts that result in refereed publications.[3]

Economics research subsidized by the NSF could also have a learning effect that enhances the ability of NSF grantees to do research addressing the important questions in the discipline which result in papers that are ultimately published in refereed economics journals.[4] Successful NSF grant applications satisfy the standards of reviewers who are in many instances scientists that establish and enforce the norms that govern publications in refereed journals. Thus, successful NSF grant applicants may benefit from learning, and having reinforced, the norm governing what standards apply for published articles, that they otherwise would not—which increases the chance of articles being published upon submission.

The remainder of this chapter is organized as follows. Section II discusses the data and conceptual framework that motivates the empirical specification of the individual economist research productivity equation. Given that the dependent variable—publications in refereed journals—is a discrete measure, research productivity equations are specified within a Poisson regression framework. The results are provided in Section III. In Section IV, we consider the implications our results have for the research productivity of black economists at HBCUs within the context of actual NSF Economics Program submission and award data. Section V concludes.

II. Data and Empirical Framework

We view the decision of an individual economist to engage in research in a manner similar to Levin and Stephan (1991). It is assumed that the individual economist has a utility function with research output as an argument. Utility is maximized by producing research output with a research production function, over a career that begins with the receipt of the Ph.D. in economics, and ends at retirement.

For the individual Ph.D. economist, the production function for research output can be viewed as having the general form $R_i = f(\theta)$, where R_i is the research output of the ith Ph.D. economist, and θ is a vector of plausible factors/inputs of research production. This is a very general functional relationship, and the econometric specification of it below presupposes that research output is separable from the utility function of Ph.D. economists. In general, for given elements of v, this specification is flexible enough to capture, where relevant, both the investment and consumption motives for research activity by individual economists [Levin and Stephan (1991)].

To estimate the parameters of econometric specifications of the research production function, data from the NSF's 1995 Scientists and Engineers Statistical Data System (SESTAT) are utilized. SESTAT is an integrated dataset containing data from three sources: the National Survey of College Graduates (NSCG), the National Survey of Recent College Graduates (NSRCG), and the Survey of Doctorate Recipients (SDR). As the interest of this paper is the research productivity of economists with doctorates, the SESTAT data utilized are those reported by individuals with an economics doctorate in the 1995 SDR.[5]

The research productivity of individual economists is measured from the response provided by 1995 SDR respondents regarding the extent to which they have authored or coauthored articles in refereed journals. It is a self-reported measure of publication activity.[6] For the 1995 Public SDR, the responses are coded for 12 categories, and each class, with the exception of respondents reporting zero publications or having more than 50, which has a width of 1, have a width of 5.

The categorical self-reported publication data were integerized to capture the natural discreteness of article counts, by assuming that for each class of width 5, the number of self-reported articles for a respondent has a uniform discrete distribution. In particular, for each respondent, the number of actual self-reported refereed publications is integerized by drawing R_i from a discrete uniform distribution implied by the category for which the respondent self-reported. For each category, the response is integerized by assuming that the R_i is generated by:

$$f(R_i) = \frac{1}{K} \quad \text{for} \quad R_i = R_1 \ldots R_K$$

where for a given category of K values, R_1 is the lowest valued integer, and R_K is the highest valued integer.

Given the integerization of the self-reported number of publications for the survey respondents, it is assumed that R_i is Poisson random variable with density:

$$\text{Prob}(R_i = n) = f(R_i) = \frac{e^{-\lambda_i} 1_i^n}{n!}$$

where R_i is the number of self-reported publications of individual economist i, $n = 0, 1, 2, \ldots N$, $e = 2.71828$, and λ_i = the expected value and variance of R_i. Viewing individual research output as a Poisson random variable seems reasonable given that research output is a count of published articles, and a Poisson distribution is a discrete probability distribution where zero is a natural outcome of the distribution.[7]

To estimate the parameters of the research production function, a Poisson regression model is utilized, which results from specifying λ_i as a function of a vector of exogenous variables:

$$\ln \lambda_i = \beta'\theta$$

where β is a coefficient vector, and θ is a vector of exogenous variables that determine the expected value of refereed publications for the ith economist.[8] The log-likelihood function $L(\beta)$ has a gradient and Hessian given by:

$$\frac{\partial L(\beta)}{\partial \beta} = \sum \left[\theta'\left(R_i - e^{\beta'\theta}\right)\right] = 0$$

$$\frac{\partial^2 L(\beta)}{\partial \beta \partial \beta'} = \sum \left[-\left(R_i' R_i\right)e^{\beta'\theta}\right] < 0$$

Equating the gradient to zero solves for β, and the negativity of the Hessian ensures a global maximum of the log-likelihood estimator of the coefficients in β.

The research productivity equation to be estimated is of a general form similar to that of Levin and Stephan (1991):

$$\lambda_i = E(R_i) = \exp(\beta_0 + \beta_1 \text{ AGE} + \beta_2 \text{ SALARY} + \beta_2 \text{ RSEVN}$$

$$+ \beta_3 \text{ RSEFF} + \beta_4 \text{ VINT} + \sum_{i=5}^{K} \beta_i X_i) \tag{1}$$

where E is the expected value operator, as λ_i is the expected value of the number of self-reported publications R_i. The first four explanatory variables are similar in spirit to those considered by Levin and Stephan (1991). AGE measures, in years, up to April 15, 1995, how old the respondent is. SALARY measures annual compensation. RSEVN and RSEFF are proxies for the individual's research environment and effort respectively. VINT is a measure of doctorate vintage.

The regression strategy of this paper is to consider the explanatory power of these variables for the research productivity of economists in a cross-section, and to augment it with other plausible determinants of research productivity, captured in the $\Sigma_{i=4}^{K} \beta_i X_i$ term. These additional variables will include dummies for racial minority status and NSF funding, along with their interaction, which will permit an assessment of the extent to which NSF funding per se, and its interaction with minority status, impact upon the research productivity of economists.

III. Results

Tables 1 and 2 report, respectively, the definitions and summary statistics (mean and standard deviation) of variables utilized for estimating various specifications of the research productivity equation in equation (1) above. The sample consists of 923 observations from SESTAT data. There are a total of 1065 observations on Ph.D. economists, however 142 were not suitable as a result of no response and/or miscoding on the publication and income/earnings measures. Minority economists constitute approximately 12 percent of the sample.

The summary statistics reported in Table 2 reveal, for the economists in the sample, some striking racial disparities. First, on average and relative to non-minority economists, minority economists report fewer publications. To the extent that tenure is driven primarily by publications, this may partially explain why the percent of non-minority economists that are tenured exceeds that of minority economists in the sample by approximately 18 percent. Finally given the focus of this paper, the percent of non-minority economists who report having had NSF research support exceeds that of minority economists by a factor of two and a half. In general, NSF support for economists in the overall sample is low, however, the disparity between non-minority and minority economists is striking.

To the extent that NSF research support is an important input into the research production function of economists, racial disparities in NSF support could potentially contribute to racial disparities in tenure across the population of economists on the faculty of colleges and universities. This is particularly likely to be true if the primary determinant of tenure is refereed publications. To examine the sensitivity of tenure to research productivity, Table 3 reports simple Probit parameter estimates of rudimentary specifications of the determinants of tenure.

Columns (1), (2), and (3) report estimates of the tenure specification over the entire sample, the subsample of non-minority economists, and the subsample of minority economists respectively. For all three specifications the coefficient on R_i is positive and significant. This suggests, not

Table 1
Definition of Variables

Variable	Definition (Survey, Question)
R_i:	Total number of authored or co-authored articles published in refereed journals between April 1990 and April 1995. (SDR.A32)
AGE:	1995 minus year of birth. (SDR.D18)
SALARY:	Annual salary (excludes wages, bonuses, overtime, commissions, consulting fees, net income from a business, and income from summertime teaching, research, and post doctoral appointments) of respondent as of the week of April 15, 1995. (SDR.A37)
TEARN:	Total earned income (includes, wages, bonuses, overtime commissions, consulting fees, net income from a business, and income from summertime teaching, research, and post doctoral appointments), of respondent for 1994. (SDR.A51)
RSEVN:	A dichotomous variable that equals one if the respondent reports that basic and applied research are his primary and secondary work activity. (SDR.derived)
RSEFF:	Total number of authored or co-authored papers prepared for presentation at regional, national or international conferences. (SDR.A31)
VINT:	Year in which the respondent earned doctorate in economics. Measured as one of 14 five-year intervals beginning with the year 1930, and ending with 1999. (SDR.derived)
MINOR:	A dichotomous variable that equals one if the respondent is a member of a racial minority group (Black, Hispanic, Native American, Alaskan Native, or Other). (SESTAT.00)
NSFSUP:	A dichotomous variable that equals one if during the week of April 15, 1995, the respondent had any work supported by a grant from the National Science Foundation. (SDR.A41)
TENURE:	A dichotomous variable that equals one if the respondent is tenured. (SDR.A17)

Notes: SDR.derived means that the response was derived from other questions reported in the SDR.
SESTAT.00 means that the response was derived from information reported in SESTAT.

surprisingly, that the probability of tenure is increasing in research productivity as measured by the number of authored or coauthored refereed publications. Moreover, the coefficients on the minority dummy variable by itself, and its interaction with R_i are insignificant. This suggests that being a minority economist per se and/or being a minority economist that is productive in research, does not affect, favorably or adversely, the probability of being tenured.[9]

That tenure probabilities increase with respect to research productivity has straightforward implications for the covariates of individual econo-

Table 2
Mean and Standard Deviation of Variables*

Variable	All Economists	Non-Minority Economists	Minority Economists
R_i	1.93	2.04	1.15
	(5.16)	(5.32)	(3.56)
AGE	49.32	49.37	48.92
	(10.13)	(10.11)	(10.33)
SALARY	67414	67645	65654
	(31080)	(31168)	(30483)
TEARN	71592	71685	70879
	(34268)	(34193)	(34990)
RSEVN	.665	.673	.607
	(.472)	(.469)	(.491)
RSEFF	6.63	6.65	6.40
	(7.34)	(7.39)	(6.93)
VINT	1977.4	1977.1	1979.7
	(9.96)	(10.04)	(9.08)
MINOR	.116	—	—
	(.320)	—	—
NSFSUP	.022	.023	.009
	(.146)	(.151)	(.097)
TENURE	.434	.442	.374
	(.496)	(.497)	(.486)
N	923	816	107

Notes:

*Standard deviations are in parentheses.

N = number of observations.

Table 3
The Impact of Research Productivity on Tenure: Probit Estimates*

Regressand: Tenure

Regressors	All Economists	Non-Minority Economists	Minority Economists
	(1)	(2)	(3)
Constant	.404	.406	.338
	(.018)[a]	(.018)[a]	(.048)[a]
MINOR	−.057	—	—
	(.050)	—	—
R_i	.018	.018	.031
	(.003)[a]	(.003)[a]	(.013)[b]
MINOR x R_i	.486	—	—
	(.489)	—	—
N	923	816	107

Notes:

*Standard errors are in parentheses.

N = number of observations.

[a]Significant at the .01 level.

[b]Significant at the .05 level.

mist research productivity. For those covariates that are crucial inputs into the research production process, tenure probabilities will also be increasing with respect to these covariates. The central concern of this paper is to what extent is NSF research support a covariate of minority and non-minority economist research productivity. If NSF is a covariate of research productivity, it will also have an effect on tenure probabilities. The individual research productivity equation specified in (1) is amenable to examining this by including suitable variables in the $\Sigma X_i \beta_i$ term.

Table 4 reports simple Poisson parameter estimates for the research productivity equation. Six specifications are reported based on two different measures of compensation (salary and total earned income), and estimated separately for the entire sample of economists, the subsample of non-minority economists, and the subsample of minority economists. To facilitate convergence of the Poisson log-likelihood function, four of the variables (AGE, SALARY, TEARN, VINT) were logarithmically transformed. For each specification two diagnostic measures are also reported. The coefficient α is the result of an auxiliary regression that tests for mean-variance equality, or overdispersion—a restriction required if the conditional mean of R_i is to be equal to $\lambda_i = \exp(\beta'\theta)$.[10] As a goodness-of-fit measure, the ratio of the number of zeros predicted by the estimated Poisson model ($\Sigma[\lambda\hat{}_i = 0]$) to the number of actual zeros ($\Sigma[R_i = 0]$), is computed and reported.

For the entire sample of economists, the parameter estimates reported in columns (1) and (2) of Table 4 are similar with respect to the measure of income. The expected value of research productivity increases with respect to effort, income, and when the environment in which the economist is employed is such that basic and applied research are dominant work activities. In contrast, the expected value of research productivity decreases with respect to age, and degree vintage. Being a minority economist, all things being equal, also lowers the expected value of research productivity, as indicated by the negative and significant sign on the MINOR dummy variable.

Given the central concern of this paper, what is instructive about the results in columns (1) and (2) is the positive and significant sign on the dummy variable for having NSF support. Having NSF research support apparently increases the expected value of research productivity. In addition, the positive and significant sign on the interaction of having NSF support and being a minority economist, suggests that NSF research support for minority economists ameliorates and offsets the adverse impact that being a minority has on the expected value of research productivity.

Table 4
Poisson Regression Parameter Estimates of Research Productivity Equation

Regressand: R_i = Total number of authored or co-authored publications.

Specification:	All Economists		Nonminority Economists		Minority Economists	
	(1)	(2)	(3)	(4)	(5)	(6)
Regressors:						
Constant	434.68	280.02	1026.8	901.40	143.72	418.88
	$(53.07)^a$	$(54.45)^a$	$(99.66)^a$	$(100.82)^a$	(353.0)	(322.94)
lnAGE	−1.32	−1.12	−3.48	−3.36	−1.07	−2.29
	$(.171)^a$	$(.172)^a$	$(.314)^a$	$(.315)^a$	(1.15)	$(1.06)^b$
lnSALARY	.174	—	.267	—	2.94	—
	$(.029)^a$	—	$(.051)^a$	—	$(.336)^a$	—
lnTEARN	—	.445	—	.606	—	2.07
	—	$(.035)^a$	—	$(.059)^a$	—	$(.309)^a$
RSEVN	.417	.406	1.16	1.15	2.10	1.73
	$(.039)^a$	$(.039)^a$	$(.083)^a$	$(.083)^a$	$(.386)^a$	$(.378)^a$
RSEFF	.027	.026	.035	.034	.083	.076
	$(.001)^a$	$(.001)^a$	$(.001)^a$	$(.001)^a$	$(.006)^a$	$(.006)^a$
lnVINT	−56.72	−36.84	−135.00	−118.03	−23.07	−57.38
	$(6.91)^a$	$(7.09)^a$	$(12.85)^a$	$(13.12)^a$	(45.73)	(41.98)
MINOR	−.202	−.236	—	—	—	—
	$(.055)^a$	$(.057)^a$	—	—	—	—
NSFSUP	.133	.124	.499	.482	1.54	1.33
	$(.074)^c$	$(.092)^a$	$(.106)^a$	$(.106)^a$	$(.369)^a$	$(.373)^a$
MINOR x NSFSUP	.675	.537	—	—	—	—
	$(.350)^a$	$(.321)^c$	—	—	—	—
α	5.14	4.86	4.98	4.71	1.49	1.85
	$(.810)^a$	$(.643)^a$	$(.845)^a$	$(.682)^a$	$(.311)^a$	$(.447)^a$
$\Sigma(\hat{\lambda}_i = 0)/$ $\Sigma(R_i = 0)$	.019	.023	.292	.306	.384	.565
N	923	923	816	816	107	107

Notes:
Standard errors in parentheses.
N = Number of observations.
[a]Significant at the .01 level.
[b]Significant at the .05 level.

The results reported in columns (3)–(6) of Table 4 are the Poisson regression parameter estimates for the subsample of non-minority and minority economists. For the relevant subset of explanatory variables, the results are similar to the parameter estimates over the entire sample. For both nonminority and minority economists, having NSF support increases the expected value of research productivity. For minority economists, the magnitude on the dummy for having NSF support exceeds that of non-minority economists. This suggests that NSF research support to minority economists results in a larger pay-off in terms of research productivity, relative to non-minority economists.

The fit of the simple Poisson model varies across the sample. For the entire sample the model successfully predicts no more than 2 percent, approximately, of the actual zero-valued publication observations. In the subsample of non-minority economists, no more than 30 percent, approximately, of the zero-valued publication observations are successfully predicted. For the subsample of minority economists, the fit is much better. For the specification in column (5), the simple Poisson model successfully predicts 56 percent, approximately, of the actual zero-valued publication observations.

Notwithstanding the variability of the goodness-of-fit across the specifications in columns (1)–(6), the positive and significant coefficient on α for each specification leads to the rejection of the mean-variance equality restriction required of the simple Poisson regression specification of research productivity. The data are characterized by overdispersion, suggesting the inadequacy of the simple Poisson specification. In this context, the poor fit of the model across the specifications in Table 4 may be a result of the inadequacy of the Poisson specification to explain the data.

An alternative to the simple Poisson specification that results in overdispersion, or mean-variance inequality, arises where there are an excess or preponderance of zero observations, and the process generating the zero observations on publications is different from the process generating the nonzero observations. There is indeed a preponderance of zeros for the sample. For the entire sample of economists, approximately 82 percent of the observations on self-reported publication are zero. For the subsample of non-minority and minority economists, the percent of zero valued publications observations are approximately 81 and 89 percent respectively.

One way to extend the simple Poisson specification so as to accommodate a preponderance of zeros is to imagine the zero observations arising from two regimes as in Lambert (1992). Suppose that R_i takes on the value of zero in regime one with probability q_i, but in regime two, R_i takes on the value λ_i with probability $(1 - q_i)$. Since a zero can occur in both regimes:

$$\text{Prob}[R_i = n = 0] = q_i + (1 - q_i)e^{\lambda_i}$$

$$\text{Prob}[R_i = n > 0] = (1 - q_i) \; \frac{e^{-\lambda_i}1_i^n}{n!}$$

If we further assume that the regime split is determined by $q(i) = z_i = F(\Sigma \gamma_i X_i)$, where $F(\cdot)$ is a normal cumulative density function, the X_i are variables that determine if R_i is in regime 1 or regime 2, and the γ_i are coefficients. This extension of the simple Poisson model is known as the Zero-Inflated Poisson (ZIP) model.[11]

Given the preponderance of zero-valued publication observations, and the rejection of mean-variance equality restriction for all the specifications in Table 4, a ZIP model is implemented by postulating:

$$z_i = F[\gamma_1 VINT + \gamma_2 NSFSUP]$$

This implies that the regime split between publications being zero and being generated by a Poisson process is a function of the year in which an individual economist earned the doctorate, and whether or not the economist has had NSF research support. The γ coefficients indicate the effect that each variable has on the probability of belonging to the zero publications regime.

The inclusion of VINT in z_i seems a plausible assumption as Levin and Stephan (1991) find evidence that the research productivity of scientists declines with the vintage of their doctoral degree. This is based upon the idea that knowledge acquired during the doctoral graduates of later vintage, is more current than the doctoral graduates of early graduates. As the knowledge base of economists of earlier vintage is more depreciated relative to those of early vintage, it seems reasonable that the probability of having zero publications varies inversely with vintage.

Two considerations motivate the inclusion of NSFSUP in z_i. First, being awarded an NSF grant may confer upon the grantee the ability and prestige to leverage other research subsidizing resources that enhance the ability to publish in refereed journals. In this context, not having NSF support could increase the probability of not having any publications, which would partially explain whether or not an observation belongs to the regime of zero-valued publications. Finally, it is quite possible that receiving NSF support is a function of the grant applicants track record as measured by refereed publications. The inclusion of NSFSUP in z_i partially resolves the possible selection and endogeneity bias associated with NSF research support by making it a determinant of whether or not a Ph.D. economist belongs to a regime in which the actual nonzero count of publications is determined by having NSF research support.

Table 5 reports the ZIP parameter estimates for the same specifications that were reported in Table 4. The parameter estimates are based upon the regime switching function $z_i = F(\cdot)$ specified as a Probit equation. As the ZIP model is not nested within the simple Poisson, Table 5 also reports v, the test statistic developed by Vuong (1986), and suggested by Greene (2000) as suitable for testing the ZIP model against the non-nested alternative of the simple Poisson model. If the absolute value of v is greater than or equal to 2, the ZIP model adequately explains the data relative to the simple Poisson model.[12]

For all the specifications reported in Table 5, the Vuong test statistic exceeds that absolute value of 2, suggesting the adequacy of the ZIP model for the data. In terms of goodness-of-fit, each specification successfully predicts approximately all of the zero-valued publication observations—a substantial improvement over the fit of the simple Poisson results reported in Table 4. For the subsample of minority economists, the constant term and the variable NSFSUP were omitted due to singularity of the covariance matrix when they were included. Thus, for the minority economist subsample, the reported parameter estimates are only suggestive, and not directly comparable to the results in columns (1)–(4) of Table 5, or to the results reported in columns (5)–(6) of Table 4.

The results reported for the ZIP specifications in columns (1)–(4) of Table 5 are in striking contrast to the simple Poisson parameter estimates reported in Table 4. Having NSF research support, and being a minority with NSF research support no longer have a significant and positive effect on research productivity for Ph.D. economists with publications. Instead, NSF research support determines whether or not a Ph.D. economist belongs to the regime of zero-valued publication observations. The coefficient γ_2 is positive and significant, suggesting that the probability of not having any publications increases with respect to not having NSF support. The positive and significant sign on γ_1 implies that the probability of belonging to the regime of zero-valued publications increases with respect to the vintage of the economics doctorate.

For the subsample of minority economists, as the specifications reported in columns (5)–(6) in Table 5 are different, the γ coefficients are suggestive. As is the case for the entire sample, and the subsample of non-minority economists, γ_1 is positive and significant. The coefficient on γ_2, while insignificant, is negative, suggesting again that not having NSF support has a tendency to assign economists to a regime of zero-valued publication observations even in a small sample of minority economists.

Table 5
Zero-Inflated Poisson Regression Parameter Estimates
of Research Productivity Equation

Regressand: R_i = Total number of authored or co-authored publications.

Specification:	All Economists (1)	(2)	Nonminority Economists (3)	(4)	Minority Economists (5)	(6)
Regressors:						
Constant	434.70	280.05	1026.6	901.17	—	—
	$(88.42)^a$	$(80.67)^a$	$(82.96)^a$	$(80.43)^a$	—	—
*ln*AGE	−1.16	−.925	−2.83	−2.58	−.62	−1.15
	$(.245)^a$	$(.232)^a$	$(.235)^a$	$(.233)^a$	(1.28)	(1.27)
*ln*SALARY	.101	—	.037	—	1.44	—
	$(.043)^b$	—	(.039)	—	$(.643)^b$	—
*ln*TEARN	—	.290	—	.189	—	.675
	—	$(.047)^a$	—	$(.043)^a$	—	(.419)
RSEVN	.234	.219	.278	.278	2.10	.067
	$(.116)^b$	$(.128)^c$	$(.091)^a$	$(.097)^a$	(2.13)	(3.78)
RSEFF	.011	.012	.013	.012	.014	.006
	$(.0007)^a$	$(.0008)^a$	$(.0007)^a$	$(.0004)^a$	(.013)	(.015)
*ln*VINT	−56.57	−36.59	−133.63	−117.45	−1.59	−.132
	$(11.51)^a$	$(10.51)^a$	$(10.80)^a$	$(10.48)^a$	(1.57)	(.976)
MINOR	−.124	−.128	—	—	—	—
	$(.072)^c$	$(.071)^c$	—	—	—	—
NSFSUP	.018	.028	.007	.008	—	—
	(.101)	(.112)	(.118)	(.128)	—	—
MINOR x NSFSUP	.172	.003	—	—	—	—
	(1.56)	(2.25)	—	—	—	—
γ_1	0008	.0007	.0008	.0008	.0009	.001
	$(.00004)^a$	$(.00004)^a$	$(.00005)^a$	$(.00005)^a$	$(.0002)^a$	$(.0002)^a$
γ_2	−.781	−.869	−1.44	−1.42	−1.61	−3.37
	$(.453)^c$	$(.450)^b$	$(.473)^a$	$(.469)^a$	(1.73)	(5.01)
v	47.91	47.22	39.19	39.69	11.78	16.74
$\Sigma(\hat{\lambda}_i = 0)/$ $\Sigma(R_i = 0)$	1.001	1.001	1.001	1.001	1.001	1.001
N	923	923	816	816	107	107

Notes:
Standard errors in parentheses.
N = Number of observations.
[a]Significant at the .01 level.
[b]Significant at the .05 level.
[c]Significant at the .10 level.

In general, the results reported in Table 5 suggest that NSF research support matters for the research productivity of economists, in a particular way. Having had NSF research support apparently matters for whether or not the number of publications is not zero. Beyond zero publications, NSF support does not seem to matter, suggesting that the receipt of NSF research support increases the probability that a Ph.D. economist crosses the zero publication threshold.

Given that minority economist research productivity is positively correlated with tenure probabilities and the number of minorities that earn doctorates in economics, an interesting science policy question is: would increased NSF research support to minority economists matter for their research productivity? This is a useful inquiry to the extent that diversity among the ranks of Ph.D. economists is a desirable science policy objective. If indeed increased NSF support could enhance the research productivity of minority economists, the payoffs would be more minority economists coming through the pipeline (Agesa, Granger, and Price, 1998) and, given the results from the tenure equations reported in Table 3, more tenured minority economists on faculties of colleges and universities.

The results reported in Table 5 do not permit a clear assessment of whether increased NSF research support to minority economists would enhance their research productivity. The significance of the minority status variable while negative, only suggests that for economists above the threshold of zero publications, being a minority is associated with lower research productivity. The results reported in Table 5 show that not having NSF research support increases the probability of having zero research productivity. If minority status also increases the probability of being in the zero research productivity regime, and minority economists are less likely to receive NSF support, increased NSF research support to minority economists could enable them to cross the zero research productivity threshold.

Table 6 reports ZIP parameter estimates over the entire sample of economists with the regime switching equation augmented to include the dummy variable for minority status.[13] The Vuong test statistic suggests the adequacy of the ZIP specification and the model explains approximately all the zero-valued publication observations. In addition to the doctoral vintage and NSF research support dummy, the dummy for minority status is positive and significant in the regime switching equation. Thus, being a minority Ph.D. economist increases the probability of being in the no research productivity regime. Moreover, the dummies for minority status, and its interaction with the dummy for NSF support are rendered insignificant by including the dummy for minority status in the regime switching equation.

As both minority status and having no NSF support increase the probability of having no research productivity, the results reported in Table 6 have a straightforward implication for the likely effects of increased NSF research support to minority economists. Given that having no NSF research support and being a minority economist increases the probability of having zero research productivity, the results in Table 6 suggest that increased NSF research support to minority economists who have never had such support would push them across the zero productivity threshold.

IV. HBCU Black Economist Research Productivity and NSF Funding

The parameter results reported in Tables 4–6 on the effects of NSF research support on minority economist research productivity are potentially useful for explaining the negative HBCU effect reported in Agesa, Granger, and Price (2000). The 1995 public SESTAT data do not allow us to determine the exact place of employment for a given economist. As such, we can only conjecture that the coefficient on being a minority economist is picking up some of the effects that being employed at an HBCU has on individual research productivity. It is certainly the case that among black economists in academia, a disproportionate number are employed at HBCUs, and among black economists in academia, a disproportionate number with zero publications are employed at HBCUs.[14] In this context, if the receipt of NSF research funding increases research productivity for minority economists, the parameter results in Tables 4–5 suggest that the research productivity of black economists at HBCUs could benefit significantly from NSF funding.

If NSF funding enhances refereed publications prospect either through conferring upon the recipient a prestige that enables favorable referee reports—the leveraging effect of Wachtel (2000)—and/or by imparting the social learning of publication norms as a result of successfully surviving the NSF peer review process (Ellison, 2000), then the receipt of NSF research funding by black economists at HBCUs could result in a significant increase in their research productivity. To explore this possibility, Table 7 reports descriptive data on NSF economics program grant submissions and awards from HBCU economists between 1980–2002, along with the average number of EconLit Journal of Eco-

Table 6
Zero-Inflated Poisson Regression Parameter Estimates
of Research Productivity Equation

Regressand: R_i = Total number of authored or co-authored publications.

Specification:	All Economists	
	(1)	(2)
Regressors:		
Constant	464.69	280.05
	$(90.75)^a$	$(80.79)^a$
lnAGE	−1.18	−.917
	$(.251)^a$	$(.233)^a$
lnSALARY	.121	—
	$(.043)^a$	—
lnTEARN	—	.282
	—	$(.047)^a$
RSEVN	.221	.217
	$(.119)^c$	$(.128)^c$
RSEFF	.013	.012
	$(.004)^a$	$(.004)^a$
lnVINT	−56.59	−36.58
	$(11.81)^a$	$(10.52)^a$
MINOR	−.090	−.117
	(.070)	(.088)
NSFSUP	.054	.029
	(.101)	(.116)
MINOR x NSFSUP	−.054	−.013
	(1.14)	(2.8)
γ_1	.0008	.0007
	$(.00004)^a$	$(.00005)^a$
γ_2	−1.65	−.872
	$(.473)^a$	$(.453)^c$
γ_3	.611	.635
	$(.334)^c$	$(.333)^c$
v	47.89	47.34
$\Sigma(\hat{\lambda}_i = 0)/\Sigma(R_i = 0)$	1.004	1.008
N	923	923

Notes:
Standard errors in parentheses.
N = Number of observations.
[a]Significant at the .01 level.
[c]Significant at the .10 level.

Table 7
HBCU NSF Economics Program Submissions/Awards and Average
Research Productivity of Black HBCU Economists

Institution	Submissions 1980–2000	Awards 1980–2000	Average Number of Publications 1969–2005
All HBCUs	32	3	4.03
North Carolina A&T State University	4	3	10.0

Notes: Submission and award data on HBCUs are based on confidential NSF administrative data obtained during the author's tenure as Program Director for Economics. HBCU black economist publication data are based upon articles indexed in the American Economic Association's EconLit electronic bibliography database. The average publication measure does not include those individuals with zero publications.

nomic Literature (JEL)-indexed publications through 2005 for black economists employed at all HBCUs, and from North Carolina A&T State University—the HBCU that accounted for all the NSF economics program awards during the period.

The relationship between black economist research productivity at HBCUs and and NSF research support in Table 7 approximates the relationship between NSF research support and minority economist research productivity suggested by the parameter estimates in Tables 4–6. The data reported in Table 7 suggest that black economists at HBCUs who have received NSF funding are less likely to have zero refereed publications relative to black economists at HBCUs who have never received NSF funding. This suggests a possibly casual link between NSF funding of black economists at HBCUs, and their later research productivity.[15] In this context, part of the adverse effect that being at an HBCU has on individual economist research productivity (Agesa, Granger, and Price, 2000) could be explained by the low levels of NSF Economics Program research funding to black economists at HBCUs.[16]

The parameter estimates in Table 6 suggest that NSF research support does not have a direct monotonic effect on research productivity for minority economists, but for minority economists it enables it them to cross a threshold of having no refereed publications. The data in Table 7 suggest that at least for minority economists at HBCUs, receiving NSF support also has a direct positive effect on research productivity. While this cannot be explored in the 1995 Public SESTAT data as there is no way to identify the type of institution (e.g., HBCU or not), the data in Table 7 suggest that the positive effects of NSF support on the research productivity of black economists at HBCUs is significant, and larger than suggested by the parameter estimates in Table 6.

V. Conclusions

The central concern of this paper was to determine the importance of NSF research support for the research productivity of minority economists—particularly black economists at HBCUs. In light of the finding of Agesa, Granger, and Price (2000) that being at an HBCU lowers economist research productivity, given that funded research is an important determinant of individual research productivity, this paper explored whether or not increased NSF funding to economists at HBCUs would increase their research productivity. Parameter estimates from a ZIP model of individual research productivity revealed that NSF research support does matter for the research productivity of economists in a particular way. NSF research support seems to matter for enabling economists to cross the threshold of zero research productivity. Once across that threshold, the results suggest that NSF research support does not matter for the number of articles published by economists.

Being a minority economist and not ever having NSF research support were among the factors that increased the probability of having zero research productivity. Descriptive data on HBCU economist submissions/awards from NSF economics and their research productivity reveal a pattern in which NSF support not only enables black economists at HBCUs to cross a threshold of zero publications in refereed economics journals, but also a continuous monotonic relationship between NSF support and research productivity. This suggests that the receipt of NSF research support by black economists at HBCUs who have never had NSF funding would increase their research productivity substantially. To the extent that black economist research productivity is correlated with black faculty tenure and the number of HBCU baccalaureate graduates who go on to earn doctorates in economics, a further implication is that an NSF policy of funding the research efforts of HBCU black economists who have never had such support would indirectly mitigate the under-representation of minority Ph.D. economists among the rank of tenured economics faculty, and the pipeline.

In general, the results reported here suggest that NSF research support enhances the research productivity of any economist, minority or non-minority, who has never had such support—being a minority economist only reduces the likelihood of receiving such support. The fact that minority status reduces the likelihood of receiving NSF support raises troubling concerns about possible bias in the manner in which the NSF awards research support. Wachtel (2000) for example, has recently provided evidence that since 1974, NSF research support has been disproportionately awarded to economics faculty at fifteen top tier research universities. This suggests that the NSF award process is not unbiased in that the distribution of awards is skewed. The results here suggest another possible bias—against minority economists. If indeed there is a bias against minority economists in the funding process, this bias undermines the NSF's officially stated commitment to enabling the careers, and mitigating the underrepresentation of minority Ph.D. economists.

The bias against minority economists, if it exists, need not be based on their current status as members of a racial/ethnic minority group. The analysis of Wachtel (2000) suggests that success in obtaining NSF research support is correlated with past success. This introduces a bias based on past success. To the extent that minority economists have little past success, as the data and results reported here suggest, minority economists may not be biased against because they are minorities, but because they have no track record of success getting NSF research support. To the extent that social capital accrued through scientific networks such as the National Bureau of Economic Research (NBER) matters for success in obtaining NSF research support (Feinberg and Price, 2004), the funding bias against minority economists could also reflect discrimination against minority economists with respect to obtaining membership in scholarly networks such as NBER.

There are some possible limitations of the results reported here. Given the other important determinants of research productivity that are not included in the model estimated here, the parameter estimates could suffer from omitted variable bias. The cross-sectional nature of the data also prevent the determination of life cycle effects on research productivity as in Levin and Stephan (1991). In all the specifications reported, however, the variable for age was always negative and significant. Notwithstanding these possible limitations, the results offer some insights into the role that NSF funding could have upon the research productivity of black economists at HBCUs. In addition to increasing submissions from black economists at HBCUs, NSF science policy goals should be mindful of any biases that may constrain awards to black economists at HBCUs. The results reported here suggest that an NSF science policy that is mindful of the research awards accruing to black economists at HBCUs would increase the productivity of black economists at HBCUs. Such a policy could also promote racial diversity among the ranks of Ph.D. scientists engaged in the research enterprise, as the research productivity of black economists is positively correlated with the number of HBCU undergraduates that go on to earn economics doctorates (Agesa, Granger, and Price, 1998).

Notes

1. Collins (2000) reports that in 1995, black, Hispanics, and Native Americans accounted for 3 percent of the economics doctorates employed by four-year colleges and medical institutions.
2. Collins (2000) reports summary statistics which reveal that among all colleges and universities in 1995, black Americans accounted for 1.6 percent of tenured faculty in economics. For colleges/universities with doctoral programs in economics, black Americans accounted for .08 percent of tenured faculty in economics.
3. Wachtel, (2000, p. 22) has recently argued that "The imprimatur of an NSF grant carries significant leverage by aiding in acceptance of articles by the major journals, receiving further grants from private foundations and other government funding agencies, and career advancement."
4. Ellison (2000) provides a theoretical account of the social norms that evolve among journal referees for the type of papers that are ultimately published in economics journals. Authors, if they are to be successful publishers, must comply with the social norm governing publishable papers. It is in this context that NSF review process is valuable, as it is a way for potential authors to learn the norm that publishable papers must be in compliance with, which could increase the probability of getting published.
5. The SDR has been sponsored by the NSF and other federal agencies since the early 1970s. The survey consists of a sample of individuals who earned science and engineering doctorates at US colleges and universities. The survey is biennial, and every two years a new sample of doctorate earners is added from another NSF sponsored survey: the Survey of Earned Doctorates.
6. In particular, question A32.2 of the 1995 SDR asks the respondent: Since April 1990, how many articles that you have authored or co-authored have been accepted for publication in a refereed professional journal?
7. Having zero as a natural outcome of the distribution generating publications is ideal as it obviates the need to employ double logarithmic regression specifications as in Bodenhorn (1997), or treating the data as being truncated at zero as in Levin and Stephan (1991). For a more detailed justification of using a Poisson probability distribution for research publications, see Agesa, Granger, and Price (2000).
8. Michener and Tighe (1992) note that the Poisson density has a history as a specification offered to explain count data. For example, L. von Bortkiewicz (1898) applied it to explain mule-kick deaths. The specific regression formulation where γ is expressed as a function of exogenous variables has been considered by Hausman, Hall, and Griliches (1984), Chappell, Kimenyi, and Mayer (1990), and more recently by Agesa, Granger, and Price (2000).
9. The insignificance of minority status as a determinant of tenure probabilities in the sample is in contrast to the findings of Ards, Brintnall and Woodard (1997),

who find that in the case of political scientists with doctorates, being a minority lowers the probability of tenure.

10. More generally, if R_i is a Poisson random variable, Cameron and Trivedi (1990) show that a test for mean-variance equality is based on the hypothesis test: H_o: var(R_i) λ_i versus the alternative H_a: var$(R_i) = \lambda_i + \alpha g(\lambda_i)$, where $g(\lambda_i)$ is a function specified to equal 1, λ_i, or λ_i^2. A test for mean-variance equality is a t-test for significance of α in the auxiliary regression: $\Sigma w_i g(\lambda_i)[(R_i - \lambda_i)^2 - R_i - \alpha g(\lambda_i)]$ = 0, where $\Sigma w_i g(\lambda_i)$ is a weight based on a consistent estimate of the coefficient vector of the exogenous variables. If the coefficient on α is insignificant, the null hypothesis of mean-variance equality cannot be rejected.

11. This extension of the simple Poisson model has also been called a "Zero-Altered Poisson" model by Greene (2000), and the Poisson "With Zeros" [Mullahy (1986)], The ZIP description, which is now more or less the convention is due to Lambert (1992). It is easy to demonstrate that for this model: $E(R_i) = (1 - q_i)$ and Var(R_i) $= \lambda_i(1 - q_i)(1 + \lambda_i q_i)$. Clearly, the ZIP model is characterized by overdispersion, as the mean and variance are no longer identical.

12. The Vuong test statistic reported in Table 5 is the version suggested by Greene (2000) and is computed as follows: let $f_1(y_i \mid x_i)$ be the predicted probability that the random variable Y equals y_i under the assumption that the distribution is a ZIP, let $f_2(y_i \mid x_i)$ be the predicted probability that the random variable Y equals y_i under the assumption that the distribution is a Negative Binomial, and let $m_i = \log[f_1(y_i / x_i)/f_2(y_i \mid x_i)]$, the Vuong test statistic is:
$$v = [n^{1/2}(1/n\Sigma m_i)/(1/n\Sigma(m_i - \bar{m})^2)^{1/2}]$$
The non-nested alternative is specified as a Negative Binomial model. This is based upon the idea that since the Negative Binomial model is essentially a Poisson model with gamma heterogeneity (Gerber, 1992), that allows for overdispersion, the Vuong test statistic permits a determination as to whether even after allowing for overdispersion, are there still excess zero observations that are adequately explained by the ZIP model.

13. In particular, the augmentation of the regime switching equation results in:
$$z_i = F[\gamma_1 V \, INT + \gamma_2 NSFSUP + \gamma_3 MINOR]$$

14. This finding is derived from data on black economist publications in refereed economics journals—publications indexed in the American Economic Association's EconLit electronic bibliography—as well as their college/university affiliation through the year 2005 compiled and maintained by Maury D. Granger, Department of Economics, Jackson State University. The data include all known black economists employed in colleges/universities, and is available upon request from the author.

15. Of course, causality could run in the opposite direction—NSF funding could be biased toward economists with a track record of already having refereed publications. However, the black economist publication data reported in Table 7 have a time window (1969–2005) with a terminal point that exceeds the terminal point of the NSF submission/award time window (1980–2002). As such, and in the absence of any awards to HBCU black economists after 2005—of which we are unaware of—post-2002 refereed publications could possibly reflect the research productivity enhancing effects of NSF funding.

16. In general, the low levels of NSF economics funding to black economists at HBCUs could be explained by some combination of bias on behalf of NSF economics, low-quality submissions by black economists at HBCUs, and low submission rates. While we cannot address the first two factors, grants submissions to NSF Economics by black economists at HBCUs have been shockingly low. The data in Table 7 report a total of 32 submissions from HBCUs over a 22-year period. To put this

in context, as of 2002, the NSF Economics Program was receiving approximately 400 submissions annually. Thus, the low submission rates by black economists at HBCUs could potentially explain the low award rates to black economists at HBCUs.

References

Agesa, Jacqueline, Maury Granger, and Gregory N. Price. 2000. "Economics Research at Teaching Institutions: Are Historically Black Colleges And Universities Different?," *Southern Economic Journal*, 67(2), pp. 427–447.

Agesa, Jacqueline, Maury Granger, and Gregory N. Price. 1998. "Economic Research at Historically Black Colleges and Universities: Rankings and Effects on the Supply of Black Economists," *Review of Black Political Economy*, 25(4), pp. 41–54.

Ards, Sheila, Michael Brintall, and Maurice Woodard. 1997. "The Road to Tenure and Beyond for African American Political Scientists," *Journal of Negro Education*, 66(1), pp. 159–171.

Arora, Ashish, and Alfonso Gambardella. 1996. "The Impact of NSF Support For Basic Research in Economics," Working Paper, Heinz School of Public Policy, Carnegie Mellon University, Pittsburgh, PA.

Bodenhorn, Howard. 1997. "Teachers, and Scholars Too: Economic Scholarship at Elite Liberal Arts Colleges," *Journal of Economic Education*, 28(4), pp. 323–336.

Bortkiewicz, L. von. 1898. *Das Gesetz Der Kleinen Zahlen*, Leipzig, Teuber.

Cameron, Colin A. and Pravin K. Trivedi. 1990. "Regression-Based Tests for Overdispersion in the Poisson Model," *Journal of Econometrics*, 46(3), pp. 347–364.

Chappell, William F., Mwangi S. Kimenyi, and Walter J. Mayer. 1990. "A Poisson Probability Model of Entry and Market Structure with an Application to U.S. Industries during 1972–77," *Southern Economic Journal*, 56(4), pp. 918–927.

Collins, Susan M. 2000. "Minority Groups in the Economics Profession," *Journal of Economic Perspectives*, 14(3), pp. 133–148.

Creamer, Elizabeth, G. 1998. "Assessing Faculty Publication Productivity: Issues of Equity," *ASHEERIC Higher Education Report*, Volume 26, No. 2. Washington D.C.: The George Washington University Graduate School of Education and Human Development.

Ellison, Glenn. 2000. "Evolving Standards for Academic Publishing: A q-r Theory," Working Paper No. 7895, National Bureau of Economic Research, Cambridge, MA.

Feinberg, Robert M. and Gregory N. Price. 2004. "The Funding of Economics Research: Does Social Capital Matter for Success at the National Science Foundation?," *Review of Economics and Statistics*, 86(1), pp. 245–252.

Gerber, Hans U. 1992. "From the Generalized Gamma to the Generalized Negative Binomial Distribution," *Insurance: Mathematics and Economics*, 10(4), pp. 303–309.

Greene, William H. 2000. *Econometric Analysis*, 4th edition, Prentice Hall, New Jersey.

Hartley, James. E., and Michael D. Robinson. 1997. "Economic Research at National Liberal Arts Colleges: School Rankings," *Journal of Economic Education*, 28(4). pp. 337–349.

Hausman, Jerry, Brownwyn H. Hall, and Zvi Griliches. 1984. "Econometric Models For Count Data with an Application to the Patents-R&D Relationship," *Econometrica*, 52(4), pp. 909–938.

Lambert, Diane. 1992. "Zero-Inflated Poisson Regression with an Application to Defects in Manufacturing," *Technometrics*, 34(1), pp. 1–14.

Levin, Sharon G. and Paula Stephan. 1991. "Research Productivity Over the Life Cycle: Evidence For Academic Scientists," *American Economic Review*, 81(1), pp. 114–132.

Michener, Ron and Carla Tighe. 1992. "A Poisson Regression Model of Highway Fatalities," *American Economic Review*, 82(2), pp. 452–456.

Mullahy, John. 1986. "Specification and Testing of Some Modified Count Data Models," *Journal of Econometrics*, 33(3), pp. 341–365.

National Science Foundation, Division of Science Resource Studies, *SESTAT: A Tool for Studying Scientists and Engineers in the United States*, NSF 99-337, Authors, Nirmala Kannankutty and R. Keith Wilson. (Arlington, VA 1999).

Stephan, Paula. 1996. "The Economics of Science," *Journal of Economic Literature*, 34(3), pp. 1199–1235.

Vuong, Quang H. 1989. "Likelihood Ratio Tests for Model Selection and Non-nested Hypotheses," *Econometrica*, 57(2), pp. 307–333.

Wachtel, Howard. 2000. "How the National Science Foundation Funds Research in Economics," *Challenge*, 43(5), pp. 20–30.

Truth, Generalizations, and Stigmas: An Analysis of the Media's Coverage of Morris Brown College and Black Colleges Overall

Marybeth Gasman

A half-century after *Brown v. Board of Education*, 40 years after Lyndon Johnson's speech endorsing the concept of affirmative action, and two years after the Supreme Court upheld racial diversity as a factor in admissions, the approximately 80 histori-cally black colleges and universities still enroll more than 10 percent of the African-American students in higher education and award close to 20 percent of degrees. These institutions have produced leaders from Thurgood Marshall to Jesse Jackson to Spike Lee. Their step shows, marching bands, and fraternities and sororities have become integral elements of African American culture. It is [common] in black churches and neighborhoods for parents to believe that their children will have better outcomes in black colleges than in mostly white ones, because the black schools provided a more nurturing, supportive environment, free of white presumptions that blacks are intellectual inferiors or expectations they should portray the role of hip-hop gangsta. But what happens when the truism appears less and less true? What happens when an education emergency is ignored except by those enduring it? (Freedman, August 3, 2004)

The above quote about the dire situation at the nation's black colleges was penned by *New York Times* reporter Samuel Freedman and is based on his visit to one historically black institution—Texas Southern University (TSU). In fact, one of the individuals interviewed for the article by Freed-man, scholar Jacqueline Fleming, was angered enough by the reporter's comments and interpretations to write a letter to the editor of the *Times*. In the words of Fleming, a faculty member and Director of the General University Academic Center at TSU,

I cannot say how disappointed I was with the article by Samuel Friedman [sic] on black colleges. . . . I do understand his assignment was to investigate low graduation rates, but that is where the problem begins. His assignment could have just as easily been to find out why TSU's one-year retention rates (the first step in graduation rates) has increased each year since 1997, even while the average test scores of incoming students have declined over this same period. (August 16, 2005)

In her criticism of Freedman, Fleming alluded to what can be seen as a larger problem in the way the media treats historically black colleges. Fleming, the author of the classic book *Blacks in College*—one of the first comprehensive, longitudinal studies comparing the performance of African American students enrolled at black colleges and historically white colleges, took Freedman to task for his approach in framing the article:

> [T]his situation reminded me that when I published the major comparative study of Blacks in College in 1984, a *New York Times* Education reporter was taken with the research and outcomes for black colleges that were more positive than anyone would have expected at that time. (It is far better understood today that nurturance and the absence of prejudice promote intellectual development among black students.) I was told when to expect the story to appear, but it never did. Apparently at the 11th hour, the Editor canceled it. Could it have been that this story about black colleges was far too positive? Perhaps only a story on a black college crisis is worthy of print. (August 16, 2005)

Of course, the recent *New York Times* story is not the first account to negatively portray black colleges. As some of the nation's black institutions have found themselves in dire financial straits—Morris Brown College, Bennett College, and Philander Smith College are a few examples—reporters covering happenings at these colleges have often painted the shortcomings with a broad brush, sometimes generalizing to include all black colleges, both private and public. The claims of these news articles have gained national attention, jeopardizing recruitment efforts, fundraising success, and in some cases, the long-term existence of the institutions (Basinger, April 17, 2003; "Morris Brown loses appeal," April 8, 2003; Poe, November 14, 2002; Simmons, October 6, 2002; Williams, October 18, 2002). After reading these newspaper articles, I sought to examine bias in the media's coverage of black colleges on a larger scale.

Morris Brown College, in particular, provides a telling example. The small, private, church supported institution lost its accreditation, is $27 million in debt, and has been convicted by the federal government of misuse of financial aid funds. This paper reports the results of a content analysis I conducted of the media's coverage of recent events at Morris Brown College in Atlanta. Content analysis allowed me to examine a large mass of written material from a range of media venues. It gave me an indication of the dominant ideas being put forth by the media on the subject of black higher education. Specifically, I was interested in the words and phrases used to describe both Morris Brown and other black colleges mentioned in the articles. I noted the possible generalizations made about black colleges as a result of Morris Brown's situation. In conducting this content analysis, I looked at local, regional, and national media outlets.

Review of Literature

Throughout American history the media and higher education have had a lukewarm relationship. Conventional wisdom and scholarship suggest that higher education has only recently come under intense and sometimes unfair scrutiny by the media due to accountability questions and corporate scandals (Jones, 2004). According to this view, prior to the 1980s the press treated most postsecondary institutions with a hands-off attitude (Stepp, 2003; McLendon & Peterson, 1999). In contrast, when one looks at the history of media coverage of black colleges and universities, it appears that these institutions have been the recipient of countless jabs and continuing skepticism since their beginnings (Willie, 1978; Jones, 2004).

In recent years, several scholars have explored the relationship between higher education and the media. Rochelle Stanfield (1998) examined the ways in which the media misleads the public with regard to tuition costs—claiming that costs are increasing at greater rates than is supported by national data. Michael McLendon and Marvin Peterson (1999) analyzed media stories pertaining to the 1995 state appropriations conflict between the University of Michigan and Michigan State University to examine the influence of the media on public policy. The authors discovered that the media had considerable influence over local and regional politics, shaping the public discourse and selectively reporting on the appropriations conflicts. When race was considered alongside higher education coverage, the results were quite interesting. For example, Jane Rhodes (1999) explored national press coverage of the Black Panther Party, finding that initially the national press had no interest in the group. However, once the organization gained momentum in cities and on college campuses, the media sharpened its portrayals of Black Panther ideologies—eventually elevating the Panthers to celebrity status. Perhaps the closest study to that undertaken here is Bruce A. Jones' (2004) study of 1980s *Chronicle of Higher Education* coverage of university scandals, including black colleges and their historically white counterparts. Jones found that between 1980 and 1989, there were twenty-five stories in the *Chronicle* on scandal and corruption. Many of these pertained to black colleges. Unlike the treatment received by historically white institutions (usually a "slap on the hand" by the media), newspapers called for the closure of some black institutions. Subsequently, state governments threatened to close some institutions. As a result, some black college administrators began to claim that the media had a dual standard of treatment toward college and university scandals.

Conceptual Framework and Method

It is not a secret that the media is attracted to controversy; however, many reporters still maintain that they operate with the heightened sense of objectivity emphasized in journalism school. According to Cohen (1963) "the pattern of news coverage . . . influences public perceptions of what current issues are important" (p. 229). Cohen referred to these patterns as the "media agenda" (Cohen, 1963; McCombs, 1992; McClendon and Peterson, 1999). Moreover, according to media scholar Iyengar (1988), "there can no longer be serious doubts over the ability of the mass media to influence the political agenda. The agenda-setting effect has proven to be quite robust, spanning a variety of issues, media channels, and target audiences" (Iyengar, 1988, p. 338). With the concept of "agenda setting" in mind, I examined the media's treatment of Morris Brown College during its recent accreditation and financial situation, looking at how the media might shape the public's understanding of the institution in both positive and negative ways. In addition, I examined the media's interpretation of the situation for black colleges overall based on their understanding of Morris Brown.

There is no single definition of content analysis as a research method. Thus, to guide this project, I borrowed from several sources (Bishop, 2003; DeVaney, 1987; Fitsgerald, 2000; Gall, Borg, and Gall, 1996; Lincoln and Guba, 1985; Tuckman, 1978; Zelizer, 2002). However, my approach was primarily informed by David Altheide's *Qualitative Media Analysis*. In his book, Altheide describes a three-part process that calls for the identification of frames, themes, and discourses within the content of written material. Specifically, he notes: "Frames focus on what will be discussed and how it will be discussed. . . ."; in other words, how the media selects the content for the article (Altheide, 1996, p. 31). According to Altheide, themes pertain to the recurring and dominant ideas that appear within the material that has been selected. Lastly, Altheide describes the discourse as the actual messages being communicated by the documents (in the case of this study the newspaper/website/television reports)—that is, the words, the images, photographs, phrases, etc. Thus, according to Altheide, the documents analyzed "carry the discourse that reflects certain themes, which in turn are held together and given meaning by a broad frame" (Altheide, 1996, p. 31).

To acquire data for this research project, I systematically collected newspaper and magazine articles, television transcripts, and web-based publications for a period of two years. In order to obtain wide reach, I subscribed to an Internet news search service that finds all of the news stories published on black colleges each day and sends a summary and corresponding Internet link to my email address. In addition, I sifted through newspapers and magazines and conducted ten Lexis-Nexis searches covering the two-year period of Morris Brown's recent financial and accreditation struggle. These efforts yielded a total of 407 news stories pertaining to Morris Brown College and/or black colleges in general. I did not include articles that were about individual black colleges other than Morris Brown. The stories that I examined were found in Atlanta newspapers, regional and national papers, as well as trade papers and magazines such as *The Chronicle of Higher Education* and *Black Issues in Higher Education.* In acquiring articles from a multitude of sources, I aimed to get a sense of the treatment of black colleges in a broad cross-section of media outlets. I read each of the articles carefully, identifying frames, themes, and discourse as described above. The resulting paper is divided into three sections according to Altheide's structure: *Frames,* which focuses on what the media discussed and how they discussed it; *Themes,* which highlights the dominant ideas that appear in the media's discussion; and *Discourse,* which emphasizes the way the media represents the issues at Morris Brown using descriptors and phrases.

Origins and Mission of Morris Brown College

In 1885, the State of Georgia issued a charter to Morris Brown College, an institution founded on the idea of serving students from low-income backgrounds.[1] Unlike most other black colleges, Morris Brown was started by African Americans, a fact that gave the institution few resources but greater autonomy.[2] As members of the African Methodist Episcopal (AME) Church, the college founders were dedicated to providing an educational experience that was inclusive of black students from diverse backgrounds. According to Morris Brown's own description, the "College not only has inspired average and better than average students to great heights of achievement in competition, but has also transformed sensitive 'high risk' students into performers far better than their credentials suggest them capable" (www.morrisbrown.edu, February 6, 2004). Although this is a noble cause, over the course of its lifetime, Morris Brown's dedication to low-income students (and hence to the receipt of fewer tuition dollars) has caused it many financial problems. The AME

Church provides some institutional support but has not been able to give enough funding to offset these diminished revenues.

During the early 1990s, Morris Brown College faced a $10 million deficit that caused students, faculty, alumni, and the local Atlanta community to question its future existence. However, the Morris Brown community refused to let the institution go under, raising $7 million dollars in donations and saving $2 million through cost-cutting strategies. Although still struggling financially during the latter part of the 1990s, the institution was able to deflect negative publicity, and even garnered some nationwide media coverage when then-president, Dolores E. Cross, announced that every first year student at Morris Brown College would be furnished with a laptop computer. Nonetheless, in the fall of 2002, the institution became mired in controversy once again. Its commitment to supporting low-income students combined with inappropriate spending and accreditation problems catapulted the small college into the national spotlight.

Framing the Situation at Morris Brown College

The media's framing of the problems at Morris Brown College manifested itself in the following questions: What are the financial problems at the institution? Will it maintain its accreditation? Who is leading the institution? And who is saving the institution? All of the media stories center on at least one of these questions and in some cases all of them. Although at first glance these frames seem quite typical for the media's coverage of higher education stories, when I looked more deeply at the questions asked within each of the frames a unique set of themes emerged.

The initial articles presented a discussion of the financial situation at the institution and tried to uncover, piece by piece, what was happening at the college, who was responsible, what changes were taking place, and what the ramifications of the financial situation were.

What Are the Financial Problems?

A November 2002 story on the *Cable News Network* (CNN) spelled out Morris Brown's financial quagmire bluntly and assigned blame directly in its "breaking news" story: "The historically Black college founded by former slaves is more than $23 million in debt and could be forced to close in a crisis that is being blamed on its past president and her ambitious efforts to enlarge Morris Brown and raise its profile" (Haines, November 1, 2002, n. p.). The article gave an overview of each financial blunder made by the institution, sometimes assigning blame and sometimes not. Of note was the media's lack of attention to the college's financial plan for the future. The story included only one line about this plan: "The school is working on a recovery plan that could include tuition increases, job cuts and cutbacks in athletics and other programs" (Haines, November 1, 2002, n.p.). Another article of note, penned by the Associated Press, detailed the efforts being made by the new president of Morris Brown:

> Charles Taylor, hired just three months ago, has been working to restructure the college's debt, which he put at $23 million—a staggering amount for an institution with an endowment that stood at only $5 million this summer. And he brought in an official from Howard University to shore up the troubled financial aid office, the root of many of Morris Brown's problems. The chairman of the board of trustees has also promised to reform the board by bringing on new members with business and financial backgrounds. ("Morris Brown May Close," November 1, 2002, p. 1A)

This article had an almost hopeful tone in its depiction of the new president and his strategies.

The Associated Press's wire service also focused on financial problems but with an eye toward their effect on the individual student. Entitled "Morris Brown College May Close," the article began by describing the "mess" at the institution: "The financial mess at Morris Brown College is so bad that the cafeteria sometimes runs out of food, computer labs carefully ration paper and laptop computers that cost students $1,500 each never arrived"(November 1, 2002, p. 1A). Another article in *The Atlanta Journal-Constitution* spoke to the financial frame in the title. Its title was "Catch-22 has Morris Brown in new bind; Pay up or lose funding, feds tell strapped school." The article gave a "play by play" of Morris Brown's financial woes and then turned to experts to discuss a way out of the financial situation (Simmons and Donsky, November 1, 2002, p. 1D).

Other articles were framed by the idea of financial instability but specifically addressed the role of federal agencies in investigating Morris Brown's financial situation. These articles detailed the federal "crackdown" on the college, widening the scope of the problems from the local to the national (Simmons, September 29, 2002; "Feds may cut off funding to Morris Brown," November 1, 2002). Of note is that the author of one of these articles also writes for Cox News Service and thus the stories were nationally syndicated.

After Morris Brown lost its accreditation, the news stories were still financially framed but focused on how the institution would "rebuild" in their "debt-ridden" state. Reporters spoke of dropping enrollments. Those members of the Morris Brown community who were interviewed talked of "eliminating short-term debt, and paying off long-term debt" (Basinger, October 19, 2003, p. 1). Still other articles focused on how the beleaguered institution would prepare for the huge reductions in the enrollment—reductions that resulted from their loss of accreditation and in turn, loss of financial aid packages for students ("Morris Brown prepares for reduced enrollments," July 29, 2003; Hoff, September 25, 2003; Rowe, April 11, 2003). The last area of emphasis is that of program and staff cuts. Many articles focused on how the financially-strapped institution was "making ends meet." For example, *Sports Illustrated* ran a story examining the suspension of the College's athletic programs and the resulting layoffs and upset students. Likewise, *The Atlanta Journal-Constitution* covered Morris Brown's struggles to collect outstanding student balances (in some cases the institution was forced to withhold diplomas, transcripts, and deny participation in graduation ceremonies) ("Morris Brown College Drops Athletics," May 6, 2003; Simmons, March 7, 2003).

Will Morris Brown Maintain Its Accreditation?

Although accreditation may not seem to be directly linked to an institution's financial stability; an institution is more likely to be held under the microscope if its financial situation is shaky. According to the Southern Association for Colleges and Schools (SACS), "The institutions [must] have a sound financial base and demonstrated financial stability and adequate physical resources to support the mission of the institution and the scope of its programs and services" (Principles of Accreditation, 2004). The organization goes on to describe the specific financial statements required as evidence of financial stability. Thus, according to SACS' principles, an institution's inability to manage its finances implies an inability to support its programs and provide adequate faculty and student services. In a looping set of circumstances, loss of accreditation by SACS leads to loss of financial aid dollars, leaving the institution even more unstable. Moreover, in the case of private black colleges like Morris Brown, the denial of academic standing means a loss of membership in the United Negro College Fund (UNCF). The UNCF provided the institution with $24 million over the past 10 years. Articles framed by accreditation focused on the details of Morris Brown's potential loss of accreditation and the possibility of regaining it.

Prior to SACS' decision to drop Morris Brown's accreditation, the media released story after story speculating as to whether or not the small college would maintain its academic standing. Each of these stories was tied to the financial problems at the institution. The *Atlanta Journal-Constitution,* for example, made a play on a popular African American-oriented movie with the headline, "Morris Brown Waits to Exhale." The article mentioned the accreditation briefly but also talked about the institution's enormous debt and meager endowment (Donsky and Jones, December 8, 2002). Likewise, *The Chronicle of Higher Education* published an article detailing the impending accreditation decision but the entire story was focused on the financial problems of Morris Brown and gave very little indication of what accreditation is and how it has an impact on a college (Williams, October 18, 2002).

Once Morris Brown lost its accreditation, the media focused on the impact of this decision on student financial situations. Most of the stories opened with news of the accreditation loss but quickly moved to the impact that this would have on Morris Brown students—80 percent of whom lost their financial aid. *ABC News,* for example, used testimonials by Morris Brown students: " 'I'm just going to have to go to another institution if this thing stands,' said Renata Robertson, who can't afford to stay if she doesn't receive half the $6,000-a-semester tuition she gets in federal financial aid" ("Morris Brown College Faces Uncertainty," December 11, 2002). A *Chronicle of Higher Education* story included another student perspective on the accreditation situation:

> "It's really breaking my heart to do this," said Tiphanie Pharris, the reigning Miss Sophomore at Morris Brown. "I believe you pledge your allegiance to one school, and that's where you stay." But the uncertainty at Morris Brown—and the risk of losing a private scholarship that can only be awarded to students at accredited colleges—prompted Ms. Pharris and her mother to discuss a possible transfer to Clark Atlanta throughout the early part of this academic year. (Williams, December 13, 2002)

The last group of accreditation-related articles pertained to how Morris Brown planned on regaining its status with SACS. These articles highlighted the institutions efforts to pay off debt. One strategy described in a story in *Black Issues in Higher Education,* called for the college to pay off its short-term debt in order to regain its accreditation. Specifically, the magazine reported,

> Morris Brown has raised more than half of the $10 million short-term debt that it owes, has maintained current notes on the long-term debt, and has restructured the board to recruit business and corporate leaders including two bank presidents. Many internal protocols have been improved and systems of accountability are being reviewed and strengthened. ("Morris Brown to Begin Process of Re-Accreditation, April 24, 2003, p. 8)

Who Is Leading the Institution?

Although this frame is not used as often as the financial and accreditation frames, it is the underlying idea of multiple articles. At the outset of Morris Brown's publicized problems, the institution chose a new president, Charles E. Taylor, a veteran educator and businessman. He had served as president of Wilberforce University in Ohio from 1976-1984 and in a senior management position with British Petroleum Company. Taylor was seen as someone who was going to go into the institution and fix it—including the college's short-term debt. The media portrayed him as an individual who was willing and had the courage to "turn the institution around" ("Morris Brown College Names Charles Taylor," October 14, 2002; "Morris Brown names educator," September 13, 2002; Donsky, September 13, 2002; Ghezzi, October 1, 2002).

As Morris Brown's troubles deepened, the media looked to Charles Taylor for leadership or the "final" word on the College's controversy and many of the articles focused on his approach to changing the institution. Typically Taylor's comments would be juxtaposed with more pessimistic statements about the school's future. For example, in an *Atlanta Journal-Constitution* article, Taylor's defense of the college is juxtaposed with a statement of doubt about the school's enrollment figures:

> The school has already seen its enrollment decrease from 2,547 in the fall to an estimated 1,130 [April 8, 2003]. But Taylor insisted that the school will survive. "Morris Brown will continue to improve, we will continue to raise funds and we will continue to meet the needs of our students," he said. "In time, we will also regain the college's accreditation." (Jones, April 8, 2003)

Not all of the media stories related to leadership focused on the president, however. Several pertained to the rejuvenation of the college's Board of Trustees. One article opened up with the statement, "Morris Brown College's board of trustees must be reorganized if the school is to recover from the worst financial crisis in its history, the board chairman says" (Donsky, October 24, 2002, p. 1F). This article and several others talked about the need to bring "new blood" into the institution so as to provide the necessary leadership ("Jackson expected to join Morris Brown," December 4, 2003). For years, members of the Atlanta community, both black and white, have criticized the small college for the heavy representation of ministers on its Board of Trustees. These critics believed it would be more effective to have individuals associated with corporations on the Board.

At the climax of the Morris Brown controversy, just eight days after SACS rejected the College's appeal for re-accreditation, the president of

the institution resigned. Focusing on leadership, the articles in the subsequent days examined why the president resigned and who would lead
the institution in the future. *BlackVoices.com, The Chronicle of Higher
Education, The Atlanta Journal-Constitution*, and many other news
venues ran stories about the resignation, each beginning with the sense
of loss felt by the institution ("Morris Brown President Quits," April 17,
2003; Basinger, April 17, 2003; Jones, April 16, 2003; "Morris Brown
Trustees," May 8, 2003; Post, April 17, 2003; "President of Morris Brown
College," April 16, 2003; "Morris Brown President Resigns," April 16,
2003). However, the media outlets quickly turned their attention to the
story behind the resignation, looking for clues as to why President Charles
Taylor left the college during its time of need. According to *BlackVoices.
com* (a subsidiary of the *Chicago Tribune*), "things apparently went sour
between Taylor and the board following the news April 7 that the school's
accreditation bid was denied. Also Taylor had been criticized by many,
including officials of the African Methodist Episcopal Church, for not
publicly putting forth a comprehensive financial recovery plan" ("Morris
Brown President Quits," April 17, 2003). Likewise, *The Atlanta Journal-
Constitution* scrutinized Taylor's leadership, noting the ways in which he
failed: "When he took office in September, Taylor promised students he
would fix massive problems in the financial aid office or quit. While he
reorganized staff positions and launched a fund-raising initiative, Taylor
never publicly presented a comprehensive financial recovery plan" (Jones,
April 16, 2003). This article appeared just seven months after the same
paper lauded President Taylor's strengths and potential for achievement.
Moreover, this paper failed to give any coverage to Taylor's financial
plan for the college.

Who Is Saving the Institution?

Many articles were framed using the question, "Who is saving the institution?" Most of these tended to focus on the financial rescue of Morris
Brown College. It is interesting to note that the media highlighted African
American agency when using this frame; however, in doing so they also
held blacks responsible for the problems and future livelihood of the institution. According to *NBC News* and *The Atlanta Journal-Constitution*,
the alumni were rallying together to support Morris Brown both in spirit
and financially. In news stories filled with quotes by prominent Atlanta
politicians, many of whom graduated from the small black college, the
media told of the swell of alumni support: "pledging $2.5 million to help
pull the school out of debt" and raising "$50 million over the next year"

(Simmons, October 26, 2002). Another story examined the Morris Brown students' efforts to raise money for the institution: "The students started the fund-raiser around 8 A.M. and by 3 P.M. collected around $2,000 that will be given to Morris Brown . . ." (Jones, March 9, 2003).

A few articles pertained to how the larger black community was saving the institution, specifically the United Negro College Fund, prominent African American celebrities, the AME church and other black colleges. Several media outlets focused on the generous support of the UNCF, of which Morris Brown was a member until it lost its accreditation. The UNCF took a vote from its 39 member colleges and decided to help "alleviate financial problems at the historically Black Atlanta school. . ." ("Morris Brown Receives Funding," March 7, 2003).

Radio personality Tom Joyner was also identified as one who might save the institution when he offered "$1 million through his private foundation to help current students at Morris Brown College complete their education" ("Joyner offers donation," August 20, 2003). The *Atlanta Journal-Constitution* ran a story about the College's close relationship with the AME church. The article, however, mainly offered a history of the relationship and neglected to talk about the current support it offers Morris Brown (Jones, December 11, 2002). Questions of whether or not an organization should take part in "saving" the college were vetted by many black colleges. Howard University, specifically, devoted several pages of its *Hilltop* to the subject of preserving the Atlanta college. According to its president, H. Patrick Swygert, "We are involved because Morris Brown is a sister institution with a great and important history and a bright future. We are involved because we at Howard take our leadership responsibilities seriously. This nation should be about the business of creating more not fewer higher education opportunities" (Hamilton, March 7, 2003, n.p.).

Common Themes in the Media's Treatment of Morris Brown College

Within the frames, which hold the media's portrayal of Morris Brown together, there are several dominant themes. These include: decline of black colleges, desertion, failure, and devotion.

Decline of Black Colleges

One of the themes receiving the most attention from the media, and perhaps the most damaging to the future of black colleges, is that of their decline. This theme most frequently appeared in articles framed by finance and accreditation. Quite often, the media generalized the experiences at Morris Brown and applied them to black colleges overall. With one exception, the wider reaching, national stories about Morris Brown seemed to give the media an opportunity to wax eloquently about the problems faced by all of these institutions. Historically, this practice of projecting the problems of one institution on the whole lot is common when one examines the history of media coverage (and scholarly analysis for that matter). For example, *USA Today* ran a story entitled "2 Black colleges may close doors: Problems at Grambling State, Morris Brown reflect trend." According to the author,

> Supporters of the nation's 105 historically Black colleges and universities are watching closely to see what happens. Over the past 26 years, the number of Black students in all colleges increased almost 60% to 1.6 million. In that time, 12 Black schools closed, most because of money problems from decreasing enrollments and inadequate endowments. Many historically Black colleges have trouble competing for students, faculty and money at a time when they're facing greater competition for Black students and teachers. Major public and private schools are aggressively recruiting Black applicants. To some, the decreasing number of Black colleges means fewer places where Black students can find a nurturing academic environment. To others, it simply represents market forces at work. Some question whether all of the schools are still needed. (Copeland, December 10, 2002, p. A3)

Likewise, *CNN* noted in their comprehensive coverage of black colleges: "The crisis at Morris Brown has put a spotlight on the United States' 103 historically Black colleges, some of which are struggling as they compete with other schools for students, faculty, and funds" ("Black colleges suffer financial strain," March 17, 2003).

In an article that aimed to show the diversity among black colleges, Audrey Williams June of *The Chronicle of Higher Education* used the Morris Brown story to introduce the idea of a mounting debate that "could shape the future of historically black colleges nationwide" (Williams, January 17, 2003). The article addressed the current economic problems at all institutions, noting that these times have been particularly difficult for small black colleges. Moreover, June claimed that "some supporters of historically Black institutions quietly question how much longer the weakest of the group can survive—and ultimately, whether they should. They say that many advocates for Black colleges are reluctant to take an honest look at some of the institutions where enrollment has dried up and cash is scarce" (Williams, January 17, 2003).

The Chicago Tribune also began its coverage of the nation's black colleges by speaking to the diversity among these institutions. However, within a few paragraphs the article shifted its focus to their problems:

"What happened at Morris Brown is tragic but not unique. Across America, many of the 103 historically Black colleges and universities are struggling to stay afloat, including some state-run institutions" (Glanton, October 21, 2002). The reporter continued by discussing the dismal state of affairs at black colleges:

> Many Black Colleges are suffering from decades of neglect, with crumbling infrastructures and antiquated facilities. They have few classrooms with computer terminals, inadequate science labs and few high-technology facilities. Conveniences that students on white campuses take for granted—email access, well-stocked libraries and inviting cafeterias—are rare at most Black Colleges. (Glanton, October 21, 2002)

Of course, the reporter failed to mention that many historically White institutions are struggling financially and do not offer their students the "conveniences" provided by their wealthier counterparts.

The title of another article, "Private historically Black colleges under stress," implied that all such institutions are suffering. However, it gives only one example of a black college "under stress" (Morris Brown) and in fact the expert interviewed in the article—James Rogers of SACS—says "The private colleges in our region, regardless of the nature of the institution [racial make-up], are the ones that are struggling the most. I don't see this as any sort of trend of the HBCUs" (Poe, December 11, 2002). Perhaps the most evenhanded national story on black colleges, and the exception mentioned earlier, is that written by Michael Fletcher at the *Washington Post*. Fletcher titled his piece "At Black Colleges, Disparate Fortunes. One Atlanta School Thrives; Another Fails"—a title that reflects the complexity of the situation described. The article examines the problems faced by many black colleges but through a wide range of interviews and hones in on the importance of these historic institutions. Fletcher commented:

> Some are enjoying unprecedented prosperity, raking in record gifts and attracting increasing numbers of top-flight applicants. But others are confronted by financial and managerial problems, declining interest from prospective students and legal and legislative mandates that are forcing them to radically rethink their missions or even shed their Black identities. (Fletcher, November 23, 2002, p. A01)

Desertion/Allegiance

Within the frames of accreditation and who would save Morris Brown, the theme of desertion/allegiance appears often. The main emphasis in this area is on students. Reporters spent time interviewing students and gauging the student response to Morris Brown's financial woes and loss of accreditation. The *Savannah Morning News*, for example, opened with "Morris Brown College promised to keep fighting after losing its accreditation this week, but many students at the historically Black school won't be around to see how things turn out. Those still on campus Tuesday said they were looking for another place to go to school next year, concluding that a diploma from an unaccredited college isn't worth the effort" (Niesse, April 9, 2003).

Likewise, *The Atlanta Journal-Constitution* interviewed disgruntled students who aimed to leave Morris Brown. According to one student who was trying to transfer to either Clark Atlanta University or Georgia State University, "I made a wrong choice when I came to Morris Brown. I'm suffering the repercussion of it. It's too bad it's gone this way. My senior year has just been a catastrophe" (Morgan in Simmons, November 7, 2002).

Students' decisions about whether or not to leave the institution were also the focal point of a Morris Brown related story in *The Chronicle of Higher Education*. The journalist detailed the conflicts that Morris Brown students were grappling with:

> Although it is exam period at Morris Brown College, students here suddenly have quite a bit more to worry about than tests. Many of them say they'll be forced to spend their winter break trying to decide whether they will remain at the institution, now that it has lost its accreditation. "I just need to think," said a junior, Michele Thompson, as she headed to take a biology examination. "I don't know what I'm going to do. Who thought it would come to this?" (Williams, December 13, 2002)

A key factor that most of the articles pointed to was the dedication of Morris Brown students to their school. This was expressed eloquently in a previously mentioned quote from *The Chronicle of Higher Education*, which described a student's attachment and loyalty to the black college: "'It's really breaking my heart to do this,' said Tiphanie Pharris, a student mentioned earlier in this article. 'I believe you pledge your allegiance to one school, and that's where you stay'" (Williams, December 13, 2002). Although the above-mentioned quotes are the words of students, the reporters chose which quotes to use, thus shaping the direction of the story. Reporters can look for the voices they want—voices that offer the perspective that fits their arguments.

Failure

Failure is a theme that is consistent in almost every article regardless of the frame. It either refers to Morris Brown's failure as a whole, the institution's former president Dolores Crosse's failure, the institution's failure to gain accreditation or failure to win its accreditation appeal, the new president's failure, or the failure of black colleges overall to manage and cope in the current economy. Initial articles about the Morris Brown situation discussed the institution's fiscal and academic failure. According to *The Chronicle of Higher Education*, for example, the "Southern Association of Colleges and Schools, the accreditation agency that put Morris Brown on probation 10 months ago because of its bad bookkeeping and lack of faculty members with advanced degrees, will determine the status of the college . . ." (Williams, October 18, 2002). Likewise, in an article that all but predicts the failure of Morris Brown, Paul Donsky and Andrea Jones of *The Atlanta Journal-Constitution* wrote, "On Tuesday, the 117-year-old private Atlanta school will learn whether it will lose its accreditation—a potentially fatal blow that would cut off the federal financial aid most students depend on to help pay their college expenses" (Donsky and Jones, December 8, 2002).

In discussing the problems at Morris Brown, the media blamed the institution's former president Dolores Cross as well as some of the Morris Brown administration for poor decision making. Most articles alluded to misuse of financial aid funds and a poor decision to change the institution's NCAA status from Division II to I (forcing an increase in the institution's athletic budget from $2.2 million to $4.3 million). For example, *The Atlanta Journal-Constitution* placed the blame squarely with Cross:

> In recent years, school officials took several steps to boost prestige and revenue that appear to have misfired. Former President Delores Cross, who resigned last February, built the school's enrollment from fewer than 2,000 students in 1998 to nearly 2,800 last year. To house the extra students, the college had to book rooms in Atlanta motels. That practice ended before this school year. In 2000, Morris Brown moved from NCAA Division II to Division I, the highest level of athletics. To compete in Division I, schools have to spend more money on scholarships and travel. . . . The school also made headlines when Cross started a program to provide a laptop computer for each student—a first of its kind for a historically Black college. But the company that supplied the computers said Morris Brown never paid the $4.2 million tab. (Donsky and Jones, December 8, 2002)

Although many of the problems described by the paper have proved accurate, it is interesting to note that just two years earlier, the media, including the *Atlanta Journal-Constitution* and *The Chronicle on Higher Education*, were lauding President Cross for her groundbreaking thinking in the decision to require students to purchase the laptops. In this instance, the same frame—leadership—was being used, but the theme was innovation rather than failure. As with Delores Cross, the media labeled new President Charles Taylor a failure both during his appeal for re-accreditation and when he resigned from the institution. A *Chronicle of Higher Education* headline summed up the way Taylor's resignation was treated by the media: "President Resigns at Beleaguered Morris Brown College" (Basinger, April 17, 2003). Many newspapers said that Taylor had "no comprehensive plan" or "no recovery plan" for the institution and this is why he failed (Jones, April 16, 2003; Basinger, April 17, 2003). One article stated Taylor's problems this way: "during his brief presidency, he said little publicly about how he might turn the problems around to save the institution" (Basinger, April 17, 2003).

Devotion

Regardless of the frame used, in many of the articles on the Morris Brown situation, one theme rings clearer than any other—namely that a kind of religious devotion marks the college's culture. Of course this may be related to Morris Brown's strong church ties or its sense of spirituality and faith in the African American religious community; regardless, it is telling (and perhaps a reflection of the colleges location in the South) how often references to religion appear in the media's portrayal of the struggling black institution. The *Atlanta Journal-Constitution*, for example, referred to a fundraising event for Morris Brown as such, "The ceremony at times felt like a church tent revival, with prayers, songs, and 'amens' shouted to comments from the podium" (Scott, March 16, 2003). Likewise, an *NBC News* story used language that compared the Morris Brown students to the Israelites fleeing Egypt—describing the "exodus" at the college and their "plight" (Hoff, September 25, 2003). The *Florida Times-Union* discussed the "faith" of the administrator, faculty and students: "A skeleton crew of faithful administrators, teachers, and students remain. They say they are devoted to restoring the reputation of the school known for educating anyone willing to work hard" (Basinger, October 19, 2003). In many ways, it appears that in the eyes of the media, the only thing that can save Morris Brown is prayer and "good old fashioned" hard work.

Discourse Resulting From the Media's Coverage of Morris Brown

According to Altheide, the frames used by the media give meaning to specific themes and carry a discourse that becomes part of our everyday language depending upon our social and intellectual circles (Altheide, 1996). In the case of the media's coverage of the recent situation at Morris Brown College, the discourse is contained in "catch" phrases that are used continuously. Looked at as a whole, these phrases can be seen to indicate either the obsolescence or the uniqueness of black colleges.

Obsolescence

Earlier I noted that the media contributes to the public's constant questioning of the future of black colleges by attributing the problems of a few to all—thus, establishing an agenda. Behind this is an assumption that black colleges are obsolete—a leftover from times of legalized segregation (Thompson, 1973). The problems of Morris Brown, which are symptomatic of the obsolescence of these institutions, can be grouped into two larger categories. First, in the post-*Brown* era, integration makes black colleges unnecessary. Consider the following examples:

> Many other Black colleges have struggled to stay afloat over the last few decades as racial integration has altered enrollment, faculty, administrations and financial support at the schools. (Poe, 2002)

> Still, the question remains: In an era that's a generation removed from Jim Crow, how many private historically Black colleges and universities does the country need? (Poe, 2002)

> It is time to face the facts: Morris Brown is among hundreds of financially weak historically Black colleges, most of which cannot survive another 20 years. Nor should they. They were born of a historic injustice—the vicious laws of segregation that kept African-American students, no matter how competent, out of historically white colleges and universities. With those laws long since repealed, scores of segregated colleges and universities are now looking for a new reason to exist. (Tucker, 2002, p. 17A)

Although this discourse creates a bleak picture for black colleges, it leaves a glimmer of hope in the possibility that these schools will indeed find a new "reason to exist."

Slightly more bleak is the notion found in many of the articles, that black colleges, created in the days of slavery and segregation, bear the taint of inferiority. According to this perspective, this condition results in poor facilities, poor finances, low standards, and inadequately prepared students:

> The college's situation speaks to a larger issue facing historically Black colleges. They need to be academically proficient, finically solvent and technologically sufficient. (Post, April 24, 2003)

> The Achilles' heel for many historically Black colleges has always been incompetence in fiscal matters. The reasons are many and varied: hiring administrative support staff who are inadequately trained for their jobs; downright indifference on the part of personnel; and autocratic management structures instituted or perpetuated

by college presidents who place a disproportionate emphasis on power and veneer. (Willis, October 21, 2002)

> Founded in 1885 by former slaves, the college has become a slave to debt that threatens to close its door. ("The Morris Brown Mess," November 11, 2002)

The implication of these statements is that racism has led to the inferiority of Black colleges overall—and that these institutions have not been able to emerge from this second-class status. (Thompson, 1973; Anderson, 1988; Brown and Lane, 2003)

Uniqueness

The second and more positive category of discourse on Morris Brown College points to the special role that it plays in the lives of African American students and the local community. One point mentioned in this discourse is that Morris Brown is a college founded by blacks for blacks—in fact, it is one a few black colleges founded by a black-controlled institution rather than northern white missionaries or philanthropists (Anderson, 1988).[3] The following quotation, for example, nicely addresses not only these points, but also the college's special commitment to the needs of black students: "With a mission to serve both high-achieving students and those 'who might not otherwise receive the opportunity to compete on the college level,' the school is the state's only college founded by Blacks." (Jones, December 11, 2002; "Morris Brown Trying to Collect," June 5, 2003). Another quotation from a Morris Brown student, included in *The Atlanta Journal-Constitution,* summarized Morris Brown's close connections to its student community: "This is my family now," he said. "I would never leave Morris Brown unless it loses accreditation" (Ghezzi, October 1, 2002).

Again, part of Morris Brown's uniqueness is the religious devotion of its community. This is made clear in a number of phrases used in the articles. Quoting an individual who was trying to raise funds on behalf of the struggling institution, one article stated: "We're doing everything we possibly can, and then we're going to pray" (Scott, March 16, 2003). Another article describes the fundraising effort as "passing the offering plate" (Simmons, October 27, 2002). And finally, referring to the Morris Brown's situation, another article quoted AME minister Michael Jones, who was invoking the college's motto: "Ain't nothing dead on Martin Luther King Drive. It's still a haven for hungry souls" (Simmons, October 27, 2002). The motto "haven for hungry souls" is indicative of the institution's close ties to the church.

Conclusion

On May 21, 2004, the *Atlanta Journal-Constitution* included an editorial entitled "Morris Brown must face financial reality and close." The following is an excerpt from the news story:

> The 42 students who received degrees from Atlanta's Morris Brown College on Sunday should be commended for completing their studies amid the turmoil that has enveloped the college since it lost its accreditation in December 2002. In return for their hard work, however, they received degrees that will be questioned by prospective employers and graduate schools. They deserve better, as do the students who have chosen to remain at the financially troubled college. . . . Morris Brown is on life support, and its leaders need to pull the plug. Morris Brown prides itself on offering a college education to students who might not otherwise have a chance to attend a four-year school because of poor academic performance. They claim that these students would be the most vulnerable to an abrupt shutdown. Dozens of small colleges have the same mission, as do two-year and technical colleges. . . . It's time to replace nostalgia with a reality check. Morris Brown officials have had years to correct poor management and massive debt. At this point, the best thing they can do is plan a graceful exit for the school and its students. (editor, May 21, 2004)

Given Morris Brown's situation, a story this bleak might be unremarkable—except that it is the culmination of two years of similarly dire articles about the institution. Moreover the discussion in these articles often spills over into black colleges as a whole, with dire predictions for the lot of them. This leads this author to wonder how much influence the media has had over the outcome of Morris Brown's efforts to recover (not its problems). How much influence should it have?

Do the media have an agenda? Many alumni feel that they do. For example, alumna Clarisa Myrick-Harris writes,

> I am told that the newspaper continues to publish its often-erroneous assessments because the editorial board is "concerned" about the welfare of the students. The paper's persistent meddling smacks of paternalism. Further, the paper's viewpoint is skewed and devoid of historical understanding about Morris Brown in particular and historically black colleges and universities in general (Myrick-Harris, May 21, 2004).

As Myrick-Harris notes, the media does not understand the mission of an institution like Morris Brown—one of racial uplift through access. Although community and technical colleges provide a kind of access, racial uplift in particular is not their mission—therefore, it is inaccurate to claim, as the *Atlanta Journal-Constitution* does, that Morris Brown could simply be replaced by these other institutions.

Of course, the media should act as a public critic, but should it direct our actions? Does the discourse produced by the media change the way the public views Morris Brown and, in effect, black colleges? Although the media does notice some of the good brought about by black colleges, do they focus on these positives aspects of black higher education less frequently? When we examine the coverage of the struggling institution over the course of a two-year period, disturbing themes indicate a media agenda that springs into action whenever a historically black college is in trouble. Morris Brown's critics may say that the institution made itself an easy target. Surely Morris Brown College deserved criticism. But one test of fair coverage is how it treats the worst cases. Does it confine criticism to the one at fault or allow it to taint the innocent as well?

A content analysis of the media's coverage of Morris Brown College's situation suggests that the media has made and continues to make generalizations about black colleges based on the faults of a few. These generalizations call into question the very existence of black colleges. Although news reports began with appropriate questions about the leadership, financial stability, fundraising ability, and quality of the board of trustees at Morris Brown, they quite frequently attributed the institution's problems to black colleges as a whole. With very little background or knowledge of the history of these institutions, the media is contributing to a discourse on black colleges, which contains catchphrases that are used continuously, picked up by politicians, policymakers, and academics, and thrust into the public domain. For example, the frame of financial problems at Morris Brown combined with the theme of the decline of black colleges easily gave rise to a discourse on the "taint of inferiority" left over from segregation. This type of material is the source of the problem of media generalizations about black colleges. Although the media have the full set of facts in front of them, they mold these facts into a form that results in a negative picture of black colleges.

In its coverage, the media rightly pointed to the unique environment at Morris Brown College. However, they neglected to use this as an opportunity to show the diversity among black colleges overall, and to point out that its situation is not representative of all of these institutions. Each black college, although dedicated to racial uplift and the education of African Americans, has its own environment, culture, and struggles (Brown, 2003; Perna 2001). Black colleges themselves need to be aware of the types of discourse embedded in past media coverage and how this can distort their stories. They must expose examples of unfair coverage, thereby forcing the media to be responsible for understanding the history and culture of these institutions. Black college administrators and faculty need to keep track of institutional data and use it to counter stories pushed forth by the media. Overall, black colleges need to be wise to the ways of the media and use an aggressive strategy. They must contribute to a national discourse on "their" institutions rather than letting the mainstream media set the agenda.

Notes

1. Although the institution was established in 1881, it did not receive a charter until 1885.
2. Due to the vestiges of slavery, African Americans did not have the resources to fund their own institutions, thus most black colleges were funded by white missionaries, the federal government, and eventually northern industrial philanthropists. This fact severely hampered institutional autonomy.
3. The majority of black colleges were founded by white northern missionaries and the Freedman's Bureau. During the late 1800s and early 1900s, white industrial philanthropists supported black colleges financially with the intention of controlling the future of black higher education.

References

Altheide, D. (1996). *Qualitative Media Analysis*. Thousand Oaks, CA: Sage Publications.

Anderson, James D. (1988). *The Education of Blacks in the South, 1860–1935*. Chapel Hill: The University of North Carolina.

Auditor Questions College's Ability to Survive. *The Associated Press*, October 18, 2002.

Basinger, J. (April 17, 2003). President Resigns at Beleaguered Morris Brown College. *The Chronicle of Higher Education*.

Basinger, B. (Sunday, October 19, 2003). Morris Brown Tries to Rebuild. *The Florida Times Union*.

Bishop, R. (2003). The World's Nicest Grown-Up: A Fantasy Theme Analysis of News Media Coverage of Fred Rogers. *Journal of Communication*.

Black colleges suffer financial strain. *CNN*, Monday, March 17, 2003, 9:59 A.M.

Brown, M. C. (Summer 2003). Emics and Etics of Researching Black Colleges: Applying Facts and Avoiding Fallacies, *New Directions for Institutional Research*, no. 118, 27–40.

Brown, M. C. and Lane, J. E. (Eds.). (2003). *Studying Diverse Institutions: Contexts, Challenges, and Considerations. New Directions for Institutional Research.* New Jersey: Wiley & Sons.

Cohen, B. (1963). *The Press and Foreign Policy*. Princeton: Princeton University Press.

Copeland, L. (December 10, 2002). 2 Black Colleges May Close Doors; Problems at Grambling State, Morris Brown Reflect Trend. *USA Today*, A03.

DeVaney, A. (1987). Reader theories and educational media analysis. Paper presented at the Annual Convention of the Association for Educational Communications and Technology, Atlanta, Georgia.

Donsky, P. (September 13, 2002). Morris Brown Chooses Chief. *The Atlanta Journal-Constitution*.

Donsky, P. (Sunday, December 8, 2003). Morris Brown to Learn its Fate Tuesday. *The Atlanta Journal-Constitution*.

Donsky, Paul (October 24, 2002). Morris Brown Seeks Business-Wise Trustees. *The Atlanta Journal-Constitution*, 1F.

Donsky, P. and Jones, A. (Sunday, December 8, 2002). Morris Brown Waits to Exhale. Accreditation to be Decided. *The Atlanta Journal-Constitution*.

Donsky, P. and Jones, A. (December 8, 2002). Morris Brown Accreditation to Be Decided. *The Atlanta Journal-Constitution*.

Editor (May 21, 2004). Morris Brown Must Face Financial Reality and Close. *Atlanta Journal-Constitution.*

Ex-Morris Brown President Says Bills Paid with Financial Aid. *The Associated Press.* October 17, 2002.

Feds may cut off funding to Morris Brown. *AccessNorthGA.com.* Friday, November 1, 2002.

Fitzgerald, M. A. (2000). Criticizing Media: The Cognitive Process of Information Evaluation. *Educational Media and Technology Yearbook.* 25, 130–140.

Fleming, J. (August 16, 2005). Re: Little-Noticed Crisis at Black Colleges. Letter to the Editor of the *New York Times* (in possession of author).

Fletcher, M. A. (Saturday, November 23, 2002). At Black Colleges, Disparate Fortunes. One Atlanta School Thrives; Another Fails. *The Washington Post,* A01.

Freedman, Samuel G. (August 3, 2005). Little-Noticed Crisis at Black Colleges. *New York Times,* www.nytimes.com.

Gall, M., Borg, W., and Gall, J. (1996). *Educational Research.* New York: Longman.

Ghezzi, P. (October 1, 2002). School president: I'll Fix It or Quit. *The Atlanta Journal-Constitution,* 1D.

Glanton, D. (October 21, 2002). Black Colleges Fight to Survive, Financial, Other Ills Beset Many Venerable Schools. *The Chicago Tribune.*

Haines, E. (November 1, 2002). Historically Black Morris Brown College in Trouble. *CNN.*

Hamilton, K. (March 7, 2003). Howard Committed to Saving Morris Brown. *The Hilltop.*

Harasin, L. (October 28, 2002). Morris Brown President to Lay Out Recovery Plan. *Action News 2.*

Hoff, V. (September 25, 2003). Morris Brown Opens with 70 Students. *News 11.*

Iyengar, S. (1988). New Directions for Agenda Setting Research. In J. Anderson (Ed.), *Communication Yearbook 11* (pp. 595–602). Thousand Oaks, CA: Sage Publications.

Jackson Expected to Join Morris Brown's Board of Trustees. *The Macon Telegraph.* December 4, 2003.

Jones, B. (2004). Toward Strategic Planning: Issues and Status of Black colleges. In Brown, M. C. and Freeman, K. (2004). *Black Colleges.* Westport, CT: Ablex Press.

Jones, A. (April 8, 2003). Morris Brown Won't Close, President says. *The Atlanta Journal-Constitution.*

Jones, A. (April 16, 2003). Morris Brown President Taylor Resigns. *The Atlanta Journal-Constitution.*

Jones, A. (March 7, 2003). College Fund Gives $1.5 Million to School. *The Atlanta Journal-Constitution.*

Jones, A. (December 11, 2002). College Has Kept Close Ties to Church. *The Atlanta Journal-Constitution.*

Jones, L. (March 9, 2003). Morris Brown Students Raise Cash. *The Atlanta Journal-Constitution.*

Joyner Offers Donation to Morris Brown. *NBC News 11.* August 20, 2003.

June, A. W. (October 18, 2002). Morris Brown College Faces Big Debt and an Accreditor's Judgment. *The Chronicle of Higher Education.* 49, no. 8, A31.

June, A. W. (December 13, 2002). At Morris Brown College, Students Grapple With a Tough Decision: Stay or Go? *The Chronicle of Higher Education.*

June, A. W. (January 17, 2003). Endangered Institutions. Morris Brown's Plight Reflects the Financial Troubles of Small, Poorly Financed Black Colleges. *The Chronicle of Higher Education.*

Lincoln, Y. and Guba, E. (1985). *Naturalistic Inquiry.* Beverly Hills: Sage Publications.

McCombs, M. (1993). The Evolution of Agenda Setting Research: Twenty-Five Years in the Marketplace of Ideas. *Journal of Communication*, 43(2), 68–67.

McLendon, M. & Peterson, M. W. (1999). The Press and State Policy Making for Higher Education, *Review of Higher Education*, 22, 3.

Morgan, D. quoted in Simmons, K. (November 7, 2002). Morris Brown Students Consider Transferring Out. *The Atlanta Journal-Constitution*.

Morris Brown College History, www.morrisbrown.edu [accessed February 6, 2004].

Morris Brown Receives Funding. *NBC News 11*. March 7, 2003.

Morris Brown Prepares for Reduced Enrollment. *The Associated Press*. Tuesday, July 29, 2003.

Morris Brown Trustees Appoint Chemistry Professor as Acting President. *Black Issues in Higher Education*. May 8, 2003, 9.

Morris Brown College Names Charles Taylor its New President. *JET*. October 14, 2002.

Morris Brown Names Educator Businessman as President. *The Associated Press*. September 13, 2002.

Morris Brown Trying to Collect Student Debt. *Atlanta Daily World*. June 5, 2003.

Morris Brown Tries to Collect Student Debt. *Macon Telegraph*. May 31, 2003.

Morris Brown President Resigns. *NBC News*. April 16, 2003.

Morris Brown President Quits. *BlackVoices.com*. April 17, 2003.

Morris Brown President Lays Out Recovery Plan. *AccessNorthGA.com*. October 28, 2002.

Morris Brown May Close. *The Associated Press*. November 1, 2002.

Morris Brown's Financial Aid Practices Investigated. *The Associated Press*. September 30, 2002.

Morris Brown to Begin Process of Re-Accreditation. *Black Issues in Higher Education*. April 24, 2003, p. 8.

Morris Brown College Faces Uncertainty. *ABC News*. December 11, 2002.

Morris Brown Alumni Raise 2.5 Million. *NBC News 11*. October 26, 2002.

Morris Brown College Drops Athletics. *Sports Illustrated*. Tuesday, May 6, 2003.

The Morris Brown Mess: The Historically Black College is in Debt and May Close. *Lee Bailey's Eurweb.com*. November 11, 2002.

Myrick-Harris, C. (May 21, 2004). Morris Brown Will Overcome Obstacles. *The Atlanta Journal-Constitution*.

Niesse, M. (April 9, 2003). Students Leaving after Morris Brown Loses Accreditation Bid. *Savannah Morning News*.

Perna, L. (2001). The Contribution of Historically Black Colleges and Universities to the Preparation of African American Faculty Careers. *Review of Higher Education*, 42, 265-294.

Poe, J. (November 14, 2002). Black Colleges Under Pressure to Change. *The Atlanta Journal-Constitution*. Front Page and F1.

Poe, J. (December 11, 2002). Private Historically Black Colleges under Stress. *The Atlanta Journal-Constitution*.

Post, C. (April 17, 2003). Morris Brown President Resigns, Supporters Press On. *Atlanta Daily World*.

Post, C. (April 24, 2003). Morris Brown President Resigns, Supporters Press on. *St. Louis American*.

President of Morris Brown College Resigns. *Tallahassee Democrat*. April 16, 2003.

Principles of Accreditation, http://www.sacscoc.org/pdf/principle of accreditation1.pdf [March 9, 2004].

Rowe, S. (April 11, 2003). Deadline for Morris Brown Transfers. *News 11*.

Scott, P. (March 16, 2003). Morris Brown Rejoices. *The Atlanta Journal-Constitution*.

Simmons, K. (October 6, 2002). Morris Brown at the Brink. *The Atlanta Journal-Constitution*. Metro Section, C2, C4, C5.

Simmons, K. (April 8, 2003). Morris Brown Loses Appeal, May Close as Aid Evaporates. *The Atlanta Journal-Constitution*.

Simmons, K. (October 28, 2002). Morris Brown at the Wall: Today May Decide School's Fate. *The Atlanta Journal-Constitution*.

Simmons, K. (October 5, 2002). Morris Brown: Laptop for Every Student is PR Boon Turned Bust. *The Atlanta Journal-Constitution*. Metro Section, 5C.

Simmons, K. (March 7, 2003). Morris Brown Wants Pay Before Graduation. *The Atlanta Journal-Constitution*.

Simmons, K. (October 16, 2002). Morris Brown Admits Use of Student Aid to Pay Bills. *Cox New Service*.

Simmons, K. (September 29, 2002). Feds: Morris Brown Misused Student Aid. *The Atlanta Journal-Constitution*. 1A.

Simmons, K. (October 26, 2002). Alumni Pledge Cash for Morris Brown. *The Atlanta Journal-Constitution*.

Simmons, K. (October 27, 2002). Today May Decide Morris Brown's Fate. *Cox Enterprises, Inc. Wire Service*.

Simmons, K. and Donsky, P. (November 1, 2002). Catch-22 Has Morris Brown in New Bind; Pay Up or Lose Funding, Feds Tell Strapped School. *The Atlanta Journal-Constitution*, 1D.

Stepp, C. S. (January/February 2003). Higher Examination, *American Journalism Review*.

Thompson, D. C. (1973). *Private Black Colleges at the Crossroads*. Westport, CT: Greenwood Press.

Tucker, C. (October 23, 2002). Morris Brown College: Ailing Institution Must Face Awful Truth: It's Time to Close. *The Atlanta Journal-Constitution*, 17A (editorial).

Tuckman, G. (1978). *Making News: A Study in the Construction of Reality*. New York: Free-Press.

UNCF to Help Fund Morris Brown College. *Macon Telegraph*. March 8, 2003.

Willie, C. (1978). *Black Colleges in America*. New York: Teachers College Press.

Willis, G. (October 21, 2002). Rescue Black Colleges from Financial Ruin. *The Atlanta Journal-Constitution*. Home Edition, 9A.

Zelizer, B. (2002) Journalists as Interpretive Communities. *Critical Studies in Mass Communications*, 10, 219–237.

Historically Black Colleges and Universities: A Bibliography

Marybeth Gasman, University of Pennsylvania

Overview and Foundations of Black Colleges

AAUP Committee (Jan–Feb 1995). The Historically Black Colleges and Universities: A Future in the Balance. *Academe*, 81(1), 49–58.

Allen, W. R. (2005). A Forward Glance in a Mirror: Diversity Challenged—Access, Equity, and Success in Higher Education. *Educational Researcher,* 34(7), 18–23.

Allen, W. R., & Jewell, J. O. (2002). A Backward Glance Forward: Past, Present and Future Perspectives on Historically Black Colleges and Universities. *The Review of Higher Education,* 25(3), 241–261.

Bonner, F. A., II, & Murry, J. W., Jr. (1998). Historically Black Colleges and Universities: Is Their Mission Unique? *National Association of Student Affairs Professionals Journal,* 1(1), 37–49.

Bowles, F., & DeCosta, F. (1971). *Between Two Worlds: A Profile of Negro Higher Education.* New York: The Carnegie Foundation for the Advancement of Teaching.

Browning, J., and Williams, J. (1978). History and Goals of Black Institutions of Higher Learning. In *Black Colleges in America: Challenge, Development, Survival,* edited by Charles V. Willie and R. Edmonds. New York: Teacher's College Press.

Buchanan, L., and Hutcheson, P. (1999). "Re-Considering the Washington-Du Bois Debate: Two Black Colleges in 1910-1911." In *Essays in 20th Century Southern Education: Exceptionalism and Its Limits,* edited by Wayne Urban. New York: Garland Press.

Bullock, H. (1967). *A History of Negro Education in the South: From 1619 to the Present.* Cambridge, MA: Harvard University Press.

Clark, F. G. (1958). "The Development and Present Status of Publicly-Supported Higher Education for Negroes." *The Journal of Negro Education,* 27(3), 221–232.

Cohen, R. T. (2000). *The Black Colleges of Atlanta.* South Carolina: Arcadia Publishing.

Drewry, H. N., & Doermann, H. (2001). *Stand and Prosper: Private Black Colleges and Their Students.* Princeton, NJ: Princeton University Press.

Du Bois, W. E. B. (1973). The Future and Function of the Private Negro College. In *The Education of Black People, Ten Critiques, 1906–1960,* edited by Herbert Aptheker. New York: Monthly Review Press.

Du Bois, W. E. B (1903). The Talented Tenth. In *The Negro Problem: A Series of Articles by Representative American Negroes of Today.* New York: J. Pott & Company, 1903, 33–75.

Garibaldi, A. (1984). *Black Colleges and Universities: Challenges for the Future.* New York, NY: Praeger.

Gasman, M. (2006). Education in Black and White: New Perspectives on the History of Historically Black Colleges and Universities," *Teachers College Record* (www.tcrecord.org).

Gasman, M. (2005). Coffee Table to Classroom: A Review of Recent Scholarship on Historically Black Colleges and Universities. *Educational Researcher,* 34(7), 32–39.

Gasman, M. (March–April 2006). Salvaging "Academic Disaster Areas": The Black College Response to Christopher Jencks' and David Riesman's 1967 Harvard Educational Review Article. *Journal of Higher Education,* 77(1), 317–352.

Goodwin, R. K. (1991). Roots and Wings. *Journal of Negro Education,* 60(2), 126–132.

Harvey, W. B., & Williams, L.E. (1989). Historically Black Colleges: Models for Increasing Minority Representation. *Education and Urban Society,* 1(3), 328–340.

Homan, L. M., & Reilly, T. (2001). *Black Knights: The Story of the Tuskegee Airmen.* New York: Pelican Publishing Company.

Injay (Ed.). (1999). *Black Colleges and Universities: Charcoals to Diamonds.* Huntsville, AL: SSSH! Enterprises.

Jackson, C. (2003). *Historically Black Colleges and Universities: A Reference Handbook.* Santa Barbara, CA: ABC-CLIO.

Jaffe, A. J., Adams, W., and Meyers, S.G. (1968). *Negro Higher Education in the 1960's.* New York: Praeger Publishers.

Jencks, C., and Riesman, D. (1967). The American Negro College. *Harvard Educational Review,* 37(1), 3–60.

Jencks, C., and Riesman, D. (1968). Negroes and their Colleges. In *The Academic Revolution Chicago*: Chicago, Illinois: The University of Chicago Press.

Jones, J. H. (1992). *Bad Blood: The Tuskegee Syphilis Experiment.* New York: Simon & Schuster.

Jones, T. J. (1969). *Negro Education: A Study of the Private and Public Higher Education Schools for Colored People in the United States.* New York: Arno Press.

Kennard, T. H. (1995). *The Handbook of Historically Black Colleges and Universities: Comprehensive Profiles and Photos of Black Colleges and Universities.* Wilmington, DE: Jireh & Associates, Inc.

Klein, Arthur (1969). *Survey of Negro Colleges and Universities.* New York: Negro Universities Press.

Lash, J. S. (1951). The Umpteenth Crisis in Negro Higher Education. *Journal of Negro Education* 22, 8.

Lefever, H. G. (2005). *Undaunted by the Fight: Spelman College and the Civil Rights Movement, 1957–1957.* Mercer, GA: Mercer University Press.

Lindsey, D. F. (1995). *Indians at Hampton Institute, 1877–1923.* Urbana-Champaign: University of Illinois Press.

Logan, R. (2005). *Howard University: The First Hundred Years, 1867–1967.* New York: New York University Press.

McGrath, E. J. (1965). *The Predominantly Negro Colleges and Universities in Transition.* New York: Institute of Higher Education, Teachers College, Columbia University.

Nettles, M. T., Perna, L. W., Edelin, K. C., & Robertson, N. (1996). *The College Fund/UNCF Statistical Report, 1997.* Fairfax, VA: College Fund/ UNCF.

Nettles, M. T., Perna, L. W., & Freeman, K. E. (1999). *Two Decades of Progress: African-Americans Moving Forward in Higher Education*. Fairfax, VA: College Fund/UNCF.

Outcalt, C. L., & Skewes-Cox, T. E. (2002). Involvement, Interaction, and Satisfaction: the Human Environment at HBCUs. *Review of Higher Education*, 25(3), 331–347.

Patterson, F. D. (1958). Colleges for Negro Youth and the Future. *The Journal of Negro Education*, 27(2), 107–114.

Patterson, F. D. (1952). The Private Negro College in a Racially-Integrated System of Higher Education. *The Journal of Negro Education*, 21(3).

Pearson, R. L. (1983). Reflections on Black Colleges. The Historical Perspective of Charles S. Johnson. *History of Education Quarterly*, 23(1), 55–68.

Redd, K. E. (1998). Historically Black Colleges and Universities: Making a Comeback. *New Directions for Higher Education*, 102, 33–43.

Reverby, S. M. (2000). *Tuskegee's Truths: Rethinking the Tuskegee Syphilis Study*. Chapel Hill: The University of North Carolina Press.

Richardson, J. M. (1980). *A History of Fisk University, 1865–1946*. University, AL: The University of Alabama Press.

Richmond, K. A. (1998). Charting a New Millennium Agenda for Historically Black Colleges and Universities. *The Negro Educational Review*, 49(3), 147–152.

Roebuck, J. B., & Murty, K. S. (1993). *Historically Black Colleges and Universities: Their Place in American Higher Education*. Westport, CT: Praeger.

Sagini, M. M. (1996). *African and the African American University: A Historical and Sociological Analysis*. New York: University Press of America.

Saunders, K. P., & Westbrook, T. S. (2001). Historically Black Colleges and Universities: Lessons from the Past, Hope for the Future. *ISPA Journal*, 13(1), 2–19.

Sekora, John. (1968). On Negro Colleges: A Reply to Jencks and Riesman. *Antioch Review*, 28, 1.

Thompson, D. C. (1973). *Private Black Colleges at the Crossroads*. Westport, CT: Greenwood.

Thompson, D. C. (1986). *A Black Elite: A Profile of Graduate of UNCF Colleges*. Westport, CT: Greenwood.

Weaver, R. C. (1960). The Negro Private and Church-Related College. A Critical Summary. *The Journal of Negro Education*, 29(3), 394–400.

Williams, J., & Ashley, D. (2004). *I'll Find a Way or Make One: A Tribute to Historically Black Colleges and Universities*. New York: HarperCollins, 2004.

Willie, C. V., & Edmonds, R. R. (1978). *Black Colleges in America: Challenge, Development, Survival*. New York: Teachers College Press.

Willie, C. V. (1981). *The Ivory and Ebony Towers*. Lexington, MA: Lexington Books.

Desegregation and Legal Issues Surrounding Black Colleges

Adams, F. (1986). Why *Brown v. Board of Education* and Affirmative Action Can Save Historically Black Colleges and Universities. *Alabama Law Review*, 47(2), 481–511.

Baxter, F. V. (1982). The Affirmative Duty to Desegregate Institutions of Higher Education: Defining the Role of the Traditionally Black College. *Journal of Law & Education,* 11(1), 1–40.

Brady, K., Eatman, T., & Parker, L. (2000). To Have or Not to Have? A Preliminary Analysis of Higher Education Funding Disparities in the Post-*Ayers v. Fordice* era: Evidence From Critical Race Theory. *Journal of Education Finance,* 25(3), 297–322.

Brown, M. C., II. (1999). *The Quest to Define Collegiate Desegregation: Black Colleges, Title VI Compliance, and Post-Adams Litigation.* Westport, CT: Bergin & Garvey.

Brown, M. C., II. (2001). Collegiate Desegregation and the Public Black College: A New Policy Mandate. *Journal of Higher Education,* 72(1), 46–62.

Brown, M. C., II, & Hendrickson, R. M. (1997). Public Historically Black Colleges at the Crossroads. *Journal for Just and Caring Education,* 3(1), 95–113.

Brown, M. C., II, Donahoo, S., & Bertrand, R. D. (2001). The Black College and the Quest for Educational Opportunity. *Urban Education,* 36(5), 553–571.

Brown, W. R. (1993). School Desegregation Litigation: Crossroads or Dead End? *Saint Louis University Law Journal,* 37, 923–937.

Brown, W. R. (1994). Race Consciousness in Higher Education: Does "Sound Educational Policy" Support the Continued Existence of Historically Black Colleges? *Emory Law Journal,* 43, 1–81.

Darden, J. T., Bagakas, J. G., & Marajh, O. (1992). Historically Black Colleges and the Dilemma of Desegregation. *Equity & Excellence,* 25, 106–112.

Conrad, C. F., & Shrode, P. E. (1990). The Long Road: Desegregating Higher Education. *Thought and Action,* 6(1), 35–45.

Fienberg, L. (1993). *United States v. Fordice* and the Desegregation of Public Higher Education: Groping for Root and Branch. *Boston College Law Review,* 34(4), 803–851.

Harley, D. A., Tennessee, W., Alston, J. R., & Wilson, T. (2000). HBCUs Desegregation Challenge: Strategies for Recruiting Traditional Majority Students Representation. *Rehabilitation Education,* 14(4), 410–423.

Harley, D. A. (2001). Desegregation at HBCUs: Removing Barriers and Implementing Strategies. *The Negro Educational Review,* 52(4), 151–164.

Jackson, J. F. L., Snowden, M., & Eckes, S. (2002). *Fordice* as a Window of Opportunity: The Case for Maintaining Historically Black Colleges and Universities (HBCUs) as Predominantly Black Institutions. *West's Education Law Reporter,* 1, 1–19.

Jenkins, M. D. (1958). The Future of the Desegregated Negro College: A Critical Summary. *The Journal of Negro Education,* 27(3), 419–429.

Johnson, A. M., Jr. (1993). Bid Whist, Tonk, and the *United States v. Fordice*: Why Integrationism Fails African-Americans Again. *California Law Review,* 81(6), 1401–1470.

Kujovich, G. (1987). Equal Educational Opportunity in Higher Education and the Black College: The Era of Separate But Equal. *Minnesota Law Review,* 72(1), 29–172.

Luti, A. N. (1999). "When a Door Closes, a Window Opens: Do Today's Private Historically Black Colleges and Universities Run Afoul of Conventional Equal Protection Analysis?" *Howard Law Journal,* 42.

McKenzie, T. L. (1993). *Unites States v. Fordice*: Does the End of "Separate and Unequal" in Higher Education also Spell the End of Historically Black Colleges. *Western State University Law Review*, 20, 735–747.

Moore, J. A. (2000). Are State-Supported Historically Black Colleges and Universities Justifiable after *Fordice*? A Higher Education Dilemma. *Florida State University Law Review*, 27.

Olswang, S., and Taylor, E. (1999). Peril or Promise: The Effect of Desegregation Litigation on Historically Black Colleges." *The Western Journal of Black Studies,* 23(2), 73–82.

Patterson, C. M. (1994). Desegregation as a Two-Way Street: The Aftermath of *United States v. Fordice. Cleveland State Law Review*, 42(3), 377–433.

Preer, J. L. (1982). *Lawyers v. Educators: Black Colleges and Desegregation in Public Higher Education*. Westport, CT: Greenwood.

Preer, J. (1990). "Just and Equitable Division": Jim Crow and the 1890 Land-Grant College Act. *Prologue*, 22(4), 323–337.

Samuels, A. L. (2004). *Is Separate Unequal? Black Colleges and the Challenge to Desegregation*. Lawrence, Kansas: The University Press of Kansas.

Smith, T. A. (1993). *United States v. Fordice*: The Interpretation of Desegregation in Higher Education and the Struggle for the Survival of the Historically Black Colleges in America. *Southern University Law Review*, 20(2), 407–439.

Snowden, M. T., Jackson, J. F. L., & Flowers, L. A. (2002). An Examination of the Efficiency of the Proposed Remedies and Settlement for Ayers: Based on a Study of Black College Students in Mississippi. *NASAP Journal,* 5(1), 7–20.

Taylor, E., & Olswang, S. (1999). Peril or Promise: The Effect of Desegregation litigation on Historically Black Colleges. *The Western Journal of Black Studies,* 23(2), 73–82.

Thomas, G. E., & McPartland, J. (1984). Have College Desegregation Policies Threatened Black Student Enrollment and Black Colleges?—An Empirical Analysis. *Journal of Negro Education*, 53(4), 389–399.

Ware, L. (1994). The Most Visible Vestige: Black Colleges After *Fordice. Boston College Law Review*, 35(3), 633–680.

Williamson, J. A. (2004). Brown, Black, and Yellow: Desegregation in a Multi-Ethnic Context. *History of Education Quarterly*, 44(1), 109–12.

Black Colleges, Policy Issues, and Society

Adebayo, A. O., Adekoya, A. A., & Ayadi, F. (2001). Historically Black Colleges and Universities as Agents of Change for the Development of Minority Business. *Journal of Black Studies*, 32(2), 166–183.

Ayadi, F. (1994). The Role of Historically Black Colleges and Universities in a Renewed Black Capitalism. *Business and Economic Review*, 8(1), 1–19.

Bart, B. D., Philbrick, J. H., & Tapp, C. D. (1993). The Impact of Newsletters on Community Attitudes: The Case of a Historically Black College. *Journal of Marketing for Higher Education,* 4(1/2), 339–350.

Billingsley, A., & Elam, J. C. (1986). *Black Colleges and Public Policy.* Chicago: Follett Press.

Brown, M. C., II, & Davis, J. E. (2001). The Historically Black College as Social Contract, Social Capital, and Social Equalizer. *Peabody Journal of Education,* 76(1), 31–49.

Brown, M. C., II, & Freeman, K. (Eds.). *Black Colleges: New Perspectives on Policy and Practice.* Westport, CT: Praeger.

Coaxum, J. (2001). The Misalignment Between the Carnegie Classifications and Black Colleges. *Urban Education,* 36(5), 572–584.

Davis, L. J., & Galloway, S. W. (1995). Prospering through Partnering: A Strategy for Historically/Predominantly Black Colleges and Universities. *The Journal of Continuing Higher Education,* 43(2), 21–26.

Elbert, M. M. (2005). *The Politics of Educational Decision Making: Historically Black Colleges and Universities and Federal Assistance Programs.* Westport, CT: Praeger.

Freeman, K., & Cohen, R. T. (2001). Bridging the Gap between Economic Development and Cultural Empowerment: HBCUs Challenges for the Future. *Urban Education,* 36(5), 585–596.

Harley, D. A. (2000). University Partnerships between Minority Institutions and Major Research Universities: Expanding Academic Opportunities and Strengthening Collaboration. *Rehabilitation Education,* 14(4), 350–360.

Hytche, W. P. (1990). Historically Black Institutions Forge Linkages with African Nations. *Educational Record,* 71(2), 19–21.

Jones, M. (1971). The Responsibility of the Black College to the Black Community: Then and Now. *Daedalus,* 100, 732–744.

Jones, B. W. (1998). Rediscovering our Heritage: Community Service and the Historically Black University. In Zlotkowski, E. (Ed.) *Successful Service-Learning Programs: New Models of Excellence in Higher Education.* Bolton, MA: Anker Publishing Company, Inc.

Payne, N. J. (1987). The Role of Black Colleges in an Expanding Economy. *Educational Record,* 68(4), 104–106.

Shaw, R. G. (1991). Forging New Alliances with Historically Black Colleges. *Community, Technical, and Junior College Journal,* 61(6), 41–43.

Simmons, H. L. (1984). The Accreditation Process as a Factor in the Improvement of Traditionally Black Institutions. *Journal of Negro Education,* 53(4), 400–405.

Stewart, T. J., Prinzinger, J. M., Dias, J. K., Bowden, J. T., Salley, J. K., & Smith, A. E. (1989). The Economic Impact of a Historically Black College Upon its Local Community. *Journal of Negro Education,* 58(2), 232–242.

Wenglinsky, H. H. (1996). The Educational Justification of Historically Black Colleges and Universities: A Policy Response to the U.S. Supreme Court. *Educational Evaluation and Policy Analysis,* 18(1), 91–103.

Wolanin, T. R. (1998). The Federal Investment in Minority-Serving Institutions. *New Directions for Higher Education*, 26(2), 17–32.

Students at Black Colleges

Allen, W. R. (1992). The Color of Success: African-American College Student Outcomes at Predominantly White and Historically Black Public Colleges and Universities. *Harvard Educational Review*, 62, 26–44.

Allen, W. R., Epps, E. G., & Haniff, N. Z. (Eds.). (1991). *College in Black and White: African-American Students in Predominantly White and in Historically Black Public Universities.* Albany, NY: State University of New York Press.

Bennett, P., & Xie, Y. (2003). "Revisiting Racial Differences in College Attendance: The Role of Historically Black Colleges and Universities." *American Sociological Review*, 68(4): 567–580.

Berger, J. B., & Milem, J. F. (2000). Exploring the Impact of Historically Black Colleges in Promoting the Development of Undergraduates' Self-Concept. *Journal of College Student Development*, 41(4), 381–394.

Bohr, L., Pascarella, E. T., Nora, A., & Terenzini, P. T. (1995). Do Black Students Learn more at Historically Black or Predominantly White Colleges? *Journal of College Student Development*, 36(1), 75–85.

Bridges, B., B. Cambridge, G.D. Kuh, and L. H. Leegwater (2005). "Student Engagement at Minority-Serving Institutions: Emerging Lessons from the BEAMS Project." *New Directions for Institutional Research*, 125, 25–43.

Brown, M. C., II (1998). African American College Student Retention and the Ecological Psychology of Historically Black Colleges. *National Association of Student Affairs Professionals Journal*, 1(1), 50–66.

Brown, T. L., Parks, G. S. and Phillips, C. M. eds. (2005). *African American Fraternities and Sororities: The Legacy and the Vision.* Lexington, KY: University of Kentucky Press.

Chism, M., & Satcher, J. (1998). African-American Students' Perceptions Toward Faculty at Historically Black Colleges. *College Student Journal*, 32(2), 315–320.

Conrad, C. F., Brier, E. M., & Braxton, J. M. (1997). Factors Contributing to the Matriculation of White Students in Public HBCUs. *Journal for a Just and Caring Education*, 3(1), 37–62.

Constantine, J. M. (1995). The Effect of Attending Historically Black Colleges and Universities on Future Wages of Black Students. *Industrial and Labor Relations Review*, 48(3), 531–546.

Constantine, M. G. (2002). Cultural Congruity, Womanist Identity Attitudes, and Life Satisfaction Among African American College Women Attending Historically Black and Predominantly White Institutions. *Journal of College Student Development*, 43(2), 184–194.

DeSousa, D. J., & Kuh, G. D. (1996). Does Institutional Racial Composition make a Difference in What Black Students Gain from College? *Journal of College Student Development*, 37(3), 257–267.

Dreher, G. F., & Chargois, J. A. (1998). Gender, Mentoring Experiences, and Salary Attainment Among Graduates of a Historically Black University. *Journal of Vocational Behavior*, 53(3), 401–416.

Fleming, J. (1984). *Blacks in College: A Comparative Study of Students' Success in Black and White Institutions*. San Francisco: Jossey-Bass.

Fleming, J. (2001). The Impact of a Historically Black College on African American Students: The Case of Lemoyne-Owen College. *Urban Education*, 36(5), 597–610.

Flowers, L. A., Jackson, J. F. L., & Bridges, B. K. (2002). Influences on Precollege Students' Use of Study Strategies. *Journal of Critical Inquiry Into Curriculum and Instruction*, 4(1), 10–15.

Freeman, K. (1999). HBCs or PWIs? African American High School Students' Consideration of Higher Education Institution Types. *The Review of Higher Education*, 23(1), 91–106.

Freeman, K. (2005). *African American College Choice and the Influence of Family and School*. Albany, SUNY Press.

Freeman, K., & Thomas, G. E. (2002). Black Colleges and College Choice: Characteristics of Students who Choose HBCUs. *Review of Higher Education*, 25(3), 349–358.

Fries-Britt, S. L., & Turner, B. (2002). Uneven Stories: Successful Black Collegians at a Black and a White Campus. *Review of Higher Education*, 25(3), 315–330.

Garibaldi, A. (1991). The Role of Historically Black Colleges in Facilitating Resilience Among African American Students. *Education and Urban Society*, 24(1), 103–112.

Giddings, P. (1994). *In Search of Sisterhood: Delta Sigma Theta and the Challenge of the Black Sorority Movement*. New York: HarperCollins.

Gurin, P., & Epps, E. (1975). *Black Consciousness, Identity, and Achievement: A Study of Students in Historically Black Colleges*. New York: John Wiley and Sons.

Gurin, P. (1966). Social Class Constraints on the Occupational Aspirations of Students Attending Some Predominantly Negro Colleges. *The Journal of Negro Education*, 35(4), 336–350.

Gurin, P., and Epps, E. (1966). Some Characteristics of Students from Poverty Backgrounds Attending Predominantly Negro Colleges in the Deep South. *Social Forces*, 45(1). 27–40.

Hall, B. (2005). When the Majority is the Minority: White Graduate Students' Social Adjustment at a Historically Black University. *Journal of College Student Development*, 46(1), 28–42.

Johnson, C. S. (1969). *The Negro College Graduate*. New York: Negro Universities Press.

Kim, M. M. (2002). Historically Black vs. White Institutions: Academic Development Among Black Students. *Review of Higher Education*, 25(4), 385–407.

Kimbrough, R. M., Molock, S. D., & Walton, K. (1996). Perception of Social Support, Acculturation, Depression, and Suicidal Ideation Among African American College Students at Predominantly Black and Predominantly White Universities. *Journal of Negro Education*, 65(3), 295–307.

Kimbrough, W. *Black Greek 101*. Fairleigh-Dickinson: Fairleigh-Dickinson University Press.

Lang, M. (1986). Black Student Retention at Black Colleges and Universities: Problems, Issues, and Alternatives. *The Western Journal of Black Studies*, 10(2), 48–53.

McDonough, P. M., Antonio, A. L., & Trent, J. W. (1997). Black Students, Black Colleges. An African American College Choice Model. *Journal for a Just and Caring Education*, 3(1), 9–36.

Miller, P. B. (1995). To "Bring the Race Along Rapidly": Sport, Student Culture, and Educational Mission at Historically Black Colleges During the Interwar Years. *History of Education Quarterly*, 35(2), 111–133.

Nettles, M. T., Wagener, U. Millett, C., and Killenbeck, A. (1999). "Student Retention and Progression: A Special Challenge for Private Historically Black Colleges and Universities." *New Directions for Higher Education*, 27(4), 51–67.

Nixon, H. L., & Henry, W. J. (1992). White Students at the Black University: Their Experiences Regarding Acts of Racial Intolerance. *Equity & Excellence,* 25(2–4), 121–123.

Rosenthal, J. (1975). Southern Black Student Activism: Assimilation vs. Nationalism. *The Journal of Negro Education*, 44(2), 113–129.

Ross, L. (2001). *Divine Nine: The History of African American Fraternities and Sororities*. New York: Kensington Publishing Corp.

Ross, M. J. (1998). *Success Factors of Young African American Men at a Historically Black College*. Westport, CT: Praeger.

Ross, M. J. (2003). *Success Factors of Young African American Women at a Historically Black College*. Westport, CT: Praeger.

Schwartz, R. A., & Washington, C. M. (1999). African-American Freshmen in a Historically Black College. *Journal of the First-Year Experience and Students in Transition*, 11(1), 39–62.

Sissoko, M. (2005). Minority Enrollment Demand for Higher Education at Historically Black Colleges and Universities From 1976 to 1998: An Empirical Analysis. *Journal of Higher Education*, 76(2), 181–208.

Wade, B. H. (2002). How Does Racial Identity Affect Historically Black Colleges and Universities' Student Perceptions of September 11, 2001? *Journal of Black Studies*, 33(1), 25–43.

Watson, L. W., & Kuh, G. D. (1996). The Influence of Dominant Race Environments on Student Involvement, Perceptions, and Educational Gains: A Look at Historically Black and Predominantly White Liberal Arts Institutions. *Journal of College Student Development*, 3(4), 415–424.

Webster, D. S., Stockard, R. L., & Henson, J. W. (1981). Black Student Elite: Enrollments Shifts of High Achieving, High Socio-Economic Status Black Students from Black to White Colleges During the 1970s. *College and University*, 56(3), 283–291.

Willie, C. V. (1994). Black Colleges are Not Just for Blacks Anymore. *Journal of Negro Education*, 63(2), 153–163.

Wilson, R. (1990). Can Black Colleges Solve the Problem of Access for Black Students? *American Journal of Education*, 98(4), 443–457.

Wolters, R. (1975). *The New Negro on Campus: Black College Rebellions of the 1920s.* Princeton, NJ: Princeton University.

Philanthropy, Fundraising, and Black Colleges

Anderson, E., & Moss, A. (1999). *Dangerous Donations: Northern Philanthropy and Southern Black Education, 1902–1930.* Columbia: University of Missouri Press.

Anderson, J. D. (1998). Training the Apostles of Liberal Culture: Black Higher Education, 1900–1935. In *The Education of Blacks in the South, 1860–1935.* Chapel Hill: University of North Carolina Press.

Anderson, J. D. (1980). Philanthropic Control over Private Black Higher Education. In *Philanthropy and Cultural Imperialism: The Foundations at Home and Abroad.* Edited by Robert Arnove. Massachusetts: G. K. Hall & Co.

Bieze, M. (2005). Ruskin in the Black Belt: Booker T. Washington, Arts and Crafts, and the New Negro. *Source: Notes in the History of Art.*

Beize, M. (2004). Booker T. Washington: Philanthropy and Aesthetics. In *Uplifting a People: African American Philanthropy and Education*, edited by M. Gasman and K. Sedgwick. New York: Peter Lang.

Boger, C., Catrelia S. H., & Enid B. J. (1999). A Study of the Relationship Between Alumni Giving and Selected Characteristics of Alumni Donors of Livingstone College, NC. *Journal of Black Studies*, 29(4), 523–539.

Brazzell, J. C. (1992). Bricks Without Straw: Missionary-Sponsored Black Higher Education in the Post-Emancipation Era. *Journal of Higher Education*, 63(1), 26–49.

Gasman, M. (2001). Charles S. Johnson and Johnnetta Cole: Successful Role Models for Fundraising at Historically Black Colleges and Universities. *The CASE International Journal of Educational Advancement*, 1(3), 237–252.

Gasman, M. (2002). W.E.B. Du Bois and Charles S. Johnson: Opposing Views on Philanthropic Support for Black Higher Education. *History of Education Quarterly*, 42(4), 493–516.

Gasman, M. (2002). A Word for Every Occasion: Appeals by John D. Rockefeller, Jr. to White Donors on Behalf of the United Negro College Fund. *History of Higher Education Annual*, 22, 67–90.

Gasman, M. (2002). An Untapped Resource: Bringing African Americans into the College and University Giving Process. *The CASE International Journal of Educational Advancement*, 2(3), 280–292.

Gasman, M. (2005). The Role of Faculty in Fundraising at Black Colleges: What is it and What Can it Become? *International Journal of Educational Advancement*, 5(2), 171–179.

Gasman, M. (2004). Rhetoric vs. Reality: The Fundraising Messages of the United Negro College Fund in the Immediate Aftermath of the *Brown* Decision. *History of Education Quarterly*, 44(1).

Gasman M., & Anderson-Thompkins, S. (2003). *Fund Raising from Black College Alumni. Successful Strategies for Supporting Alma Mater.* Washington, DC: CASE Books.

Gasman, M., & Epstein, E. (2004). Creating an Image for Black Colleges: A Visual Examination of the United Negro College Fund's Publicity, 1944–1960. *Educational Foundations*, 18(2), 41–61.

Holloman, D., Gasman, M., & Anderson-Thompkins, S. (2003). Motivations for Philanthropic Giving in the African American Church: Implications for Black College Fundraising. *Journal of Research on Christian Education*, 12(2), 137–169.

McPherson, J. M. (1970). White Liberals and Black Power in Negro Education, 1865–1915. *The American Historical Review*, 75(5), 1357–1386.

Patterson, F. D. (1959). Foundation policies in Regard to Negro Institutions of Higher Learning. *Journal of Educational Sociology*, 32(6), 290–296.

Peeps, J. M. S. (1981). Northern Philanthropy and the Emergence of Black higher Education: Do Gooder's, Compromisers, or Co-conspirators? *Journal of Negro Education*, 50(3), 251–269.

Pike, G.D. (1973). *Jubilee Singers, and their Campaign for Twenty Thousand Dollars*. London: Hodder and Stoughton.

Sav, T. (2000). Tests of Fiscal Discrimination in Higher Education Finance: Funding Historically Black Colleges and Universities. *Journal of Education Finance*, 26(2), 157–72.

Stuckert, R. (1964). The Negro College—A Pawn of White Domination. *The Wisconsin Sociologist*.

Trent, Jr., W. J. (1955). Cooperative Fund Raising for Higher Education. *Journal of Negro Education*, 24(1), 6–15.

Trent, Jr., W. J., and Patterson, F.D. (1958). Financial Support of the Private Negro college. *Journal of Negro Education*, 27(3), 398–405.

Tucker, S. K. (2002). The Early Years of the United Negro College Fund. *The Journal of African American History*, 87(4), 416–432.

Urban, W. J. (1989). Philanthropy and the Black Scholar: The Case of Horace Mann Bond. *Journal of Negro Education*, 58(4), 478–493.

Ward, A. (2000). *Dark Midnight When I Rise: The Story of the Jubilee Singers, Who Introduced the World to the Music of Black America*. New York: Farrar, Straus, and Girioux.

Watkins, W. (2001). *White Architects of Black Education: Ideology and Power in America*. New York: Teachers College Press.

Black College Presidents

Benjamin, L. (2004). *Dreaming No Small Dreams: William R. Harvey's Visionary Leadership*. Arlington: Tapestry Press.

Brown, L. (1998). *Long Walk: The Story of the Presidency of Willa B. Player at Bennett College*. Greensboro: Bennett College's Women's Leadership Institute.

Carter, L. (1998). *Walking Integrity: Benjamin Elijah Mays, Mentor to Martin Luther King Jr.* Mercer: Mercer University Press.

Davis, L. (1998). *Clashing of the Soul: John Hope and the Dilemma of African American Leadership and Black Higher Education in the Early Twentieth Century.* Athens: The University of Georgia Press.

Engs, R. (1999). *Educating the Disfranchised and Disinherited: Samuel Chapman Armstrong and Hampton Institute*. Knoxville: The University of Tennessee Press.

Gasman, M. (1999). Scylla and Charybdis: Navigating the Waters of Academic Freedom at Fisk University during Charles S. Johnson's Administration (1946–1956). *American Educational Research Journal*, 36(4), 739–758.

Gasman, M. (2001). The President as Ethical Role Model: Instilling an Ethic of Leadership at Fisk University During the 1950s. *Journal of College and Character*, 2. Retrieved January 17, 2006 from http://www.collegevalues. org/articles.cfm?a=1&id=510.

Gilpin, P. J., & Gasman, M. (2003). *Charles S. Johnson. Leadership Behind the Veil in the Age of Jim Crow*. Albany, NY: SUNY Press.

Goodson, M. G., ed. (1991). *Chronicles of Faith: The Autobiography of Frederick D. Patterson*. The University of Alabama Press: Tuscaloosa, Alabama.

Manley, A. (1995). *Legacy Continues: The Manley Years at Spelman College, 1953–1976*. New York: The University Press of America.

Mays, B. (2003). *Born to Rebel*. Athens: University of Georgia.

McKinney, R. (1997). *Mordecai, the Man and his Message: The Story of Mordecai Wyatt Johnson*. Washington, DC: Howard University Press.

Robbins, R. (1996). *Sidelines Activist: Charles S. Johnson and the Struggle for Civil Rights*. Jackson: University of Mississippi Press.

Smith, G. (1994). *Black Educator in the Segregated South: Kentucky's Rufus B. Atwood*. Lexington: University of Kentucky Press.

Urban, W. J. (1994). *Black Scholar*. Athens, Georgia: University of Georgia.

Watson, Y., and Gregory, S. T. (2005). *Daring to Educate: The Legacy of Early Spelman College Presidents*. Sterling, VA: Stylus Publishing.

Williamson, J. A. (2004). "This Has Been Quite a Year for Heads Falling": Institutional Autonomy in the Civil Rights Era. *History of Education Quarterly*, 44(4).

Faculty at Black Colleges

Billingsley, A. (1982). Building Strong Faculties in Black Colleges. *Journal of Negro Education*, 51(1), 4–15.

Edgcomb, G. S. (1993). *From Swastika to Jim Crow: Refugee Scholars at Black Colleges*. Malabar, FL: Krieger.

Foster, L. (2001). The Not-So-Invisible Professors: White Faculty at the Black College. *Urban Education*, 36(5), 611–629.

Foster, L., Guyden, J. A., & Miller, A. L. (1999). *Affirmed Action: Essays on the Academic and Social Lives of White Faculty Members at Historically Black Colleges and Universities*. Lanham, MD: Rowman & Littlefield.

Johnson, B. J. (2001). Faculty Socialization: Lessons Learned from Urban Black Colleges. *Urban Education*, 36(5), 630–647.

Johnson, B. J., & Harvey, W. (2002). The Socialization of Black College Faculty: Implications for Policy and Pactice. *Review of Higher Education*, 25(3), 297–314.

Meier, A. (1992). *A White Scholar in the Black Community, 1945–1965.* Amherst, Massachusetts: University of Massachusetts Press.

Minor, J. T. (2004). Dilemmas of Decision-Making in Historically Black Colleges and Universities: Defining the Context. *Journal of Negro Education,* 73(1), 40–52.

Paddon, A. R., & Cobb, L. (1990). Overlooked Faculty Resource in Historically Black Colleges. *Journalism Educator,* 45(1), 64–70.

Perna, L. (2001). The Contribution of Historically Black Colleges and Universities to the Preparation of African Americans for Faculty Careers. *Research in Higher Education,* 42(3), 267–294.

Phillips, I. P. (2002). Shared Governance on Black College Campuses. *Academe,* 88(4), 50–54.

Smith, S. L., & Borgstedt, K. W. (1985). Factors Influencing Adjustment of White Faculty in Predominantly Black Colleges. *Journal of Negro Education,* 54(2), 148–163.

Thompson, C. J., & Dey, E. L. (1998). Pushed to the Margins: Sources of Stress for African-American College and University Faculty. *Journal of Higher Education,* 69(3), 324–345.

Gender Issues at Black Colleges

Bonner, F. B. (2001). Addressing Gender Issues in the Historically Black Colleges and Universities Community: A Challenge and Call to Action. *Journal of Negro Education,* 70(3), 176–191.

Fleming, J. (1983). Black Women in Black and White College Environments: The Making of a Matriarch. *Journal of Social Issues,* 39(3), 41–54.

Tabbye, C., A. Harris, D. Rivas, L. Helaire, & L. Green. (2004). Racial Stereotypes and Gender in Context: African Americans at Predominantly Black and Predominantly White Colleges. *A Journal of Research,* 51(1–2), 1–16.

Williams, L. A. (1986). Chief Academic Officers at Black Colleges and Universities: A Comparison by Gender. *Journal of Negro Education,* 55(4), 443–452.

Conducting Research on Black Colleges: Methodological Concerns and Approaches

Brown, M. C. (2003). Emics and Etics of Researching Black Colleges: Applying Facts and Avoiding Fallacies. *New Directions for Institutional Research,* 118, 27–40.

Brown, M. C., & Lane, J.E. eds. (2003). *Studying Diverse Institutions: Contexts, Challenges, and Considerations. New Directions for Institutional Research.* New Jersey: Wiley & Sons, 2003.

Hossler, D. (1997). Historically Black Public Colleges and Universities: Scholarly Inquiry and Personal Reflections. *Journal for Just and Caring Education,* 3(1), 114–126.

Curriculum

Agingu, B. O. (2000). Library Web Sites at Historically Black Colleges and Universities. *College & Research Libraries*, 61(1), 30–37.

Curtin, M., & Gasman, M. (2003). Historically Black College MBA Programs: Prestige, Rankings, and the Meaning of Success. *Journal of Education for Business*, 79(2), 79–84.

Davis, A. L. (1985). The Role of Black Colleges and Black Law Schools in the training of Black Lawyers and Judges: 1960–1980. *The Journal of Negro History*, 70(1/2), 24–34.

Davis, J. J., & Markham, P. L (1991). Student Attitudes Toward Foreign Language Study at Historically and Predominantly Black Institutions. *Foreign Language Annals*, 24(3), 227–237.

Epstein, E., & Gasman, M. (2005). A Not-So-Systematic Effort to Study Art: Albert Barnes and Lincoln University, *History of Higher Education Annual*, 24.

Gasman, M. (2001). Passport to the Front of the Bus: The Impact of Fisk University's International Program on Race Relations in Nashville, Tennessee. *49th Parallel—The International Journal of North American Studies*, 7. Retrieved January 12, 2006 from http://www.49thparallel. bham.ac.uk/back/issue7/gasman.htm.

Gasman, M., & Epstein, E. (2002). Modern Art in the Old South: The Role of the Arts in Fisk University's Campus Curriculum. *Educational Researcher*, 31(2), 13–20.

Hudgins, J. L. (1994). The Segmentation of Southern Sociology? Social Research at Historically Black Colleges and Universities. *Social Forces*, 72(3), 885–893.

Jarmon, C. (2003). Sociology at Howard University: From E. Franklin Frazier and Beyond. *Teaching Sociology*, 31(4), 366–374.

Johnson, C. (2002) *African Americans and ROTC: Military, Naval, and Aeroscience Programs at Historically Black Colleges, 1916–1973*. Jefferson, NC: McFarland and Company, Inc.

Jones-Wilson, F. C. (1984). The Nature and Importance of the Foundations of Education in a Teacher Education Program at a Black University. *Teacher Education Quarterly*, 11(2), 41–45.

Medford, G. S. (1998). A View of Curricula in Educational Theatre from Seven Historically Black Colleges and Universities, 1900–1990. *The Negro Educational Review*, 49(3–4), 139–146.

Powell, R. J., & Reynolds, J. (1999). *To Conserve a Legacy. American Art from Historically Black Colleges and Universities*. Cambridge, MA: Massachusetts Institute of Technology.

Price, G. N. (1998). Black Colleges and Universities: The Road to Philistia? *Negro Educational Review*, 49, 9–21.

Price, G. N. (2000). The Idea of the Historically Black University. *Negro Educational Review*, 51(3), 99–113.

Trent, W., & Hill, J. (1994). The Contributions of Historically Black College and Universities to the Production of African American Scientists and

Engineers. In Pearson, W., Jr., & Fechter, A. (Eds.), *Who Will Do Science?: Educating the Next Generation.* Baltimore, MD: Johns Hopkins.

Verharen, C. C. (1993). A Core Curriculum at Historically Black Colleges and Universities: An Immodest Proposal. *Journal of Negro Education,* 62(2), 190–203.

Watkins, W. (1990). Teaching and Learning in the Black Colleges: A 130-year Retrospective. *Teaching Education,* 3(1), 10–25.

Recruitment Issues at Black Colleges

Harper, S. R. (2001). On Analyzing HBCU Admissions and Recruitment Material. *National Association of Student Affairs Professionals,* 4(1), 55–64.

Hendrix, W. F., & Javier, W. (1986). Recruitment: A Significant and Overlooked Component of Black College Survival. *The Western Journal of Black Studies,* 10(2), 55–58.

Diversity at Black Colleges

Harrington, E., & DiBona, J. (1993). Bringing Multiculturalism to the Historically Black University in the United States. *Educational Horizons,* 71(3), 150–156.

Jewell, J. (2002). To Set an Example: The Tradition of Diversity at Historically Black Colleges and Universities. *Urban Education,* 37(1), 7–21.

Kranz, P. L., Lund, N. L., & Johnson, B. O. (1996). Enhancing Racial Understanding: A Class Visit to a Black University, *The Journal of Experiential Education,* 19(3), 152–157.

Sims, S. J. (1994). *Diversifying Historically Black Colleges and Universities: A New Higher Education Paradigm.* Westport, CT: Greenwood Press.

Wingard, E. (1982). Experience of Historically Black Colleges in Serving Diversely Prepared Students. *New Directions for Experiential Learning,* 17, 29–36.

Grading for Effort: The Success Equals Effort Policy at Benedict College

Omari H. Swinton

1. Introduction

Many students and professors believe that the more effort a student puts forth in a class, the better grade that student will earn. This paper will describe the Success Equals Effort (SE^2) policy, formerly known as the SEE policy, at Benedict College. The SE^2 policy gives explicit grades for effort and knowledge to all students taking freshman and sophomore-level courses. This policy was implemented to increase the preparedness of Benedict College's students by emphasizing the importance of effort. By focusing on effort, Benedict College hopes to increase learning, retention and graduation rates, and the value of the degree its students receive.

This paper is organized as follows. The second section describes the SE^2 policy. The third section discusses the assumptions that are necessary for the policy to be successful. This will be followed by a discussion of who Benedict College's students are and how they compare with college students in general. Then the fifth section discusses the actual outcomes of the policy by looking at grade observations. The last section will discuss my future research.

2. Benedict College and the SE^2 Policy

Benedict College was founded in 1870 on an 80-acre plantation in Columbia, South Carolina. Under the auspices of the American Baptist Home Mission Society, Mrs. Bathsheba A. Benedict, of Pawtucket, Rhode Island, provided $13,000.00 to purchase the land to open Benedict Institute on December 12, 1870. This new school was established for recently emancipated people of African descent. Benedict College remains a Historically Black College and University (HBCU) with 2,770 students as of Fall 2004. Benedict is an open-admissions college.

Benedict College implemented the Success Equals Effort (SE[2]), formerly known as the SEE policy, in the spring of 2002. The policy emerged out of dissatisfaction with learning outcomes due in part to a lack of preparedness of students for the rigors of college. The unique aspect of this policy is that for freshman- and sophomore-level courses effort is an explicit part of a student's grade.[1] The aim of the policy is to increase learning, retention and graduation rates, and the value of the degree its students receive. Although the policy was implemented in the spring of 2002, it was not strictly enforced until Fall 2004.[2] The SE[2] policy requires that a professor report to the registrar two grades for students taking freshman- and sophomore-level courses: effort and content learning (knowledge). The administration weights the two grades differently for freshman and sophomore courses. The policy is designed such that freshmen are guaranteed a minimum passing grade of "C" if they earn the maximum effort grade of an "A" even if they fail content learning. Final grades are reported on a 4 point scale where an A = 4, B = 3, C = 2, D = 1, and F = 0. The following tables give the 25 possible combinations of effort and knowledge grades and the final grade that the student will receive. Table 1 gives the possible outcomes for freshman-level courses, and Table 2 gives the possible outcomes for sophomore-level courses. The tables are calculated roughly using a weight of 60–40 for effort to knowledge in freshman-level courses. In the sophomore-level courses, the weight used is roughly 40–60 effort to knowledge. In the junior- and senior-level courses, professors submit only a final grade; as in college courses throughout the United States, professors may or may not take effort into consideration when determining the final grade.

The method for measuring effort and knowledge is defined for each class by the individual professor. Measures that are used in defining effort range from homework, attendance, class participation, and attendance of office hours. Content learning (knowledge) is measured by

Table 1
Freshman Level

		Knowledge Grade				
		A	B	C	D	F
	A	A	A	B	C	C
Effort	B	B	B	B	C	D
Grade	C	B	C	C	C	D
	D	C	C	D	D	F
	F	C	D	D	F	F

Table 2
Sophomore Level

		Knowledge Grade				
		A	B	C	D	F
Effort Grade	A	A	B	B	C	D
	B	A	B	C	C	D
	C	B	B	C	D	D
	D	B	C	C	D	F
	F	C	C	D	D	F

tests, quizzes, and/or term papers. Under this policy, the professor may have to put in more effort, if his original grading policy did not consider effort. The student has much more control of the effort grade than of the content learning grade. The content learning grade is usually an attempt to demonstrate knowledge with questions that are unknown beforehand, while effort is work that is performed throughout the class without as stringent a time constraint. Another aspect of this policy is that students who can earn high grades with little or no effort must now put forth effort to achieve the same high mark. Therefore, for these students, it is harder to earn the highest possible marks.

3. Assumptions

For the SE^2 policy to increase learning, retention and graduation rates, and the value of the degree its students receive, some assumptions must hold. To better think about these assumptions, a student's and professor/administrator's choices will be discussed. The students want to maximize the grade that they receive in a class. The goal of the professor/administrator, hereafter called the professor, will be to assign grades that maximize the informational learning of the students. The grade is a signal to future employers about the student's ability. Students want to put in the least effort to earn a given grade, which is a measure of the knowledge that the student has mastered in the class.[3] The professor wants to maximize the signal that the grade gives to future employers, i.e., to have the student earn the highest grade, but does not want to lower the amount of knowledge that the students are tested over.

The conflict that exists is how do professors motivate students to put forth more effort. The following examples illustrate the conflict. Suppose a professor decides to maximize students' grades by giving all students the best possible grade. If the professor does this, students will have no incentive to put forth effort. Even worse, the signal, which is just the grade, will not tell future employers anything about a student's ability. If a professor decides instead to maximize the effort given, the professor will give all the credit to effort as opposed to knowledge. This will maximize effort given by students; however, the signal will only tell workers how good the student is at giving effort and not what the student knows. If a professor instead decides to give credit only for knowledge as opposed to effort, this may cause students below a certain ability level to give no effort. This policy will signal to future employers which students have low or high ability. However, the policy will not induce all students to give effort.[4] Therefore, the problem is to induce all students to give effort, while minimizing the weakening of the signal that is sent to future employers and not lowering the amount of knowledge gained by the students.

Assume a student's ability is the main factor in determining the grade a student will receive. This ability is known by the student. The student with a certain ability level will be guaranteed a minimum grade. This minimum grade is increasing in the ability of the student. Each professor determines how much knowledge to teach in each class. The more knowledge that is taught, the harder it will be to receive a given grade in a class. It is easier to earn a higher grade for a given ability level, the lower the amount of knowledge taught.

For the SE^2 policy to increase learning, retention and graduation rates, and the value of the degree its students receive, these are the assumptions that I believe must hold.

Assumption 1. Effort affects the knowledge grade positively. If this were not the case, causing students to give more effort would only increase the effort grade. Without this assumption, the SE^2 policy would automatically lower the value of the final grade to future employers.

Assumption 2. Effort today has permanent effects on a student's ability to earn higher grades tomorrow. This assumption can be justified if more effort will lead to better student work ethic, motivation, and attitudes, which should increase the ability of the student to receive a higher grade in the future. Without this assumption, the SE^2 policy will just delay a student flunking until the student is no longer subject to the policy.[5]

Assumption 3. Professors will implement the policy wholeheartedly. A problem that comes with such a policy is that professors might not truly report the grades. A professor could either under report effort grades or knowledge grades to make sure the student receives the grade that the professor feels they deserve, not the grade the policy would assign. If this were to occur, the policy would not work.

Assumption 4. The professor defines effort, and this definition of effort is known by the student. The professor designs an effort grading policy such that more effort results in better performance on tests.

4. Benedict College's Students

According to "High School Academic Curriculum and the Persistence Path Through College" August 2001,[6] only 61.2 percent of students with an SAT score from 400–790, 62.1 percent of black students, 56.9 percent of students with parental education level of high school or less, and 56.1 percent of students attending a less selective private school will stay enrolled continuously in their first school. The demographic data that follows will show why Benedict College implemented the SE^2 policy.

Benedict College is an HBCU—at least 97 percent of its students are black. In Fall 2004, there were 2,433 students who were subject to this policy. My demographic data, which comes from Benedict College, is limited to students who enrolled at Benedict College from Fall 1999 to Fall 2004. The data set includes information on SAT math and verbal scores, ACT composite score, high school rank, high school grade point average, and high school size as well as demographic variables such as mother's education level, father's education level, number of siblings, number of siblings in college, parental taxable income (PTI), and expected family contribution to the student's education (EFC). A drawback of the data is that mother's education level, father's education level, number of siblings, number of siblings in college, PTI, and EFC are reported only for students who were enrolled in Fall 2004. Therefore, for students who entered school in Spring 2005, no demographic information is available. There are also many students with missing SAT, ACT, and high school grade point averages. These students can be thought of as those who decided to attend college late.

Table 3 gives the summary statistics for students in Fall 2004 who are affected by the SE^2 policy. The mean SAT score for a student attending Benedict College is 782. The mean ACT score of 15 is approximately equivalent to a score on the SAT of 750.[7] These scores are below the national average of all students from the years 1998 to 2003, which range from 1016 to 1026, and are also below the mean for blacks for the year 2003, which is 857. The mean high school grade point average for those Benedict students with reported SAT scores is 2.37, which is below the mean of black SAT takers for the year 2003, 2.95.[8]

Table 4 shows that the mean of the parental taxable income is $25,210.35. This leads to a mean expected family contribution to the student's education of $2,353. The mean EFC is above the national average for families in the lowest income quarter, $1,300, but is well below the national average for families in the lower middle quarter, $4,900.[9] The students are likely to be the only child in school, and come from a

Table 3
Summary Statistics of Those Students Affected by the SE^2 Policy

Variable	Number of Obs.	Mean (Std. Dev)	Min	Max
SAT verbal	960	390.27 (94.33)	200	780
SAT math	960	392.36 (97.29)	200	800
ACTCOMP	667	15.17 (2.77)	5	28
H.S. GPA	1769	2.37 (0.62)	0.67	5.05
H.S. RANK	1769	150.81 (111)	1	711
H.S. SIZE	1769	232.3 (132.08)	5	1247

Table 4
Family Characteristics of those Affected by the SE^2 Policy

Variable	Number of Obs.	Mean (Std. Dev)	Min	Max
Expected Family Contribution	2518	2352.81 (6342.95)	0	64585
Parental Taxable Income	2518	25210.35 (32001.3)	–13000	222949
Number of Children in College	1931	1.26 (0.55)	1	5
Number of Children in Household	1978	3.59 (0.55)	1	11

family with 3.6 kids. The current fertility rate is close to 2 children per woman in the United States. Benedict College students tend to come from larger than average families.

Table 5 gives details about the parental education. Of the students with non-missing parental education information, 51 percent do not have parents who attend college. This suggests that a little more than half of Benedict students are first-generation college students. If I assume that unknown parental education means that a student is estranged from that parent, then roughly 33 percent of Benedict students with parental education data are estranged from one of their parents. This will also proxy for the number of students from a single-parent home.

Table 5
Family Education of Those Students Affected by the SE² Policy

		Father's Education				
		Middle School/ Jr. High	High School	College or Beyond	Unknown/ Missing Obs.	Total
	Middle School/ Jr. High	63	46	4	54	165
	High School	90	761	156	210	1220
Mother's Education	College or Beyond	28	390	351	143	·912
	Unknown/ Missing Obs.	2	40	16	476	534
	Total	183	1241	526	885	2831

This section shows that Benedict College's students possess characteristics of students not likely to finish school. By focusing on effort, Benedict College hopes to increase its students' chances of graduating.

5. Policy Impact

5.1 Grades

The grades that are earned under the policy range from A to F for the knowledge and effort grades. If a student withdraws from a course, no knowledge or effort grades are recorded. Table 6 shows the total of withdrawals before and after the policy. The total percentage of with-

Table 6
Number of Withdrawals for Freshman and Sophomore-Level Courses

Term	Number of Observations	Percentage of Withdrawals
Fall 1999	11,166	22.10
Spring 2000	11,124	22.14
Fall 2000	12,468	20.81
Spring 2001	11,841	21.00
Fall 2001	12,318	14.73
Spring 2002	11,834	19.71
Fall 2002	12,662	14.40
Spring 2003	11,816	12.29
Fall 2003	12,602	16.10
Spring 2003	11,052	15.35
Fall 2004	11,800	13.49
Spring 2005	10,499	8.25

drawals in freshman- and sophomore-level courses is at its lowest for fall semesters in Fall 2004. The percent is at its lowest for spring semesters in Spring 2005. This indicates that given explicit credit for effort at least causes more students to complete a class that before they would have withdrawn. Additionally, this indicates that those students that withdrew either had an event occur that made attending school not as important to them, or that they did not respond to the incentives given.

For freshman- and sophomore-level courses, the final grade is a combination of a knowledge and effort grade. There are 9,953 grade observations for the 2,433 students who are subject to the SE^2 policy in the Fall 2004, and 9,631 grade observations for the 2,334 students who are subject to the SE^2 policy in Spring 2005. There are 5,532 grades for freshman-level classes in the Fall of 2005 and 5,200 grades for freshman-level classes in the Spring of 2006. There are 4,421 for sophomore-level classes in the Fall of 2005 and 4,431 for sophomore-level classes in the Spring of 2006.

Tables 7 and 8 give the outcomes for freshman-level courses. Students are more likely to earn an "A" for an effort grade than the knowledge grade. For freshman-level courses, we see heavy concentration when the effort grade equals the knowledge grade, for Fall 2004 45.9 percent and for Spring 2005 55.32 percent. In freshman-level courses in Fall 2004, 15.24 percent of the final grades are lower than the knowledge grade. In freshman-level courses in Spring 2005, 7.06 percent of the final grades are lower than the knowledge grade.

The fact that some students actually earn a final grade less than their knowledge grade shows that the policy is not just a grade booster. In

Table 7
Grade Distribution by Freshman-Level Courses for Fall 2004

| | | Knowledge Grade | | | | | |
		A	B	C	D	F	Total
	A	A	A	B	C	C	
		17.77	8.5	5.53	2.78	1.79	36.37
	B	B	B	B	C	D	
		3.22	9.38	6.4	3.9	1.55	24.45
Effort	C	B	C	C	C	D	
Grades		1.48	2.37	9.35	4.18	2.22	19.60
	D	C	C	D	D	F	
		0.69	1.17	1.61	3.45	1.99	8.91
	F	C	D	D	F	F	
		0.81	0.78	1.74	1.37	5.95	10.65
	Total	23.97	22.2	24.63	15.68	13.5	

Table 8
Grade Distribution by Freshman-level Courses for Spring 2005

| | | Knowledge Grade | | | | | |
		A	B	C	D	F	Total
	A	A	A	B	C	C	
		20.5	8.71	5.08	2.44	1.48	38.21
	B	B	B	B	C	D	
		1.21	11.02	6.62	2.94	1.17	22.96
Effort	C	B	C	C	C	D	
Grades		0.46	1.77	9.96	4.85	2.75	19.79
	D	C	C	D	D	F	
		0.17	0.42	0.88	3.88	1.58	6.94
	F	C	D	D	F	F	
		0.06	0.25	0.71	1.12	9.96	12.10
	Total	22.4	22.17	23.25	15.23	16.94	

freshman-level courses in Fall 2004, 36.85 percent of the final grades are higher than the knowledge grade. In freshman-level courses in Spring 2005, 36.04 percent of the final grades are higher than the knowledge grade. This shows that the vast majority of students either earn the same final grade or benefit by receiving a higher final grade.

Tables 9 and 10 give the outcomes for sophomore-level courses. In sophomore-level courses, we see the same pattern of heavy concentration where the effort grade equals the knowledge grade, 51.19 percent in Fall 2004 and 62.18 percent in Spring 2005. As in freshman-level courses, students are more likely to earn an "A" for their effort grade than their knowledge grade. In sophomore-level courses in Fall 2004, 4.61 percent of the final grades are lower than the knowledge grade. In sophomore-level courses in Spring 2005, 2.37 percent of the final grades are lower than the knowledge grade. This pattern is similar to freshman-level courses.

This shows that students who are better prepared, i.e., those in sophomore-level courses are better at earning higher effort grades. In sophomore-level courses in Fall 2004, 15.45 percent of the final grades are higher than the knowledge grade. In sophomore-level courses in Spring 2005, 11.67 percent of the final grades are higher than the knowledge grade.

From final grades alone, it is difficult to say whether the policy harms or helps students, where harmed means the policy caused the student to receive a lower final grade and helped means the policy caused the student to receive a higher final grade. Extreme cases concern students who

Table 9
Grade Distribution by Sophomore-level Courses for Fall 2004

		Knowledge Grade					
		A	B	C	D	F	Total
	A	A	B	B	C	D	
		23.12	8.41	6.13	1.81	1.06	40.53
	B	A	B	C	C	D	
		2.92	9.86	5.02	3.64	1.27	22.71
Effort	C	B	B	C	D	D	
Grade		1.47	3.82	9.09	3.94	1.54	19.86
	D	B	C	C	D	F	
		0.61	0.93	1.74	2.87	2.24	8.39
	F	C	C	D	D	F	
		0.88	0.34	0.38	0.66	6.24	8.50
	Total	29	23.57	22.37	12.92	12.25	

Table 10
Grade Distribution by Sophomore-level Courses for Spring 2005

		Knowledge Grade					
		A	B	C	D	F	Total
	A	A	B	B	C	D	
		22.55	5.91	4.85	1.76	0.36	35.43
	B	A	B	C	C	D	
		2.57	13.68	4.33	2.05	1.08	23.72
Effort	C	B	B	C	D	D	
Grades		0.41	3.25	11.78	2.01	1.56	19.00
	D	B	C	C	D	F	
		0.14	0.74	2.75	5.17	1.62	10.43
	F	C	C	D	D	F	
		0.07	0.27	0.74	1.33	9.00	11.42
	Total	25.73	23.85	24.46	12.32	13.63	

have an "A" for effort and a "D" or "F" for knowledge in freshman-level courses and have an "A" for effort and a "D" for knowledge in sophomore-level courses. Those students, who can be thought of as being helped by the policy, represent less than 13 percent. Therefore, there were not many students who received the safety net "C" under this policy.

The other extreme cases, where students have a "F" for effort and an "A" for knowledge in freshman-level courses and have a "F" for effort and an "A" or "B" for knowledge in sophomore-level courses, are less than 3 percent in both years. Therefore, there were not many students who were harmed by the policy.[10]

Table 11 presents the percent of "A" and "F" effort grades earned by types of students. The types are first-generation and non-first-generation college students, quartile of parental taxable income, quartile of SAT and missing SAT, quartile of high school grade point average and missing high school grade point average.

First-generation college students are more likely to earn an "F" for effort, and less likely to earn an "A." As a student's parental income quartile increases, the percent of "As" for effort increases. The incidence of "Fs" decreases as quartile of parental taxable income increases. Students with no SAT score are least likely to earn an "A," and also are most likely to earn an "F" for effort. The higher the quartile of the SAT score, the more likely a student is to earn an "A." Students in the lowest quartile are less likely to earn an "F" than students in the 25–50th quartile. Other than that oddity, as the quartile of the SAT score increases, the students become less likely to earn an "F." Students with no high school grade point average are the second most likely to earn an "A," and the second least likely to earn an "F." As you increase the quartile of high school grade point average, a students becomes more likely to earn an "A" and less likely to earn an "F." The data show that effort earned does vary across student characteristics in a way that shows effort is not a given grade. The students who you think would be better prepared for college are more likely to earn "As" for effort than the other students.

Table 11
Percent of "A" and "F" Effort Grade by Types of Student

Group	A	F
First Gen	35.45	10.82
Not First Gen	37.27	10.15
No PTI	51.96	11.12
>25th Quartile PTI	32.02	13.19
25–50th Quartile PTI	35.43	11.17
50–75th Quartile PTI	37.62	9.55
>75th Quartile PTI	39.00	9.41
No SAT	34.62	11.68
<665 SAT	34.65	9.68
760–665 SAT	36.16	10.62
860–761 SAT	42.46	8.74
<860 SAT	57.03	5.88
No HSGPA	41.36	10.76
<1.87 HSGPA	25.88	14.55
2.31–1.87 HSGPA	29.71	13.30
2.76–2.32 HSGPA	36.15	10.80
>2.76 HSGPA	51.48	5.44

Table 12 presents the percent of "A" and "F" knowledge grades earned by each type of student. First generation college students are more likely to earn an "F" for effort, and less likely to earn an "A." As a student's parental income quartile increases, so does the percent of "As" for effort except for the 50–75th percentile. The incidence of "Fs" decreases as quartile of parental taxable income increases. Students with no SAT score are least likely to earn an "A," and also most likely to earn an "F" for effort. The higher the quartile of SAT score, the more likely a student is to earn an "A." As the quartile of the SAT score increases, the student becomes less likely to earn an "F." Students with no high school grade point average are the second most likely to earn an "A," and the second least likely to earn an "F." As you increase the quartile of high school grade point average, a student becomes more likely to earn an "A" and less likely to earn an "F." These show that effort does vary across student characteristics in a way that shows effort is not a given grade. The students who you think would be better prepared for college are more likely to earn "As" for knowledge than the other students.

5.2 What the SE² Policy Means

On Benedict College's website, there is a list of what the SE² means and doesn't mean.[11] Given these grade observations, I can say that the SE²

Table 12
Percent of "A" and "F" Knowledge Grade by Types of Student

Group	A	F
First Gen	22.52	14.92
Not First Gen	25.13	12.80
No PTI	41.51	13.84
>25th Quartile PTI	20.00	18.06
25–50th Quartile PTI	23.91	14.76
50–75th Quartile PTI	23.80	13.39
>75th Quartile PTI	25.88	11.50
No SAT	22.01	16.08
<665 SAT	20.43	15.17
760–665 SAT	20.52	13.03
860–761 SAT	30.69	9.94
>860 SAT	48.74	5.34
No HSGPA	29.36	14.39
<$1.87 HSGPA	15.72	19.37
2.31–1.87 HSGPA	18.4	18.03
2.76–2.32 HSGPA	22.03	13.33
<$2.76 HSGPA	37.08	7.40

policy is doing some of the things it is supposed to. "Students can earn an A, B, C, D, or F grade." As shown by the grade observations, students still earn all possi-ble grades. "It is more difficult to earn a satisfactory grade." This statement is true for at least some of the students. The grades show that some students might have earned a better grade before the policy. "Only Freshmen receive a warranty to receive a satisfactory grade, if they make an 'A' in effort." The grades show that less than 7 percent of freshman with a failing knowledge grade earn the minimum passing grade of a "C." "An incentive is provided for students to put forth maximum effort in learning." Students are responding to the incentives to give maximum effort since many students earn "As" for effort. By definition of the policy, since junior- and senior-level courses are not subject to the policy, "No student could earn a degree solely because of effort." "An enhancement of academic freedom; Faculty determine how effort is defined." This statement is by definition partially true. The professors do define effort, but they do not determine the weight given to effort in the final grade.

"A quality academic process with increased student learning"; "Positive work ethics, motivation, attitudes, study habits, and responsibility"; "A potential increase in the value of the Benedict College degree and the employability of graduates"; and "Greater faculty efforts and more serious evaluation and instructional techniques" are parts of the SE^2 policy that cannot be answered by just looking at the grade observations. The increased learning will be looked at in my future research.

6. Future Research

My future research will analyze whether or not the SE^2 policy leads to increased learning, retention, and graduation rates, and whether students who earn an "A" for effort learn more in future classes. To begin testing whether the SE^2 policy leads to increased learning, I will look at the returns to the knowledge grade due to effort. This policy provides a data set in which the amount of effort that a student chooses to give in a class matters. I will be able to investigate the effects that more effort given has on the returns to learning.

To see if students who earn an "A" for effort learn more than those with lower effort levels and the assumption that effort today has some positive effects tomorrow, I will compare grades that students earn in two-part courses, i.e., Freshman Composition 1 and 2. If the assumption holds true, then students who give more effort in the first part of the course should experience higher returns to their knowledge grade in the second part, all else equal. For example, if you have two students with the same "ability" level, the student who gave more effort in part one of the course should learn more in part two of the courses. Using syllabi, I will be able to construct what "grades" students would have earned in classes pre-SE^2 if their classes had been subject to the policy. This will help show which type of students benefit or are hurt by the policy and whether learning has increased. Once the freshmen of Fall 2004 begin to take other classes besides freshman and sophomore-level courses, I will also be able to test whether the students who were subject to the SE^2 policy outperform those who were not subject to the policy.

It cannot be answered whether the SE^2 policy increases graduation until the freshman entering the Fall 2004 and Fall 2005 classes begin to graduate. However, using the full data set, I will be able to test whether the policy leads to an increased probability that particular types of students reach the continuation requirements and to higher retention rates. If the policy leads to more students reaching the continuation requirement and to higher retention rates, then it is working toward higher graduation rates. For the policy's effects to be fully testable, it must stay in effect till Spring 2010.

7. Appendix

7.1 List of What the SE^2 Means and Doesn't Mean

The SE^2 means:
1. A quality academic process with increased student learning.
2. Positive work ethics, motivation, attitudes, study habits, and responsibility.
3. Students who earn an A in effort are more likely to learn.
4. Students can earn an A, B, C, D, or F grade.
5. It is more difficult to earn a satisfactory grade.
6. An incentive is provided for students to put forth maximum effort in learning.
7. Only freshmen receive a warranty to receive a satisfactory grade, if they make an A in effort.
8. No student could earn a degree solely because of effort.
9. A potential increase in the value of the Benedict College degree and the employability of graduates.
10. An enhancement of academic freedom; Faculty determine how effort is defined.
11. Greater faculty efforts and more serious evaluation and instructional techniques.

The SE^2 does not mean:

1. A watered-down academic process with decreased learning.
2. Poor work ethics, motivation, attitudes, study habits and responsibility.
3. Students who earn an A in effort are least likely to learn.
4. Students automatically earn a grade of C.
5. Satisfactory grades are easier to earn.
6. An incentive is provided for students who do not earn their grade.
7. There is a guarantee for satisfactory grades after the freshman year.
8. The Benedict College degree will be awarded to unqualified students.
9. A devalued Benedict College degree or the reduced employability of graduates.
10. A diminishing of academic freedom; The administration determines how effort is defined.
11. Lessened faculty efforts and less serious evaluation and instructional techniques.

Notes

1. According to Benedict College, no other college or university has such a policy.
2. The administration checked the grades that professors were assigning, and noticed that the policy was not being followed by all. The policy initially did not require professors to submit both the effort and knowledge grade. As a result, two professors were eventually dismissed for insubordination. This leads to the assumption that beginning in the Fall of 2004 the SE^2 policy was being strictly enforced.
3. This assumes that a student's outside option is not better than attending school.
4. See Betts and Grogger (2003).
5. Another way to state this assumption is to say that effort today lowers the cost of effort tomorrow.
6. See Horn, Kojoku and Carroll (2001).
7. Source: ACT concordance study of 103,525 students taking both the ACT and SAT I between October 1994 and December 1996. 8/1997.
8. College Entrance Examination Board, "2003 College-Bound Seniors: A Profile of SAT Program Test Takers."
9. Wei, Christina Chang Li, Xiaojie, and Berkner, Lutz. (2004). A Decade of Undergraduate Student Aid: 1989–90 to 1999–2000, (NCES 2004-158). U.S. Department of Education, National Center for Education Statistics. Washington, DC: U.S. Government Printing Office.
10. Both extreme cases do not consider the effects that the policy may have on the grades of the students.
11. The list can be found in the appendix.

References

Betts, Julian R. and Jeff Grogger, "The Impact of Grading Standards on Student Achievement, Educational Attainment, and Entry-Level Earnings," *Economics of Education Review*, (22:4), August 2003, pp. 343–352.

College Entrance Examination Board, "2003 College-Bound Seniors: A Profile of SAT Program Test Takers," College Entrance Examination Board, 2003.

Horn, Laura, Laurence Kojoku, and C. Dennis Carroll, High School Academic Cur-
    riculum and the Persistence Path Through College," U.S. Department of Education,
    Office of Educational Research and Improvement, National Center for Educational
    Statistics, NCES 2001-163.
Wei, Christina Chang Li, Xiaojie, and Berkner, Lutz. (2004). A Decade of Undergradu-
    ate Student Aid: 1989–90 to 1999–2000, (NCES 2004-158). U.S. Department
    of Education, National Center for Education Statistics. Washington, DC: U.S.
    Government Printing Office.

Contributors

Charles L. Betsey is a graduate professor in the Department of Economics at Howard University, Washington, DC.

Marybeth Gasman is assistant professor, Higher Education, Graduate School of Education, University of Pennsylvania.

Gregory N. Price is Charles E. Merrill Professor and Chair, Morehouse College.

Dr. Valerie Rawlston Wilson is senior resident scholar at the National Urban League Policy Institute in Washington, DC.

Omari H. Swinton is assistant professor of economics at Howard University.

Printed in the United States
206606BV00001B/199-300/P

9 781412 807821